FUGITIVE SCIENCE

AMERICA AND THE LONG 19TH CENTURY

General Editors: David Kazanjian, Elizabeth McHenry, and Priscilla Wald

Fugitive Science

*Empiricism and Freedom in Early
African American Culture*

Britt Rusert

NEW YORK UNIVERSITY PRESS
New York

NEW YORK UNIVERSITY PRESS
New York
www.nyupress.org

References to Internet websites (URLs) were accurate at the time of writing. Neither the author nor New York University Press is responsible for URLs that may have expired or changed since the manuscript was prepared.

Library of Congress Cataloging-in-Publication Data
Names: Rusert, Britt, author.
Title: Fugitive science : empiricism and freedom in early African American culture / Britt Rusert.
Description: New York : New York University Press, [2017] | Series: America and the long 19th century | Includes bibliographical references and index.
Identifiers: LCCN 2016041810| ISBN 9781479885688 (cloth : acid-free paper) | ISBN 9781479847662 (paperback : acid-free paper)
Subjects: LCSH: African Americans—Intellectual life—19th century. | African American intellectuals—History—19th century. | African Americans—Civil rights—History—19th century. | Racism—United States—History—19th century. | Science—Social aspects— United States—History—19th century. | Science—United States—History—19th century. | Empiricism—History—19th century. | Knowledge, Sociology of—History—19th century. | United States—Intellectual life—19th century. | United States—Race relations—History— 19th century.
Classification: LCC E185.89.I56 B78 2017 | DDC 323.1196/07309034—dc23
LC record available at https://lccn.loc.gov/2016041810

New York University Press books are printed on acid-free paper, and their binding materials are chosen for strength and durability. We strive to use environmentally responsible suppliers and materials to the greatest extent possible in publishing our books.

Manufactured in the United States of America

10 9 8 7 6 5 4 3 2 1

Also available as an ebook

Research is formalized curiosity. It is poking and prying with a purpose. It is a seeking that he who wishes may know the cosmic secrets of the world and they that dwell therein.
—Zora Neale Hurston, *Dust Tracks on a Road* (1942)

CONTENTS

ACKNOWLEDGMENTS

This book is the result of several years of research and writing, and throughout that process, I often wondered if I had erred in taking on such a large and ambitious topic. Now, on the other side, I'm proud of the risk I took to follow the path of a story I felt needed to be told, and so happy to reflect on all of the relationships that were made, confirmed, and strengthened through its writing.

My teachers at Duke University profoundly influenced my thinking. I owe thanks and gratitude to Cathy Davidson, Karla Holloway, Maurice Wallace, Mark Anthony Neal, Fred Moten, Matt Cohen, Robyn Wiegman, Wahneema Lubiano, Ranjana Khanna, and Charmaine Royal, as well as Barry Saunders and Timothy Morton. Priscilla Wald has been a tireless advocate, and I have so much to thank her for. Bob Cook-Deegan supported me when he didn't have to; he's the type of cheerleader we all need in our corner. I have *Polygraph* and Summer Study to thank for two formative intellectual experiences. Michelle Koerner, Alex Ruch, Luka Arsenjuk, Beatriz Llenín Figueroa, Lissette Rolón Collazo, Abe Geil, Églantine Colon, Corinne Blalock, Amalle Dublon, and Russ Leo: I'm still proud of what we made together. At the Futures of American Studies Institute at Dartmouth, Donald Pease and Elizabeth Maddock Dillon made me feel that my work might matter. Time at the Clinton Institute of American Studies, University College Dublin was similarly transformative (thanks to Liam Kennedy and again to Don Pease).

And before all of that there was the Department of English at Allegheny College, a place that introduced me to the strange, wonderful idea that one could think and write for a living. I am indebted to Ben Slote, Susan Slote, David Miller, Jennifer Hellwarth, Laura Quinn, James Bulman, Karin Quimby, and Paige Schilt.

I am lucky to be part of a department filled with smart people who care about the right things and don't take themselves too seriously. Thanks to Jim Smethurst, Steve Tracy, Yemisi Jimoh, Manisha Sinha, Bill Strickland,

Amilcar Shabazz, Kym Morrison, Dania Francis, Toussaint Losier, and Traci Parker. John H. Bracey, Jr., has advocated for me time and again, and I am so grateful for his support. I look forward to receiving photocopied items from his personal archive (office) for many years to come. Tricia Loveland: everyone knows the place would fall apart without you. Also at UMass, thank you to my colleagues who read parts of the manuscript or talked with me about the project: Randall Knoper, Jord/ana Rosenberg, Nick Bromell, Laura Doyle, Emily Lordi, Hoang Gia Phan, Asha Nadkarni, Whitney Battle-Baptiste, Laura Briggs, Ron Welburn, Kirsten Leng, and of course, Tanisha Ford. Banu Subramaniam, Jennifer Hamilton, Angie Willey, and the rest of the Five College Feminist Science and Technology Studies Initiative have been long-time supporters of this project. I am especially appreciative of the students who have taken my graduate seminar on Early African American Print Culture.

At the University of Massachusetts Amherst, I gratefully acknowledge the Office of Research and Engagement for a Healey Endowment/ Faculty Research Grant and a publication subvention grant, the Center for Teaching and Faculty Development for a Mellon Mutual Mentoring Grant, and the Interdisciplinary Studies Institute (ISI) for a faculty fellowship. The ISI's director, Stephen Clingman, must be acknowledged for creating such a collegial and intellectually stimulating environment for faculty at UMass. I also thank members of the ISI's 2014–2015 Faculty Seminar for their valuable feedback. The College of Humanities and Fine Arts provided generous research funds and leave-time while I was completing the manuscript.

A number of colleagues and friends supported the project in various ways, from reading drafts, to helping with research questions, sending along citations, inviting me to share my research, providing models of scholarship and collegiality, or just offering their support and friendship. Many thanks to Robert Levine, Michael Ziser, Daphne Brooks, Adrienne Brown, Sonya Posmentier, Michelle Coghlan, Erica Fretwell, Rachel Price, Nigel Smith, Anne Anlin Cheng, Diana Fuss, William Gleason, Susan Scott Parrish, Eduardo Cadava, Patrick Jagoda, Khalil Gibran Muhammed, Nihad Farooq, Vin Nardizzi, Alisha Gaines, Kadji Amin, Margaux Cowden, Laura Levitt, Jennifer Brody, Rizvana Bradley, Janet Neary, Anna Mae Duane, Arika Easley-Houser, Lara Langer Cohen, Danny LaChance, Sari Altshuler, Lauren Klein, Brian Connolly,

Allison Lange, Jonathan Senchyne, Brigitte Fielder, Peter Jaros, Kinohi Nishikawa, Jessica Linker, John Tresch, Edlie Wong, Alex Black, Leif Eckstrom, Andrew Cole, Cathy Dailey, Lauren Klein, Ann Fabian, Keith Wailoo, Andy Russell, Dirk Hartog, Ruha Benjamin, and Kirsten Pai Buick. I am grateful to Alondra Nelson and Gene Andrew Jarrett for their mentorship and guidance. One of the great joys of this project has been connecting with other scholars who have a deep passion for the recovery and preservation of African American texts and histories, in all of their complexity and detail. For their expertise and enthusiasm, I thank Carla Peterson, John Ernest, Eric Gardner, P. Gabrielle Foreman, Lisa Baskin, Ellen Gruber Garvey, Alan Rice, Bridget Bennett, Randall Burkett, Claire Parfait and Reginald Pitts.

The early stages of my research were supported by postdoctoral fellowships at the Duke University Center for Public Genomics (A Center of Excellence for ELSI Research, funded by the National Human Genome Research Institute and the Department of Energy, CEER Grant P50 HG003391), under the directorship of Robert Cook-Deegan, and at the Center for the Humanities at Temple University (CHAT), under the directorship of Peter Logan. Thanks are also owed to Heather Ann Thompson, then Associate Director of CHAT. Additional short-term fellowships further supported and expanded my research, while providing important forms of intellectual community rooted in shared obsessions with old, decaying things. My own personal "archival turn" happened during a short-term visiting fellowship at the American Antiquarian Society and there, thanks are due to Ellen Dunlap, Paul Erickson, Elizabeth Pope, Marie Lamoureux, Jackie Penny, and the rest of the library staff. An earlier fellowship at the Robert H. Smith International Center for Jefferson Studies helped me conceptualize how a new project on fugitive science might emerge from an old one on plantation ecologies. A National Endowment for the Humanities postdoctoral fellowship at the Library Company of Philadelphia allowed me to finish my research and writing. Any views, findings, conclusions, or recommendations expressed in this publication do not necessarily reflect those of the National Endowment for the Humanities. At the Library Company, I have James Green, Erica Armstrong Dunbar, Krystal Appiah, Connie King, Erika Piola, and Nicole Joniec to thank. Many thanks as well to Phil Lapsansky for coming out of retirement to talk about Robert Benjamin Lewis and the friendship albums.

I received crucial assistance from generous librarians and other staff members in collections and institutions across the country, including the Schomburg Center for Research in Black Culture, the David M. Rubenstein Rare Book and Manuscript Library at Duke University, the Albert and Shirley Small Special Collections Library at the University of Virginia, the Historical Society of Pennsylvania, the Wisconsin Historical Society, University Special Collections and Preservation at the University of Rochester, and the Moorland-Spingarn Research Center at Howard University. I am also indebted to William David Barry at the Maine Historical Society; Stephen Ferguson, David Platt, Gabriel Swift, Eric White, and AnnaLee Pauls of Princeton University Libraries; Aslaku Berhanu of the Charles L. Blockson Afro-American Collection at Temple University; Matthew Herbison of the Legacy Center, Drexel College of Medicine Archives and Special Collections; Ruth Bowlers of the Walters Art Museum; and Jim Kelly, Isabel Espinal, Anne Moore, and Jeremy Smith of the UMass Amherst Libraries.

The anonymous readers of the manuscript provided feedback that was both supportive and substantial, and I have benefited greatly from their thoughtful engagement and careful reading. Their confidence in the project inspired me to write a bolder book. At New York University Press, I have been fortunate to work with Eric Zinner, Alicia Nadkarni, Alexia Traganas, and series editors David Kazanjian, Elizabeth McHenry, and Priscilla Wald.

I gratefully acknowledge *African American Review*, *American Quarterly*, and *Common-place: The Journal of Early American Life*, for permission to reprint material that originally appeared in their publications.

I must thank Jim Rusert, Diane Mauger Rusert, and Lindsay Rusert Bjorhus for supporting every single decision in my life, even when they weren't sure where it would lead me. Russell Leo, Jr., and Debbie Markham Leo are the hardest working grandparents in show business. The Houle School in Northampton, Massachusetts, and the YMCA in Princeton, New Jersey, provided childcare and peace of mind.

To my comrade and co-parent, Russ Leo: this book is for you and Lucy, the ones who make it all worth it.

Introduction

The first volume of Edward Strutt Abdy's *Journal of a Residence and Tour in the United States of North America* (1835) contains a surprising anecdote about the practice of science by African Americans in the early nineteenth century. Abdy was part of a delegation sent by the English government to tour American prisons. His journal intersperses accounts of the prison system with a narrative of his travels, especially as they reflected the author's observations about race and slavery in the United States. During an account of his time in New York City, Abdy writes about his visit to St. Philip's Episcopal Church in Lower Manhattan, whose members included many of the most prominent black families in the city.[1] Given the popular dissemination of ethnographic accounts of slavery in transatlantic travelogues and newspapers, British readers would surely be interested to hear details about an Episcopal church run by free African Americans in the US North. But before taking readers into the pews of St. Philip's to hear a sermon by the Reverend Peter Williams, Abdy dwells in the graveyard that belonged to the congregation on Chrystie Street, taking a surprising detour from black theology to black craniology.

There in the graveyard, Abdy recounts, he had a conversation with St. Philip's sexton, the warden of the church's cemetery and its head gravedigger. He is keen to relate the sexton's own observations about the remains under his stewardship, especially his claim that the skulls that had been buried for many years in his graveyard—those, Abdy interjects, that "it may fairly be assumed" were the "remains of native Africans"—were "both thicker and more depressed in the front than those of recent interment." The cemetery's gravedigger further "believes that there is some difference between the European and African skulls."[2] Throughout the scene, Abdy refers to the sexton/gravedigger as his informant and establishes his expertise, not through class, social status, or education, but rather through his labor and proximity to the bodies and skulls under his care. And just as white editors assured white readers about the reliability of black autobiographical writing in the antebellum period, Abdy notes that the sexton was a man of "highly respectable character" who would not assert a "falsehood" to satisfy a "favorite theory."[3] But the author's concern with establishing the sexton's legitimacy as a source of racial knowledge and as an informant on black skulls has at least one additional, and unintended result: Abdy effectively turns the sexton into a practicing scientist and the graveyard into his laboratory.

In addition to figuring the sexton as a vernacular craniologist, Abdy's account of the observable differences between native African and European skulls also reinforces white supremacist theories of civilization from the period, in which African Americans were believed to be further evolved than native Africans because of their contact with European culture and influence in the New World. While seemingly abolitionist through its expressions of moral outrage over slavery and prejudice in the United States, Abdy's book is ultimately built upon a characterization of Africans as intellectually deficient and uncivilized. But beyond reinforcing the typical anti-black views of a British anti-slavery sympathizer, what else does Abdy's graveyard story reveal? Carla Peterson notes that St. Philip's cemetery was established after the destruction of the African Burial Ground in 1795 and was intended to serve as a resting place not just for Episcopalians, but also for all black New Yorkers regardless of denomination or class.[4] In Abdy's account, the sexton emerges as a protector of the departed, a duty that included protecting skulls from the hands of doctors, medical students, and others interested in exploiting African American bodies for the benefit of science, medicine, or politics.[5] His account also raises important questions about the sexton's access to different forms of knowledge in his capacity as warden to the church's cemetery—questions about his on-the-ground scientific training through his labor with corpses and skeletons and how such work possibly shaped his interests in fields like craniology and phrenology.

Curiously, Abdy goes on to undercut the sexton's scientific authority and reliability as an informant by relaying "an amusing trick [the sexton played] against the late Dr. Paschalis—a physician in the city." He recounts a scene in which Paschalis was pointing out to a small crowd those "peculiarities of form which he said distinguished the two races."

The sexton then proceeded to walk up and present the "learned physiologist" with "a cranium from the cemetery under his care."[6] We then come to the heart of the sexton's trick: the skull was "immediately pronounced [by Dr. Paschalis] to have belonged to a white," but then, "the other [the sexton], who had taken off some hair that happened to be sticking upon it when he took it up, produced the woolly locks, and turned to laugh against the phrenologist."[7] In addition to questioning the expertise of the white physiologist while exposing the dubiousness of scientific claims that root racial difference in anatomy, the sexton's joke makes a direct intervention into the discourse—and public performance—of racial science. The use of "against" twice in this short anecdote, as a trick played "against" Paschalis and the sexton's laugh as directed "against" the doctor, also hints at the sexton's oppositional use of craniology, pitted against racist science. After recognizing the sexton's scientific knowledge and expertise, Abdy goes on to place him in the role of a "trickster." This comic anecdote is thus also entangled with the history of minstrelsy, and it is worth pointing out that Adby's travel narrative was published in 1835, amid the growing popularity of minstrel shows in New York City and across the Northeast.

Despite the author's attempt to discipline the sexton's actions and appropriate his knowledge, the sexton's joke ultimately escapes the disciplining grid of minstrelsy, revealing his trick to be a dead serious one. Stripped of Abdy's trickster frame, the scene is recast as one of scientific exchange, in which an expert (the vernacular craniologist) presents alternative evidence (the skull) to another expert (the physician). Given these instabilities in the text, we might finally return to an important inconsistency in the passage: Abdy's initial claim that the sexton believed there was "some difference between the European and African skulls." By citing a black authority on skulls who supposedly believes in the anatomical differences between black and white people, Abdy authenticates his own position. However, the subsequent retelling of the craniological trick threatens to undo that very position, since the joke turns on the fact that the doctor is unable to tell the difference between a "white" and a "black" skull. The sexton's laugh, cutting through the scene, ultimately confirms, not the "difference between the European and African skulls," but rather the absolute absurdity of that position, as well as the program of research behind it. Moreover, through his craniological trick,

Paschalis is exposed as both a shoddy performer—unable to provide correct skull "readings" in public—and a quack scientist. Thus, while Abdy works hard to make the sexton ventriloquize his own theories, the text also briefly glimpses the sexton's resistance to the use of his voice to authorize scientific racism.

This sketch of a black vernacular craniologist in the 1830s United States is part of a neglected story about race and science in the antebellum period. Historians have meticulously documented the regimes of scientific racism that emerged alongside the transition from natural history to comparative anatomy in the late eighteenth century.[8] However, in this same moment, the popularization of phrenology, anatomy, and physiology—as well as fields with no explicit connection to race science—created opportunities for African Americans both to critique racist science and to mobilize scientific knowledge in anti-slavery activism and adjoining forms of struggle. Natural science also provided a rich speculative terrain for African Americans in the period. *Fugitive Science* excavates this story, uncovering the dynamic scientific engagements and experiments of black writers, performers, artists, and other cultural producers who mobilized natural science and produced alternative knowledges in the quest for and name of freedom. Literary and cultural critics have a particularly important role to play in uncovering this scientific history since these engagements and experiments often happened, not in the laboratory or the university, but in print, on stage, in the garden, church, parlor, and in other cultural spaces and productions. Routinely excluded from institutions of scientific learning and training, black actors transformed the spaces of the everyday into laboratories of knowledge and experimentation.

As a concept and a window onto an alternative history, *fugitive science* is intended to accommodate a wide array of actors: professional and nonprofessional scientists, enthusiastic amateurs, eccentric experimenters, and wayward dabblers in many fields, from natural history and geology to astronomy, anatomy, and beyond. Fugitive science names a dynamic and diverse archive of engagements with, critiques of, and responses to racial science, as well as other forms of natural science. Fugitive science is not restricted to scientific practices by former slaves or fugitives in the act of escape, although those stories also find their way into this study. My definition of science is purposefully broad, and it veers closer to "praxis" and "experiment" than to the specialized study of the natural world in institutional and academic contexts.

The very definition of science was capacious and flexible in early to mid-nineteenth-century contexts, and neither science nor medicine was professionalized in the United States until later in the nineteenth century. Across the early nineteenth century, science was legitimately claimed by a surprisingly broad range of practitioners and practiced in a number of nonacademic and noninstitutional spaces, from the parlor to the workshop, the church to the park.[9] In this way, fugitive science refers to African American experiments with natural science, but it simultaneously describes the itinerancies and flexibilities of antebellum science more broadly. Thus, it is poised to intervene in the characterization and periodization of nineteenth-century science within the history of science. Fugitive science may not be completely reducible to the experiments of African Americans, but it is certainly the case that black interlocutors deployed fugitive science with the most sophistication and urgency in the period.

While the history of racial science is the story of knowledge built on the brutal exploitation of racialized subjects, it was not without its opponents. While scholarship that highlights "agency" and "resistance" has thoroughly shaped the study of slavery and its aftermath, accounts of racial science have been largely untouched by that model. Rather, the history of racial science has been understood primarily as one of unchallenged regimes of violent exploitation and near total subjection.[10] This study is not interested in naively chronicling examples of resistance to racial science, but it does seek to tell a different story about race and science in the nineteenth century. Thus, it resists the "object" status of black subjects, doubly objectified as legal commodities under slavery and as frequent subjects of scientific exploitation, by focusing instead on the active *practice* of science by African Americans from the late eighteenth century through the coming of the Civil War. At the same time, black practitioners did not primarily use science to affirm their status as liberal subjects, as citizen(-scientists), or even, as white abolitionists would do for them, as fully human, though that fact sometimes served as the starting point for practitioners of fugitive science. More often, natural science served African Americans as a springboard for complex meditations on being, subjectivity, and existence. Fugitive science both aspired to and enacted freedom in terms that challenged possessive individualism just as often as it asserted that black people were not, in fact, objects, but people. More than simply establishing the fact of black humanity, African Americans used natural science to profoundly meditate on the category of the human itself—on its possibilities, limits, and its complex relationship to blackness, a concept that exceeds a simply biological or even transparently empirical relationship to race. Fugitive science is thus what Michel Foucault calls a "counter-science," a form of knowledge that "unmake[s]" the very human who is "creating and recreating his positivity in the human sciences."[11]

While working with an expansive definition of science that both reflects the diversity of nineteenth-century science and accommodates the many different ways in which African Americans engaged with science, I do not use *pseudoscience* to describe any of the fields discussed in the book since that term obscures the emergence of scientific fields out of nonscientific contexts as well as the processes by which those fields are legitimated as science. Too often, the term *pseudoscience* has been used to detach natural science from its nonscientific contexts, its roots in popular science, and its indebtedness to lay and folk knowledge. For example, while phrenology is today considered a pseudoscience, in the early and mid-nineteenth century, it was a legitimate and respected field that both relied on and contributed to developments in comparative anatomy.[12] Phrenology also anticipated key concepts in early brain science, including the idea that localized sections of the brain correspond to particular faculties.[13] Just as "quackery" was used in the nineteenth century to distance university-trained doctors from supposedly antiquated forms of lay practice and healing, the deployment of *pseudoscience* tries to imagine a scientific present unencumbered by an embarrassing scientific past.

Perhaps even more problematically, the term *pseudoscience* routinely works to exclude both nonprofessional and non-white practitioners from the field of knowledge production while discrediting valuable knowledge systems of the indigenous and the enslaved, including conjuring, astrology, and other forms of mysticism. Susan Scott Parrish has traced the significant role played by enslaved and indigenous peoples, as well as Anglo-American women, in the production of British metropolitan scientific knowledge about the New World in the seventeenth and eighteenth centuries. Because of the Baconian method's emphasis on repeated, accreted observations, experts in native environments were particularly valuable to British scientists, gentlemen travelers, and amateur naturalists who had no prior knowledge of the flora and fauna of the Americas. Parrish reveals that New World subjects were not simply exploited objects of British science and natural history, but were active agents who regularly used their technical expertise and knowledge about local environments to negotiate, navigate, and resist British encroachment on their lands and control of their bodies. Moreover, she reveals black and indigenous knowledge production in the New World to be central to the "discoveries" of the Scientific Revolution in the seventeenth century.[14]

Following Parrish's understanding of black and indigenous knowledge production as a crucial, animating force of the New Science, I consider a number of fields, from phrenology and mesmerism to conjuring and astrology, as legitimate knowledge systems since they were valued and taken seriously by the writers, intellectuals, and performers under discussion. Early African American practitioners repeatedly questioned the very definition of science, radically expanding its borders while presenting themselves as vital scientific agents who had the power to manipulate and experiment with the objects of the natural world.[15] *Fugitive Science* focuses on a set of early African American writers, visual artists, and performers—some canonical, others lesser known—who participated in scientific debates, conducted eccentric experiments, and incorporated science into their writings and performances. Some of these figures were interested in building evidence and crafting arguments against racist science, while others were interested in how sciences with no particular connection to the science of race could be used to enact a radical concept of freedom. Examining the rich cross-fertilizations between natural science and early African American writing, *Fugitive Science* chronicles early African American and Afro-Native writing as a response to the racism of the American school of ethnology; the influence of astronomy on Martin Delany's serial novel *Blake; or, The Huts of America* (1859–1862); Frederick Douglass's reprinting and repurposing of scientific texts; the scientific-artistic cultures of black women's education in antebellum Philadelphia; and the use of popular science in transatlantic abolitionist performance cultures. It stitches together a dynamic genealogy of African American science writing in the antebellum period and chronicles the influence of natural science on the origins of African American literary production. In what follows, I resituate racial science within its Atlantic and extra-institutional dimensions in order to clear a space for fugitive science in the existing historiography, outline the import of fugitivity and empiricism for this project, and provide an overview of the book's trajectory and archive, as well as—to follow Kevin Young's concept of the "shadow book" —the "shadow archives" of enslaved and working-class science that existed alongside the scientific production of black intellectuals in the US North and in transatlantic spaces.[16]

Atlantic Race Science

Although written accounts of physical differences among humans have their origin in classical antiquity, such theories were not used as ideological artillery in the defense of slavery in any sustained way until the eighteenth century. The modern science of race emerged alongside the spread of European imperialism, the rise of the slave trade, and the emergence of the Scientific Revolution in the seventeenth century. It secured its status in the eighteenth century under the auspices of natural history. During that period, European naturalists began to include the "varieties" of man in their taxonomies of animal and vegetable life. In *Systema Naturae* (1735), Carolus Linnaeus turned his binomial taxonomic system to the categorization of humans, defining five discrete races based on skin color and geographical origin. Among Europeans in the age of natural history, climatic, monogenetic theories of race prevailed: all humans were believed to be descended from Adam and Eve, but different races developed over time because of exposure to varying geographic climates. Climatologists presented a surprisingly flexible conception of race in their belief that the lower races could become more "white" and hence more civilized over time. Theories of monogenesis, which upheld scriptural authority on the unity of the races and viewed the "lower races" as degenerations of Caucasian peoples, prevailed in the early republic of the United States, and were the topic of major treatises like Samuel Stanhope Smith's *An Essay on the Causes of the Variety of Complexion and Figure in the Human Species* (1787). The prominent

physician Benjamin Rush also subscribed to the theory of racial degeneration, arguing that blackness was produced by leprosy, and since it
was caused by a degenerating disease, he believed that blackness could
be "cured."[17] While the monogenetic theory of race maintained the unity
of humankind and spoke of the eventual elevation of all races, it was
marred by a deep condescension toward the "lower" races, the equation
of whiteness with civilization, and the belief that blackness was produced through climatic degeneration.

Comparative anatomy became an attractive tool for categorizing and
managing a motley population of European settlers, indentured servants,
Africans, and Native Americans in the early republic. The transition from
natural history to comparative anatomy had a dramatic influence on
the classification and ordering of the races, making fungible, yet highly
problematic, racial categories increasingly rigid and hierarchical. Martin
Bernal observes that the "period from 1800 to 1850 in general was one of
intense activity to find anatomical bases for the racial differences which
every cultivated European 'knew' existed."[18] By the early nineteenth century, ideological presuppositions motored scientific investigations into
race, and this was especially true in the United States. In the 1830s, racist,
polygenetic theories—forwarded and promoted by a zealous group that
Stephen Jay Gould and other scholars have called the American school
of ethnology—began to gain traction amid anxieties over the rise of the
abolitionist movement and the strengthening political mobilization of
free black communities in urban areas across the Northeast.[19] Departing
from the theories of climatism and monogenesis that were dominant during the early national period, the polygenetic theory of the separate and
unequal evolution of the races gained influence throughout the 1850s as a
justification for the institution of slavery as well as the political disenfranchisement of free African Americans. Polygenetic theories of creation,
which asserted that the races were different types of humans produced
by separate divine creations, were buttressed by investigations in comparative anatomy that sought to explain differences among racial groups
through the comparison of anatomical structures. Placing Caucasians at
the apex of the evolutionary ladder, peoples of African descent were figured as physiologically and intellectually inferior to whites. While natural
history mapped out geographical and environmental influences on morphology, comparative anatomy went deeper, seeking out the sources of

human difference and inequality in internal structures of the body that remained unseen to the untrained observer.

Katy Chiles has written about the surprising flexibility of race in eighteenth-century racial theory: a wide range of texts, both literary and scientific, featured scenes in which subjects could actually change their race.[20] Such scenes of "transformable race" are almost unimaginable within the scientific regime of ossified racial categories and anxiety over miscegenation that would come to define the nineteenth century. In the early national period, scientific theories of race were also just as interested in the origins and descent of the country's indigenous population as they were about an exponentially growing population of African captives. Works like Samuel George Morton's *Crania Americana* (1839), which focused on the cataloguing of indigenous skulls from North and South America, both contributed to and were embedded in a popular obsession with Native American life and culture among Anglo-Americans, who were interested in making grand generalizations about "Indian character" at the same as they obsessed over the differences among tribes and nations.

Anglo-Americans flirted with models of Native incorporation while they feared becoming Black, and this dynamic shaped the theorization of race *across* the epistemic divide between natural history and comparative anatomy.[21] From the beginning, Anglo-American settler-colonists were more confident in their ability to contain and assimilate Native Americans into the national body politic (and later, of separating them from it). Early national racial theory also engaged in a comparative ethnology, a discourse that contrasted and hierarchized "Blacks" and "Natives" against one another. For example, Thomas Jefferson's *Notes on the State of Virginia* (1785, 1787) enquires into the state of race in the new nation by contrasting the faculties and capacities of Africans and Natives. Like uses of ethnology for pro-slavery agendas as well as various efforts aimed at restricting the rights of African Americans who were not enslaved, ethnological investigations of Native peoples helped to justify regimes of violence and dispossession at the hands of the US government.[22] But ethnology focused on Native peoples never reached the ideological power of anti-black ethnology, and as Sean Harvey notes, Native ethnology was largely rooted in arguments about linguistic rather than biological difference.[23] With the "Indian problem" supposedly solved through the large-scale displacement of indigenous peoples by mid-century, racial science largely left behind its roots in comparative ethnology to fully commit to anti-Black theories that had political expediency in the struggle over slavery's future in the US South. A quick glance at Charles De Wolf Brownell's *The Indian Races of North and South America* (1854), published the same year as Josiah Nott and George Gliddon's *Types of Mankind*, reveals the differences between ethnological approaches to African and Native peoples by the 1850s.[24] While Nott and Gliddon's *Types of Mankind* (1854) contains countless characterizations of the degeneracy of Africans and Afro-diasporic peoples, especially when these groups mixed with other races, *The Indian Races of North and South America* proceeds largely as a quaint ethnographic account of Native customs and habits. Another way to understand this distinction is to say that if Africans had no history and were forever relegated to their "primitive" physicality in an eternal present, Native Americans had only history and were an always disappearing people forever relegated to the past.

Although scientific defenses of slavery were widespread in the South, especially during the 1850s and early 1860s, the production and circulation of racial science was neither insular nor regional in scope. In his foundational study, *The Mismeasure of Man* (1981), Stephen Jay Gould reminds readers that the major advocates of polygenesis were classed together as the *American* school of ethnology by European scientists and polygenesis was itself celebrated as the first truly "indigenous" scientific theory to emerge from the young nation.[25] However, the so-called American school cannot be reduced to a distinctively Southern or even national science since this school and its polygenetic theories emerged out of a series of transatlantic networks and avenues of exchange. Throughout the nineteenth century, the American school of ethnology was part of a network of scientists, theories, and experiments that spanned the globe and were conducted in places including Latin America, the Caribbean, Western Europe, and North and West Africa.

The leading figures of American polygenesis were not Southern, and in some cases, not even American. Gould points out that many of the Southern figures associated with the movement, including the Louisiana physician Samuel Cartwright, were actually considered fringe figures in their own time.[26] The most important publications in the field, including Samuel George Morton's *Crania Americana* (1839), as well as Nott and Gliddon's *Types of Mankind* (1854), which sought to popularize and extend Morton's writings after his death, were published in the North. These texts were actually not widely cited by Southerners because of polygenesis's rejection of scriptural teachings on the creation. Furthermore, pro-slavery arguments rooted in experimental science were primarily produced in the North and in Europe. Louis Agassiz, the most famous "American" race scientist of the period, was a Swiss immigrant who first came to the United States from France in 1846 to deliver the Lowell Lectures at Harvard, where he then became a professor geology and zoology in 1848. His notorious photographic experiments with Southern plantation slaves were part of transatlantic investigations into the "races of man" that also brought him to Brazil in 1864, at the close of the Civil War, to observe "the natives" in a desperate attempt to refute Darwinian evolution and its upholding of monogenesis.[27]

Thus, even as it was used to affirm the sectionalist aspirations of the US South, nineteenth-century racial science was embedded in the production and circulation of scientific ideas and experiments across the Atlantic World. Scientific knowledge about the Black as well as the Native American body was produced and circulated through channels of expertise, collaboration, and exchange that flowed between the North and the South, especially between two major scientific metropoles in the United States: Philadelphia and Charleston. Moreover, these North-South exchanges were embedded in a larger transatlantic network, which linked Philadelphia, Charleston, Boston, and even Mobile, Alabama, to scientific metropoles like Edinburgh, London, and Paris, as well as to European colonial outposts in the Pacific, Caribbean, and South America. Darwin's *Voyage of the Beagle* (1839) is perhaps better than any other work of nineteenth-century natural history in showing how ethnological and proto-evolutionary science was produced through the networks of European imperialism and the slave trade itself. American race science was also influenced by a growing cultural obsession with Egypt, which was opened to Western scientists, adventurers, and archaeologists after the Napoleonic campaign in Egypt in 1799. The first modern excavation of an ancient sphinx occurred in 1818, and Americans and Europeans would continue to pillage Egyptian sphinxes, tombs, and other sites for decades to come. In this way, nineteenth-century racial science was indebted not only to earlier histories of European colonization in the New World, but also to ongoing forms of imperialism and conquest in places like North Africa.

Important variations in racial science also existed between different settler-colonial societies in the Americas. For example, theories of race developed differently in Brazil's complicated colonial context.[28] Science in the Deep South and in the Caribbean often resisted the anthropomorphism of ethnology and comparative anatomy, pointing instead to the porousness among humans, animals, and plants in the American "tropics."[29] Although rarely acknowledged in their work, European and Anglo-American naturalists most certainly learned about indigenous and African theories of creation and group identity. Finally, Native Americans and Africans reconceptualized theories of their own origin, descent, and ancestry in the wake of the slave trade, Native removal, and other forms of racial dispossession and forced migration.

The reorientation of US racial science as a deeply Atlantic science not only illuminates a more global and diverse network of experiments, theories, and practitioners, but also counters the misunderstanding of these sciences as nothing other than hegemonic mouthpieces for the state. Racial science was actually composed of a wide variety of scientific fields, including comparative anatomy, craniology, phrenology, and ethnology, along with mesmerism, magnetism, and geology. Approaching racial science through its many subfields, including those usually associated with popular science rather than racial science, reveals a new set of interlocutors who regularly engaged in scientific debates and countered the tenuous claims, in Douglass's words, of "the Notts, the Gliddons, the Agassiz[es], and Mortons."[30] Moreover, by the 1850s, racial scientists were touting their autonomy from the closed circuits of academic institutions. In the preface to their second edition of *Types of Mankind* (1857), Nott and Gliddon go so far as to present theirs as a science issued "from the people," a noninstitutional, populist science dis-identified from the nation-state:

The frank concurrence of Messrs. LIPPINCOTT, GRAMBO & Co. has removed every obstacle to effective publication: and thus, through the liberality and thirst for information, so eminently characteristic of American republicanism, "Types of Mankind," invested with abundant signatures, issues into day as one among multitudinous witnesses [showing] how, in our own age and land, scientific works can be written and published without solicitation of patronage from Governments, Institutions, or Societies; but solely through the co-operative support of an educated and knowledge-seeking people.[31]

Nott and Gliddon's presentation of polygenesis as a noninstitutional science is important, even if it is an exaggerated claim, since it illuminates the ways in which racial science was largely a popular science disseminated through the print sphere and emerging forms of mass culture. The popularization of racial science clearly unleashed a set of harmful racist theories among the masses and contributed more generally to the pathologizing of both enslaved and free African Americans and other subjugated groups, including Native Americans, as well as some white ethnic groups. But at the same time, the wide dissemination of race science through pamphlets, newspapers, lectures, theater, and other performance venues opened the field to an unlikely set of actors who not only critiqued scientific racism, but also constructed their own antiracist science.

The noninstitutional status of racial science in the antebellum period thus produced horizontal networks of circulation and exchange that linked racist science and anti-racist critique. Publishing histories provide further evidence of overlapping circuits of dissemination, circulation, and reception. For example, when Douglass's speech on "The Claims of the Negro, Ethnologically Considered," a vicious attack on the American school of ethnology, was printed as a pamphlet in 1854, it entered the same popular print sphere as Nott and Gliddon's just published *Types of Mankind*. Both "Claims of the Negro" and *Types of Mankind* were printed with easy and wide circulation in mind.[32] In other words, black responses to ethnology often circulated in the same publishing and lecture circuits as ethnology itself. The popularity of race science allowed African Americans to regularly intervene in the field and change the terms of debate.

The Atlantic dimensions of racial science, especially the global discourse of race in ethnology, were also mobilized by David Walker, Frederick Douglass, Martin Delany, and later, Pauline Hopkins, to develop a rich diasporic imaginary. In addition to creating a global imaginary of emancipation, the transatlantic dimensions of racial science allowed black interlocutors to forge more material connections to industrial workers outside of the United States (see Chapter 3 on Henry Box Brown's performances in England). Ironically, the transatlantic networks mapped out by ethnologists in the defense of slavery became central to the articulation of an anti-racist science oriented toward transatlantic racial solidarity and the global abolition of slavery.

The rise of racial science under the banner of comparative anatomy was also part of a broader period of scientific discovery in the early nineteenth century. Thomas Kuhn argues that this period witnessed a second scientific revolution, which included paradigm-shifting developments in a number of scientific fields and broader technological transformations that were part of the industrial revolution.[33] Abetted by technological improvements and the widespread uptake of Baconian, or empirical, methods, the second scientific revolution included the growth of geology, modern chemistry, and biology, alongside important developments in the study of electricity, heat, and magnetism.[34] Natural science, which includes the five branches of science that investigate the natural world—biology, astronomy, earth science, chemistry, and physics—provided, in the words of Ian Frederick Finseth, rich representational "affordances" to anti-slavery activists and thinkers.[35] While white abolitionists tended to ignore science or simply rejected racial science's claim that Africans were not human, African Americans largely embraced the "new sciences" of the early nineteenth century, including fields that overlapped with racial science. They often made careful distinctions between the biased science of race and science as a whole, and put natural science to work in various practical, experimental, and speculative contexts. Throughout this book, "racial science" is usually interchangeable with "racist science," though practitioners of fugitive science held out hope that a science of race could be forged that was unburdened by white supremacy.

Empiricism and Freedom

This book's capacious definition of science is meant to capture the Atlantic currents of racial science, to match the diversity of scientific practice before professionalization occurred later in the nineteenth century, and to accommodate the many different ways that African Americans produced knowledge in the period. *Fugitive Science* dovetails with more recognizable efforts at uncovering "African Americans in science," but it also suggests a less familiar trajectory of ambitious but obscure experiments, of knowledges tried, frustrated, and aborted, and of scientific practices that cannot be accommodated within narratives of black professionalization and upward mobility.

In some ways, antebellum science seems a world away from the production of science in our own moment, deeply embedded as it is in global capital and the neoliberal university.[36] At the same time, this is a period when natural science starts to look closer to what we in the twenty-first century also recognize as science. While in earlier centuries science (as *scientia*) referred to knowledge writ large, the nineteenth century witnessed the narrowing of science to those empirically driven fields engaged in the investigation of the natural world.[37] That transition is reflected in the fact that *scientist* entered the English lexicon sometime around 1830. Science in the nineteenth century is thus a transitional and fraught category. Similarly, while antebellum racial science can seem antiquated and obsolete from a twenty-first century perspective, it was at the absolute center of a new regime of knowledge organized around the human that emerged in the period, one that continues to shape contemporary structures and institutions of knowledge.[38] Today, racial science is being reanimated under new forms of appearance, especially in population genomics and other fields that investigate human difference, at the same time as it is wished away as a relic of an embarrassing past.[39] In his 1919 essay, Sigmund Freud describes the uncanny (*unheimlich*) as "that class of the frightening which leads back to what is known of old and long familiar"; the uncanny registers a return of the repressed.[40] The history and present of racial science are rife with such hauntings of earlier, repressed histories, especially eugenics. In this way, the characterization of racial science as a pseudoscience might also be understood as a disavowal of the uncanny feeling it exerts on the present.

Linked to its expansive concept of science, *Fugitive Science* works with a broad definition of empiricism, one that is related to but not reducible to science itself. More specifically, it seeks to theorize empiricism and fugitivity together, as concepts that are individually situated in the history of science and philosophy and in African American studies, respectively, but also share important points of intersection and overlap. In recent years, *fugitivity* and the attendant category of the fugitive have been rich sites of theorization for scholars of black literature and culture.[41] This concept signifies in diverse and sometimes divergent ways for different scholars, whose studies address unique contexts and forms, including law, performance, poetry, visual culture, music, and the slave narrative tradition. Taken collectively, this body of scholarship makes a number of important contributions. First, it challenges grand emancipation narratives, showing the many similarities between the age of slavery and the age of emancipation. Second, it reveals fugitivity to be a practical, philosophical, and artistic method deployed both before and after Emancipation by people enslaved, fugitive, and nominally free. Third, it unhinges black escape from the grip of criminality, transforming "the fugitive" from solely a criminal or legal category to a kind of radical comportment to the world, a subterranean politics and furtive insurgency against both the Southern slaveholding power and Northern liberalism that does not necessarily end when one successfully escapes from slavery or when slavery is legally abolished. Finally, fugitivity names a critical method, or a particular mode of study that experiments with new ways of reading and analyzing texts and contexts from the nineteenth century to the contemporary moment.[42]

Fugitive science stiches together two perhaps unlikely concepts, emerging at the intersection of scholarship on fugitivity and the theorization of minor science in the philosophy of Gilles Deleuze and Félix Guattari. Looking back to the privileging of heterogeneity, becoming, and "flux as reality" in the ancient atomism of Lucretius and Democritus (an atomism echoed in Martin Delany's writings on astronomy), Deleuze and Guattari affirm the existence of an "eccentric science" that "seems very difficult to classify, whose history is even difficult to follow."[43] This eccentric science is a "minor science" that rejects the theorems, metrics, and categorizations of state science. Minor sciences refuse to count or to be held accountable. They "pose more problems than they solve": problematics are their only mode.[44] Minor science proceeds by a radical empiricism that, instead of selecting and reducing experience into static epistemological categories, works to *amplify* experiences and build ever-proliferating connections and relations. State science captures and appropriates minor science, but minor science, which also goes under the name of "nomad" and "itinerant" science for Deleuze and Guattari, continually escapes the sovereignty imposed on its inventions. While state science establishes itself as a rigid and autonomous domain, minor science is constantly on the move, linking up nonscientific collectivities, marking and extending a territory, and tracing a line of flight. In other words, minor science is animated by the praxis of fugitivity. Oriented toward ongoing experiments in mapping, movement, and escape, minor science might also go under the name of fugitive science.

Fugitive science thus illuminates a history of science on the move in the antebellum period, a furtive, subterranean history of experiments and practices that both linked racial science to abolitionism across the Atlantic and mobilized popular science in more fleeting acts of resistance. Excluded from the ranks of professional science, the popular stage also became a key space upon which African Americans challenged the ascendency of racial science, while enacting a fugitive science—a furtive science and praxis—that suggested ways that a wide array of popular sciences might be linked to emancipation struggles.

Across this study, I categorize three forms of fugitive science: oppositional, practical, and speculative. *Oppositional forms of fugitive science* are composed of explicit critiques of racial science that aim to make a direct intervention into scientific discourse. *Practical fugitive science* seeks to "instrumentalize" science and technology in the struggle for emancipation, as, for example, in the widespread promotion of the compass as a trusty tool for slaves escaping slavery. Finally, *speculative fugitive science* uses the rich imaginative landscape of science to meditate on slavery and freedom, as well as the contingencies of black subjectivity and existence. This speculative tradition is interested in large, existential questions about the self, the world, and the cosmos and may not explicitly reference race at all. Frederick Douglass's 1854 speech "The Claims of the Negro, Ethnologically Considered," is an excellent example of oppositional fugitive science since it takes shape through a direct critique of racist ethnology. Martin Delany's writings on astronomy display the deep philosophical and existential dimensions of the speculative tradition of fugitive science. And David Walker's surprising treatment of

Jefferson's *Notes on the State of Virginia* as a book to be both reviled and studied, as well as his transformation of Jefferson's text into a tool of emancipation, like the compass, reveals the practical genealogy of fugitive science. Walker's *Appeal to the Coloured Citizens of the World* (1829) was a text written out of necessity and social contingency, not a writerly practice of slow meditation and expression. It is itself a practical tool that begs to be thrown into the cogs of slavery. This fact raises important questions about what kinds of critical reading practices best attend to the complexities of early African American texts, which were produced under conditions of urgency and contingency. Following John Ernest's theorization of early African American writing's emergence out of highly unstable social and political contexts, *Fugitive Science* experiments with a reading method that attempts to run alongside and keep up with the frenzied and dynamic experiments of early black writing and performance.[45]

The fugitive history of empiricism thus offers new materialist approaches and critical reading practices to both black science *and* literature. Through fugitivity, science emerges as a dynamic domain of practice, stretching from scientific to artistic domains. And practice shifts our attention to the various actions and activities of the oppressed that were excluded from politics proper in the contexts of enslavement and its aftermath. *Practice*, in Saidiya Hartman's terms, marks a subterranean, insurgent politics "without a proper locus," a politics that questions what has been recognized as the political in the contexts of liberalism and racial subjection.[46] Forcibly removed from the polis—the space of rights, recognition, and personhood—the resistances of the enslaved and the disenfranchised often register in seemingly nonpolitical domains. Practice thus turns our attention to the diverse forms of what Paul Gilroy calls, following Ralph Ellison, the "politics of a lower frequency," or what we might term, following Bruno Latour, a "politics by other means."[47]

Furthermore, a focus on practice shifts the history of empiricism from one unduly focused on the production of knowledge to one constituted by ongoing, active experiments. This study is particularly interested in the various *uses* of science that are made en route to the production of knowledge. For example, enslaved and indigenous peoples regularly used scientific expertise and knowledge about local environments to negotiate relationships with colonial agents, to gain political power, and to increase agency in the contexts of enslavement and colonialism.[48] While empiricism is traditionally defined as a theory of knowledge production that emerges from repeated sensory experiences, work by Deleuze as well as theorists of feminist standpoint theory has outlined ways of thinking about empiricism that instead highlight its role in the construction of subjectivity itself.[49] In his 1952 book on the philosophy of David Hume, *Empiricism and Subjectivity*, Deleuze argues that while empiricism is normally understood as the use of experience and observation to solve a problem or reach a final conclusion, the empirical method, in its continual process of shuttling back and forth between experience and its theorization, interminably posits and reiterates the very problem of experience.[50] In so doing, Deleuze transforms empiricism from a theory of knowledge to a theory of subject formation. Empiricism finds us always in the middle, in a line of flight or a line of escape—at the level of praxis and ongoing experiments—in the material realm of sensation and subjectivity rather than in the metaphysical plane of knowledge production. Such an approach necessarily widens empiricism from a narrow method within the sciences to include a broader set of experimental practices and modes of becoming in the world. In Deleuze's terms, empiricism is a nomadic practice. As a method that depends on sense perception, continual observations, and a mobile, searching orientation toward the world, there is indeed something fugitive about empiricism itself.

Fugitive science makes good on the active experimentalism of experience that lies at the heart of empiricism: it reanimates the Latin sense of experiment, *experior*: to test or to try. Instead of hardening observations and trials into theorems and facts, it tarries in the multitude of experience, continually poses problems (for the state and the state of slavery), and transforms the passivity of knowledge production into the activity of invention. Fugitive sciences are ongoing experiments in freedom, radical empiricisms.

In addition to opening up the contours of nineteenth-century science, fugitive science transforms our understanding of black cultural production in the Atlantic World. Indeed, scholars have been perhaps too apt to suggest a rigid divide between cultural and scientific production during the period, obscuring, for our purposes here, rich genealogies of black engagements with natural science. Fugitive science, as critical genealogy and as method, turns our view to a concept of experimentation that traverses African American science, art, and physical expressivity. This then, is finally an appeal for new, transdisciplinary, and perhaps also undisciplined approaches to the study of black literature and culture, approaches traversing traditional divides between the natural sciences, the social sciences, and the humanities in order to excavate neglected genealogies of experimentation across the Black Atlantic. By taking science more seriously in African American studies, and by recognizing the dynamism of natural science in the antebellum period, new light may be shed on the origins and contours of early African American cultural production, particularly the permeable boundaries of and surprising cross-fertilizations between what we today rigidly categorize as "art" and "science."[51]

A fugitive understanding of empiricism also helps to illuminate experimental aesthetic practices like assemblage, collage, and juxtaposition, which populated the antebellum African American print sphere. For example, William Wells Brown's *Clotel; or, The President's Daughter* (1853) liberally lifts material from Lydia Maria Child's "The Quadroons" (1842), published slave narratives, newspaper accounts, and abolitionist tracts. In the context of fugitive science, *Clotel* comes alive as a deeply experimental novel, a collage of different texts and contexts that draws on the Baconian method in its incorporation and accumulation of different factual sources and forms of empirical evidence.[52] In the final chapter, Brown notes that he composed his novel by reading widely and drawing on his own experiences as well as the experiences of other fugitive slaves he encountered during his travels. He then, in his words, "combined" these sources in order to make his own story.[53] Brown's daring experiment in "combination," in searching out and gathering together a number of different sources and texts, animates the sense of fugitivity that lies at the heart of empiricism. "Combination" echoes both the method of empiricism and a nineteenth-century language of seditious gathering with the intent to revolt: fugitive science stands at that very intersection, at the cross-section of science and struggle. Ultimately, nineteenth-century fugitive science and literature activated the radical implications of Francis Bacon's motto for the empirical method, drawn from Daniel 12:4: "Many shall run to and fro, and knowledge shall be increased."[54] In so doing, empiricism was loosed from the grasp of antebellum racial science, linked to a radical politics of fugitivity, and set to work in the struggle for emancipation, a struggle that included but also exceeded the abolitionist movement.

Fugitive Science and Fugitive Literature

Recent scholarship has invigorated the study of African American literature before the twentieth century. This work includes studies that employ a book history approach, theoretical work on the significance of the return to the compromised and fragmented archives of slavery and freedom, burgeoning interest in race and nineteenth-century visual culture, and explorations of the dynamic relationship between black performance and literature.[55] Studies of early African American print cultures, of literacy in its various forms (including alphabetic, oral, and social), of black literary societies and periodical cultures have all suggested that rather than further narrowing our definition of what counts as African American literature, scholars should be radically ramifying the definition of "literature" itself to accommodate all of the forms of writing and print with which people were engaged, from pamphlets and newspapers to broadsides and common-place books. This work is also drawing attention to African American editors, printers, compositors, engravers, illustrators, book-sellers, subscription agents, and the many others actors involved in the processes of print production, distribution, circulation, and reception.[56] Both Elizabeth McHenry and Eric Gardner note that for African Americans in the nineteenth century, "literature" referred not just to fiction and other forms of imaginative prose, but to a wide variety of genres.[57] *Fugitive Science* builds on this scholarship by revealing science writing to be a key genre of early African American print culture. In periodicals and newspapers, for example, scientific treatises routinely appeared alongside serial novels, short stories, and poetry, producing a dynamic space for cross-fertilization and exchange between literary and scientific texts.

In addition to chronicling the productive interanimation of black literary and scientific production across the antebellum period, *Fugitive Science* recovers a variety of neglected scientific writings in the early African American print sphere, while restoring some better-known texts to their original, dialogic publishing contexts. During the 1960s and 1970s, the Black Arts/Black Power movement produced a demand for publishers to reprint classic texts of black literature, history and politics, including texts that anticipated the freedom movement of the twentieth century and those that served as aesthetic antecedents to the prose, poetry, and drama of the era.[58] These foundational publishing initiatives set the stage for the emergence of African American literary studies as a distinct field within the academy during the 1980s. In the late 1980s and into the 1990s, the field was once again invigorated by the recovery of a number of texts, including little-known works written by African American women in the nineteenth century, which were made available to scholars through the publication of the *Schomburg Library of Nineteenth-Century Black Women Writers*, a thirty-volume set published by the Schomburg Center in conjunction with Oxford University Press, and edited by Henry Louis Gates, Jr. The excavation of poetry, short stories, and serial novels from early African American newspapers provided a particularly rich and expanded archive for literary scholars. However, in the enthusiastic search for these literary texts, especially in periodicals and newspapers, early works of black fiction and poetry were often severed from their original publishing contexts, in which a heterogeneous array of political writings, news stories, histories, and scientific treatises were regularly printed alongside fiction and poetry. *Fugitive Science* reconnects some of this writing in order to restore the dynamic fluidity and exchange between black scientific and literary production during the period.

Across five chapters, *Fugitive Science* brings attention to several figures who are little-known in literary studies, including Robert Benjamin Lewis, Hosea Easton, James W. C. Pennington, and Sarah Mapps Douglass, all of whom produced texts, speeches, and other cultural artifacts marked by a careful engagement with natural science. It also sheds new light on better-known figures—including Frederick Douglass, William Wells Brown, Henry Box Brown, and Martin Delany—by highlighting the scientific attunements of their writing and activism. In addition to excavating a rich body of science writing produced by black writers, this book reveals the fundamental role that natural science and empiricism, more generally, played in shaping the form and content of early African American literature.

Fugitive Science relies on a set of print sources that are themselves important documents of fugitive science at the same time as they help in the reconstruction of a dynamic set of scientific practices that have often eluded scholars. In other cases, print actually obscures science that appeared only in manuscript or oral forms. Thus, print is not a transparent container or transmitter of fugitive science: it is also a medium as well as an ideology that filters, shapes, and even censors information; it can obscure fugitive science just as often as it illuminates it. Cognizant of the "ideology of the book" and of the printed word, more generally, *Fugitive Science* thus also turns to performance, manuscripts, and other archives to chronicle a broader genealogy of black experiments with natural science.[59] Attentive to Diana Taylor's distinction between the archive of "supposedly enduring materials" and that of a more ephemeral repertoire, this book includes several speculative readings of "embodied practice/knowledge" to capture traces of the fleeting gestures, everyday acts, and embodied performances that have not been recorded in the annals of fugitive science but that have surely served as "vital acts" in its "transfer" across time."[60]

While *Fugitive Science* analyzes a number of lesser-known figures, texts, and performances, it turns out that it is difficult to tell this story without Thomas Jefferson. Indeed, in the early national and early antebellum period, fugitive science largely took shape as a response to Jefferson's "speculations" on African deficiency and degeneracy in his widely cited book of natural history, *Notes on the State of Virginia*. The history of black critique of *Notes* began with Benjamin Banneker's rejoinder to Jefferson's racial theories in both his 1791 correspondence with Jefferson and his own almanacs. Banneker inaugurated a tradition of critiquing, revising, and appropriating *Notes* that shaped black writing into the mid-nineteenth century. Turning to black ethnology—texts by African Americans that explore the origin, history, and ancestry of African and Afro-diasporic peoples—Chapter 1 surveys the rich responses to Jefferson's *Notes* from across the antebellum black print sphere, including David Walker's pamphlet *Appeal to the Coloured Citizens of the World* (1829), James W. C. Pennington's *A Text Book of the Origin and History, &c. &c. of the Colored People* (1841), and James McCune Smith's 1859 essays on *Notes* in the *Anglo-African Magazine*. Together with the widespread memorializing of Banneker by African Americans in the period, black responses to Jefferson carried Banneker's legacy into the nineteenth century, claiming him as the founder of a rich scientific age among black practitioners and writers of science. While writers like Walker, Pennington, and McCune Smith crafted sophisticated and varied responses to Jefferson, they nonetheless presented *Notes* as an important object of study and research. Walker viewed *Notes* as an extremely dangerous book that nonetheless should be put in the hands of each and every "son" in the black community (the question of black women readers and practitioners of natural history is taken up in Chapter 5). This ambivalence toward Jefferson and his text also captures fugitive science's complicated relationship to racial science across the decades of the antebellum era.

Chapter 2 continues to investigate the interventions and complexities of ethnologies produced by people of African descent, a body of writing that used the Bible, ancient and modern history, and proto-evolutionary discourses to respond to emerging regimes of racist ethnology and the denigration of blackness in popular culture more broadly. Chapter 2 focuses on how Black and Afro-Native ethnologies of the 1830s and early 1840s resisted the visual cultures of racist science and popular print. Where US ethnology as well as forms of antebellum visual culture, especially political cartoons and minstrelsy, sought to tether black bodies to the scientific knowledge of race through the field of the visual—showing how inferiority was marked on bodies and visible to the naked eye—the ethnologies of Robert Benjamin Lewis, Hosea Easton, and James W. C. Pennington produced ekphrastic re-visions of the Black, Native American, and Afro-Native body.

Taking a cue from such bold refusals of racist visual regimes, this book does not reproduce the visual sources of nineteenth-century race science, including the notorious images of ape-like physiognomies in *Types of Mankind* and the images of Sarah Baartman, the so-called Hottentot Venus, which circulated widely in the transatlantic press in the period. Rather, I replace the visual archive of racist science and its adjoining representations in popular culture with a series of what Shawn Michelle Smith calls "counterarchives."[61] For example, Chapter 2 considers antebellum black portraiture and ekphrastic writing as critical modes of resistance to the crude visual taxonomies and typologies of ethnology. At times, my decision not to reproduce images from racist science may prove inconvenient. However, I contend that this inconvenience is important as is the experience of having such images withheld from view. This strategy of *not visualizing* blackness is mirrored in black women's refusal to represent their bodies in the friendship albums I discuss in Chapter 5.[62] Finally, the discussion of visual images without their actual representation parallels the text-rich, image-poor context of the black antebellum print sphere, which deployed techniques of ekphrasis to attend to the visual in and through text. The ekphrastic dimensions of black ethnology are further explored in Chapter 2.

While historical images of racist science might be harnessed in a project of "remembering history so we don't repeat it," the historical violences of forced visibility must be also remembered. Saidiya Hartman and Christina Sharpe have both sounded warnings about the reproduction of scenes of black suffering and misery, scenes that reproduce racialized violences of the past, but also feed into (neo)liberal logics that traffic in the spectacle of suffering black subjects.[63] Moreover, the seemingly endless reproduction of race science's iconic images across different forms of printed (and today, digital) media points to the dangers of reproducing a visual archive that has itself helped to disseminate racial science across space and time.

Since racist science has long benefited from its dissemination through the reproduction of its most memorable images, this study presents an alternative visual archive of black-produced images and ekphrastic texts. At the same time, it follows Jasmine Nichole Cobb's argument that invisibility is both part of the social condition of blackness in modernity as well as an important representational tactic for people of African descent.[64] Chapter 2 explores that dialectic of calculated visibility and strategic invisibility as it shapes black ethnology's theorization of the visual in and against race science. Chapter 3 considers another counterarchive deeply rooted in acts of strategic visibility and opacity as it traces the embodied movements of black performers who challenged racial science's restriction of blackness to the biological body. Turning to the history of fugitive science in transatlantic performance, this chapter maps a critical genealogy of overlap and exchange between popular scientific lecture circuits and early black performance in both the United States and Great Britain from the 1830s through the 1850s. This chapter rethinks the history of racial science through the lens of performance, chronicling how Frederick Douglass, William Wells Brown, William and

Ellen Craft, and Henry Box Brown countered the widespread circulation of racist science in popular entertainment and print culture through dynamic performances of fugitive science in transatlantic spaces. Here, fugitive science marks the productive eccentricity of anti-racist sciences and their sometimes surprising connection to other forms of black cultural production, including music, performance and drama, as well as their movement across national boundaries.

The itinerancies and transatlantic movements of fugitive science foregrounded in Chapter 3 also inform Chapter 4's treatment of Martin Delany's serial novel, *Blake; or, The Huts of America* (1859–1862). That chapter rethinks Martin Delany's *Blake* by constelling the text with the many scientific fields with which Delany engaged in his fiction, nonfiction, and lectures. In addition to attending medical school for a short time, lecturing on scientific topics, leading a scientific expedition to West Africa, and presenting at the International Statistics Congress in London, Delany also published essays on astronomy that appeared next to installments of his similarly "cosmic" fiction, *Blake*, in the *Anglo-African Magazine*. Delany's substantive engagements with natural science offer new and exciting ways to think about *Blake*. Chapter 4 casts *Blake* as a deeply experimental, highly ambitious, speculative fiction, a proto–science fiction that challenged the impoverished conception of the human found in both racial science and writings by white abolitionists. While scholars have rightly delineated the novel's complex mapping of transnational spaces, the novel also forwards a truly grandiose vision of fugitivity, a cosmic and existential model that not only spans the US South and Cuba, but stretches across the globe and galaxy.

If Chapter 3 and Chapter 4 reveal the history of fugitive science through alternatively spectacular and furtive forms of movement, the fifth and final chapter explores the forms of fugitive science practiced by black women in the tight spaces of the parlor and the classroom. This chapter introduces the life and work of the African American educator, activist, poet, scientific lecturer, and Quaker, Sarah Mapps Douglass. Douglass's work beautifully represents the kinds of scientific and literary cross-fertilizations that are at the heart of this book: she taught both literature and science in the Female Preparatory Department of the Institute for Colored Youth in Philadelphia, contributed natural history discourses and paintings to the friendship albums of her friends and students, published poetry in abolitionist publications, and traveled as a lecturer on physiology and anatomy. In addition to surveying her scientific work in the semi-private space of the black classroom and parlor, Chapter 5 considers how her lectures on physiology for audiences of black women opposed the public staging of black women's supposed biological inferiority in various forms of scientific and popular spectacle. While Douglass has been situated primarily in the context of Philadelphia's vibrant community of the "black elite," this chapter speculatively places her in a more Atlantic context in order to connect her teaching, body, and performances to the global networks of race science and to figures like Joice Heth, Sarah Baartman, and other black women whose persons were subjected to various experiments, scientific and otherwise.[65]

While diverse sources and archives are explored throughout this book, it is the *Anglo-African Magazine* that perhaps best captures the spirit, force, and eclecticism of fugitive science. The *Anglo-African Magazine* (1859) was a short-lived, though extremely important early African American periodical: published monthly, it was founded and edited by Thomas Hamilton, an African American printer, book-seller, and newspaper man whose office was located in the heart of New York's printing district in Lower Manhattan. While scholars have culled the pages of the *Anglo-African* for some of the period's earliest works of African American fiction and poetry, the *Anglo-African* was by no means focused on literature: intended as a high-brow intellectual magazine for African Americans, it included contributions from well-known black intellectuals, activists, educators, and theologians on statistics, history, philosophy, and diverse inquiries into natural science. The *Anglo-African Magazine* has served as an ongoing form of inspiration for this study, and many of the figures addressed in the subsequent chapters contributed to this periodical: the first chapters of Martin Delany's *Blake* were serialized there alongside Delany's and George Vashon's essays on astronomy; James Pennington's essay on the slave trade in the *Anglo-African* incorporates ethnological theories on the origin and descent of the races; James McCune Smith's essays on Jefferson's *Notes on the State of Virginia* were published in the magazine; and even Philadelphia's Sarah Mapps Douglass contributed a short essay on education, a publication likely arranged while Douglass was in New York City lecturing on anatomy and physiology.[66]

At the same time as the *Anglo-African* represents the culmination of scientific writing in antebellum black intellectual culture, it also reflects some of the limits of excavating fugitive science through the productions of the period's most prominent black intellectuals in the urban Northeast. Returning to the case of St. Philip's craniologist-sexton with which I opened this introduction further illuminates this critical and archival lacuna. Abdy's account of the sexton humbly working with and in proximity to corpses in the cemetery suggests a rich history of black workers, free and enslaved, engaging with natural science and medicine, though the sources for this history are less likely to be found in newspapers, books, organizational records, letters, and other print and manuscript materials. Even this account of the black craniologist comes from a white-authored narrative, rather than from the sexton himself, a fact that points to the difficulty of recovering the vernacular dimensions of fugitive science in the nineteenth century. The sexton's laugh, then, as an act that exceeds and escapes Abdy's disciplining of black expertise and knowledge, might also stand in for the histories of fugitive science that did not find their way into books, newspapers, images, performance records, and other forms of historical documentation. Indeed, we can imagine the many jokes, comments, and conversations about the dubious character of racial science that surely occurred in church, at the dinner table, on the front step, or even in the field, but were not recorded in the archives of antebellum black life.

In addition to chronicling the vibrant engagements with natural history among well-educated and well-known African Americans—those with access to books, printing presses, stages, and podiums—*Fugitive Science* meditates on moments like the sexton's laugh in order to point to a more ephemeral, elusive history: a vernacular, perhaps doubly fugitive science. This underbelly of fugitive science—the science of the enslaved and the working poor—was also present at St. Philip's church, which was governed by New York's most prominent African American community but included members of the black working class among its congregants. Indeed, St. Philip's bore many connections to the history of fugitive science: James McCune Smith was a church member and leader; church minister, Peter Williams, was one of the founders of *Freedom's*

Journal; his daughter was Amy Williams Cassey, the anti-slavery activist, friendship book author, and friend to Sarah Mapps Douglass, whom I discuss in Chapter 5. In addition to their religious education, the elite members of St. Philip's routinely displayed learning and knowledge of natural science which they put to use in various scientific, social, and political settings. The church membership of this group also marks the interanimation of natural science and religion in black communities in the period. But outside the doors of St. Philip's, and somewhat removed from the community of the elite members of the congregation, the sexton—in communion with the deceased bodies of the congregation—also practiced his own form of fugitive science.

The figure of St. Philip's sexton further illuminates some of the key antagonisms that divided the so-called black elite from both the black working poor and enslaved people, a dynamic that will occasionally come to the fore in the following chapters. Of course, free-born people regularly articulated their solidarity with slaves, especially since slavery limited black freedom in the North and many free African Americans had relatives and acquaintances still held in slavery. Black activists in the North organized on their own behalf, but also fought for the cause of slaves down South. And yet, important antagonisms between these groups nonetheless persisted in forms of tension and difference that cannot be resolved through recourse to homogenizing narratives about black solidarity, agency, or resistance. Formerly enslaved activists like Frederick Douglass, William Wells Brown, and Henry Box Brown routinely pointed to the fact that they were born slaves in order to, among other things, mark their *difference* from those who were one or more generation away from slavery. Freedom in the North was an attenuated condition, to be sure, but it was clearly superior to the experience of chattel slavery.

Some of these antagonisms are registered in the records of fugitive science. For example, an installment of McCune Smith's "Heads of the Colored People" series parodies the very same sexton who appears in Abdy's account of his visit to St. Philip's Church. But while Abdy narrates a presumably benign trick that the sexton played on a white physician, McCune Smith casts the sexton in a much more sinister role, portraying him not as a respectable protector of the community's departed, but rather as a horrible, profit-driven man who carelessly packed deceased parishioners into the graveyard, sold them to the tallow factory next door when he ran out of room, and was even discovered to be feasting on the remains of the bodies put under his care before he was run out of town by church members.[67] Here, the sexton is transformed into a dangerous, maniacal member of the black underclass, a terrifying figure who also enables McCune Smith to experiment with both horror and the gothic, genres with deep roots in New York literature, from Washington Irving's gothic sketches to the supernatural stories that ran in *Freedom's Journal*, the first black newspaper published in the United States.[68] As a writer who was constantly experimenting with different writing styles and genres, McCune Smith ultimately capitalized on the sexton's tale as an opportunity for both ethnographic and literary innovation.

McCune Smith's characterization of the sexton as a dangerous, gothic protagonist also registers the antagonisms that existed between St. Philip's elite black leaders and the laborers in and at the fringes of the church's congregation. It further suggests the threat posed by knowledges and experiments undertaken outside of universities, laboratories, and other legitimated spaces of scientific learning and experimentation. Fascinatingly, both Abdy's and McCune Smith's accounts express anxieties about experimental science produced outside of institutions of scientific authority. McCune Smith's account also raises the horrifying possibility that black amateur scientists could exploit and abuse members of their own community. Were there differences between black and white uses of corpses in the pursuit of science? And did it matter if those experiments were conducted in a graveyard rather than in a laboratory or medical school? An answer of "no" to either of these questions posed serious problems for McCune Smith, who operated his own medical practice and pharmacy in the city, not too far from the sexton's graveyard laboratory.

While it is not this book's task to deliberate over questions about medical ethics in the nineteenth century, it does follow how practitioners of fugitive science negotiated the boundaries of scientific authority, legitimacy, and professionalization. Black intellectuals and university-trained physicians like McCune Smith and Martin Delany sometimes reinforced the class- and education-based demarcations that sought to exclude amateur and folk practitioners from the ranks of science and medicine. In the installment of the "Heads of the Colored People" series in which the sexton emerges as a Dr. Frankenstein-like figure, ensconced in the gothic aesthetic that also characterizes Mary Shelley's narrative, McCune Smith ultimately falls back on his own professional training to establish the difference between his own clinical work and the autodidactic forms of science and medicine practiced in the community. These included the practices of black women who worked as healers in the city and competed with McCune Smith's own practice. He also uses the periodical sketch to separate the sexton's profligate abuses of black bodies from his own clinical investigations into race, disease, and illness, investigations that took shape through observations on his patients.

Although forms of working-class and enslaved science are not always the focus of my study, I hope they remain in the reader's mind throughout, along with the qualification that the print archive does not always capture scientific activity in everyday contexts. Thus, the scientific practices of working free people up North and enslaved people down South should be thought of as "shadow archives" for the forms of fugitive science chronicled in what follows: James McCune Smith's writings on coral insects shadowed by enslaved conchologists in coastal regions of the South; Sarah Mapps Douglass's natural history cabinet shadowed by enslaved collectors of natural history specimens; the earliest professionally trained black doctors shadowed by generations of enslaved healers in the Americas; both McCune Smith's and Mapps Douglass's "legitimate" experiments with bodies and bones shadowed by St. Philip's sexton's apparently abusive experiments with the dead.[69] In other cases, the experiences of enslavement and escape fomented scientific interest and learning. Henry Box Brown's work as an enslaved "tobacconist" in a Virginia tobacco factory helped him to connect his experience to that of cotton mill workers in northwest England and to the forms of science that were popular among Britain's working class. James W. C. Pennington talked about how his use of the North Star to guide his escape from slavery sparked his interest in studying astronomy once he was settled in the North. These shadow archives, which are also the fragmented, fractured archives of enslavement and racial dispossession, stand behind and often animate this study's account of fugitive science practiced by nominally free people in the United States and across the Atlantic World.

1

The Banneker Age

Black Afterlives of Early National Science

In many ways, Thomas Jefferson's *Notes on the State of Virginia* (1785, 1787) is the ur-text against which fugitive science defined itself in the early national and antebellum periods. Jefferson's *Notes* served as the touchstone for anti-racist science stretching from Benjamin Banneker's correspondence with Jefferson in 1791 to James McCune Smith's formative essay "On the Fourteenth Query of Thomas Jefferson's Notes on Virginia" in 1859.[1] Gene Andrew Jarrett argues that *Notes* is the founding text of a rich political genealogy of African American literature.[2] Henry Louis Gates, Jr., has long argued that early African American writing took shape as a refutation of Jefferson's claims about African inferiority and that *Notes* also loomed large over the criticism of early black writing.[3] This chapter shows that *Notes* also served as the "founding text" for a vibrant genealogy of black scientific discourse in the United States, which, like the political history of early African American literature, sought to wrench science and philosophy from white supremacists and slavery apologists in order to "represent the race"[4] on different terms. I place this genealogy of black writing on *Notes* in an extended early national period to bring attention to a history of black engagements with Jefferson and Jeffersonian science that persisted from the 1790s until the eve of the Civil War. Indeed, from its continued engagement with Jeffersonian science to its ongoing commitments to climatic, monogenetic theories of evolution in the face of the rise of American polygenesis, early national science was kept alive in a somewhat surprising place—namely, antebellum black culture.[5] Eighteenth-century theories about the flexible and changeable nature of race—what Katy Chiles calls "transformable race"—while not without their own problems, were clearly superior to polygenetic theories that sought to, in Frederick Douglass's words, echoing David Walker, "read the negro out of the human family."[6] The perceived need among African Americans to continue fighting against *Notes* long after its publication speaks to both the cultural power of this text and the ways that Jefferson's theories, while somewhat idiosyncratic in the 1780s, found an ally in the American school of ethnology's enthusiasm for polygenesis and the pro-colonization debates of the nineteenth century. Paradoxically, Jefferson's black interlocutors were also at least partly responsible for keeping *Notes* alive into the antebellum period. But rather than preserving *Notes* as a sacrosanct founding document, black writers mobilized *Notes* as an object of critique and as a continual impetus to engage in what Fred Moten and Stefano Harney call "black study."[7]

This chapter draws attention to black writing that took aim at Jeffersonian science across several decades, particularly the sophisticated and sometimes surprising interventions of James McCune Smith. McCune Smith's stunningly artful writing on science and medicine also stands as an exemplar of the consistent creativity and occasional eccentricity of fugitive science. While some African American responses to *Notes* took the form of essays, letters, and pamphlets, black writers also turned to the genre of ethnology itself to rewrite Jefferson's ethnological theories of race in his natural history of Virginia. This chapter thus begins a two-chapter focus on the complex ways that black intellectuals responded to American ethnology and crafted their own ethnological texts. In broad terms, ethnology is the natural history of the human race, a subfield of natural history devoted to the classification of humans rather than nonhuman fauna and flora. Nineteenth-century ethnology was connected to the origins of anthropology, but it did not rely on the sustained empirical observation of specific groups and cultures to ground its claims. In this way, ethnology is much more theoretical—discussing the groupings of people in various climates in broad strokes—than the ethnographic mode found, for example, in Darwin's detailed description of various peoples and tribes in Latin America, Africa, and the Pacific in *Voyage of the Beagle* (1839).[8] This first chapter includes treatment of black ethnologies whenever they explicitly responded to Jefferson's *Notes*. In the next chapter, I delve into ethnology more deeply to explore how this hybrid genre enabled rich speculative theorizations of kinship as well as a means through which black writers challenged the visual evidence of race science. The discussion below of James W. C. Pennington's efforts to reconstruct the lines of kinship denied by Jefferson, who linked Africans to apes rather than to other humans, also serves as a bridge to Chapter 2's more sustained focus on speculative kinship in black ethnology.

Jefferson's *Notes* holds a complicated place in early African American culture. While antebellum black newspapers routinely lambasted Jefferson for his damaging comments on African inferiority, contributors were just as likely to cull *Notes* for remarks on the despotism of slavery and the eventual inevitability of "total emancipation" for the enslaved, thus making Jefferson an unlikely prophet for the coming of abolition.[9] More broadly, Jefferson was an important figure for black activists and writers because he embodied the contradictions that lay at the heart of the American republic: the author of the Declaration of Independence, a document that insisted on the injustices of American "enslavement" to the British crown, he was at the same time among the founding fathers who maintained their positions as slaveholders. A fierce critic of black equality, he took one of his slaves, Sally Hemings, as a concubine and manumitted the children she had for/with him. In this way, Jefferson stood in for the hypocrisy of American democracy, of a freedom-loving nation that kept people in chains.

At the same time as black intellectuals like David Walker, James W. C. Pennington, and James McCune Smith crafted critiques of *Notes on the State of Virginia*, they also presented themselves as heirs to Jefferson's scientific legacy. While the Jefferson as "father" trope is hard to shake in the history of fugitive science, this chapter suggests that the black afterlives of early national science might be also understood as a rich inheritance from Benjamin Banneker, who was also being widely cited and memorialized by African Americans in the antebellum period. In an 1837 issue of the *Colored American* that reprinted Banneker's famous letter to Jefferson under the title "Slander Refuted," a subsequent editorial note celebrates Banneker's contributions, saying that his letter is "worthy the age of Washington, of Jefferson, of Adams and of Franklin—AND WE ADD OF BANNEKER."[10] From the many recirculations of Banneker's letter to a rich genealogy of black responses to *Notes* that built on and extended Banneker's critique of Jefferson, African Americans in the antebellum period imagined a new scientific era: the Banneker Age.

Beginning in the early nineteenth century, African Americans took Banneker's limited archive and began contributing to it. Such nineteenth-century contributions to the Banneker archive—a type of retrospective, but also supplemental archive—might be understood as a form of archival redress that also inaugurated a vibrant history of black science writing in the antebellum period.[11] The diachronic approach to the Banneker archive in this chapter, one that is attentive to the black afterlives of early national science as well as the robust antebellum memorializations of Banneker, also invites new stories about Banneker himself, both within and beyond the Banneker-Jefferson exchange.

Jefferson, Banneker, and the Origins of Fugitive Science

The history of African American science before the Civil War often begins and ends with Benjamin Banneker. And yet, documentation surrounding the life and work of the most important black American man of science in the eighteenth century is quite scarce: he is, at this point, a well-known figure about whom we know relatively little. Existing artifacts and documents, including Banneker's famous almanacs, the wooden clock he constructed, and his carefully crafted letter to Jefferson, all remain important and rich resources, but the lack of additional original sources points to the fact that the silences and gaps that define the archive of slavery are also constitutive of the archives of nominal freedom. The slimness of the Banneker archive further points to the elusiveness of African American science in the eighteenth century, a science that clearly existed in many vernacular forms, ranging from the practice of enslaved healers on Southern plantations to the maritime science practiced by black sailors, but had not yet been captured by an emerging print sphere.

Some of what is known amounts to this: Banneker, the Baltimore County, Maryland, freeman, tobacco farmer, astronomer, surveyor, and polymath answered Thomas Jefferson's skepticism about the intellectual capabilities of the African race in *Notes* by sending Jefferson a copy of his recently prepared almanac in manuscript, accompanied by a letter.[12] The letter also petitions Jefferson, then Secretary of State, to end his silence on the slavery question and to take up the cause of the country's black population in earnest. Banneker addresses Jefferson as a friend to "those of my complexion," a comrade to the cause against the censure and abuse of black people, but then proceeds to boldly embed his own response to Jefferson's Query XIV within the niceties and formalities of the eighteenth-century letter. In Query XIV of *Notes*, that most incendiary section of an otherwise uncontroversial text of natural history, Jefferson famously argued that blacks were inferior to whites in reason and seemed to completely lack imagination. Citing the poetry of "Phyllis Whately" and the letters of Ignatius Sancho, he notes that while Native Americans naturally produce works of art that display their capacity for reason and imagination, the Africans have shown no such examples. He writes, "But never yet could I find that a black had uttered a thought above the level of plain narration; never see even an elementary trait of painting or sculpture." According to Jefferson, peoples of African descent lacked the ability to elevate sensation into sentiment and to sublimate desire into love: "They are more ardent after their female: but love seems with them to be more an eager desire, than a tender delicate mixture of sentiment and sensation."[13] These views are presented in order to forward Jefferson's primary hypothesis in this section of the text: as beings of sensation, not sense and reason, the enslaved masses were unfit for self-government and could not be trusted to bear the responsibilities of freedom. This, perhaps unsurprisingly, was the central argument against which African American interlocutors built evidence and crafted their own arguments.

In response to Jefferson's comments on the "distinctions" of nature that seemed to define the human race, as they did in the entire animal kingdom, Banneker's letter reminds Jefferson of something with which he, as a Christian, must certainly agree: that our "one universal Father hath given being to us all, and that he hath not only made us all of one flesh, but that he hath also without partiality afforded us all the same sensations, and end[ow]ed us all with the same faculties, and that however variable we may be in society or religion, however diversifyed in situation or colour, we are all of the same family, and stand in the same relation to him."[14] Undercutting his opening address of Jefferson as a "friend," a later clause asks Jefferson to "wean" himself from his anti-black prejudice. Banneker also answered Jefferson's comments on black difference and inferiority. In Query XIV, Jefferson famously requested further evidence of black intelligence, and Banneker sent the almanac as

such a "proof." It is further likely that Banneker was responding specifically to Jefferson's comment in *Notes* that "one [African] could scarcely
be found capable of tracing and comprehending the investigations of
Euclid."[15] Here, Banneker suggested, and the almanac proved, was one
who could. In response to Jefferson's glib comment that he simply could
not find an African endowed with the capacities for reason and imagination, Banneker urged him to look harder.

Since scholars have often returned to the same set of documents to
recover Banneker's contributions, the archive seems to reproduce the
same story about Banneker, again and again. The Banneker archive, in
this way, fits with Michel Foucault's understanding of the archive as first,
a "law" that determines and limits what can be said, a discursive system
that establishes its own rules of enunciability.[16] For Foucault, the *possibility* of the archive is the fact that its discourses have just "ceased to
be ours": "its threshold of existence is established by the discontinuity
that separates us from what we can no longer say, and from that which
falls outside our discursive practice; it begins with the outside of our
own language."[17] As an encounter with difference rather than identity,
discontinuity rather than continuity, this is where the possibility of the
archive resides. The Banneker-Jefferson encounter has been rehearsed
and restaged, often at the expense of other narratives. "At once close
to us, and different from our present existence,"[18] the task here is to
see what other stories might be told beyond the archive's already au-
thorized statements and how antebellum black interlocutors themselves
approached the Banneker archive from their own historical position,
just on the other side of that archive's discursive practice and language.

In her biographical sketch of Banneker from 1854, Martha Ellicott
Tyson, the daughter of Banneker's Quaker benefactor and collaborator
Andrew Ellicott, notes that Banneker would frequently receive mathematical problems from scholars across the country who wanted to test
his intellectual capacities.[19] According to Tyson, Banneker would never
fail to return a correct solution, and his answers were often accompanied
by additional "questions of his own composition composed in rhyme."
Tyson includes one such rhyme drawn from the memory of one of the
"first agriculturalists in our state," a man who "enjoyed many opportunities of seeing Banneker" in his youth: "Now, my worthy friend, find out
if you can / The vessel's dimensions, and comfort the man."[20] Tyson also

refers to a "poetical letter," in rhymed verse, that Banneker received from a woman named Susanna Mason. The poem circulated through local newspapers and in response to Mason's encomium, Banneker penned an apologetic letter a year later stating that he was sorry he had been too ill to "gratify your curiosity" with one his poems.[21] These elliptical, yet provocative comments from Tyson's biographical sketch reveal that Banneker's scientific writing was embedded in a network of poetic composition and letter exchange with white women, as well as the circulation of mathematical problems and answers in verse with white men.[22] A 1791 letter from Andrew Ellicott's son Elias to James Pemberton, president of the Pennsylvania Abolition Slavery, also includes a set of "Lines by B. Banneker":

> Behold ye Christians! And in pity see
> Those Afric sons which nature formed free
> Behold them in a fruitful country blest,
> Of nature's bounties see them rich possest.
> Behold them here from torn by cruel force,
> And doomed to slavery without remorse.
> This act America, thy sons have known–
> This cruel act remorseless they have done.[23]

This short poem echoes Phillis Wheatley's 1773 "To the Right Honourable WILLIAM, Earl of Dartmouth" ("I, young in life, by seeming cruel fate / Was snatch'd from *Afric's* fancy'd happy seat") as well as other abolitionist poems of the period that contrasted the happy, bucolic lives of Africans in their native home with the miserable situation of African captives in America.

While the abolitionist framing of Banneker illuminates the connection between his scientific learning and the Quaker education he received alongside the paternal guidance of the male members of the Ellicott family, scholars have recently emphasized Banneker's autodidacticism as well as his likely inheritance of knowledge on astronomy from his African grandfather and other family members. Evidence suggests that Banneker's paternal grandfather came from the Wolof in Senegal or the Dogon in Mali. Both ethnic groups were known for their expertise in astronomy and numerology.[24] Into the late eighteenth century, African scientific knowledge—especially in astronomy, mathematics, and agriculture—continued to shape black scientific thought and practice in the Americas.[25]

Beyond family and local history in Maryland, Banneker largely disappeared from the radar of white America after his death in 1804. However, his legacy was kept alive in black print and oral culture throughout the early decades of the nineteenth century and on into the second half of the century. Beyond the recirculations of Banneker's actual letter, his legacy is perhaps most apparent in the ongoing engagement with *Notes on the State of Virginia* in early African American writing. From the 1820s to the eve of the Civil War, the African American print sphere produced sophisticated and artful responses to Jefferson's theories of race, slavery, and the problem of freedom. Other book-length publications, including William Wells Brown's 1863 study of black biography, history, and ethnology, *The Black Man: His Antecedents, His Genius, and His Achievements*, reprinted the 1791 letter exchange between Banneker and Jefferson and contained a lengthy biography of Banneker. Brown's 1853 novel *Clotel; or, The President's Daughter*, indirectly critiqued Jefferson's hypocrisy in *Notes* by further circulating the rumors about Jefferson's relationship to Sally Hemings. Other works drew on these details about Jefferson's personal life to strengthen more analytical critiques of his devaluation of blackness in *Notes*. Rather than reproducing a world in which Banneker can only ever speak to Jefferson (and a world in which Jefferson bothers to respond with only a formulaic one-paragraph letter), the rest of this chapter places Banneker in dialog with black writers who, in speaking back to Jefferson's "suspicions" about black inferiority in *Notes*, carried Banneker's voice into the antebellum period and beyond. The black afterlives of early national science, from Walker and Pennington to McCune Smith, made important supplemental contributions to the original Banneker archive.

David Walker was one of the first contributors to the Banneker archive in the nineteenth century. Walker's extended treatment of *Notes* appeared in his 1829 *Appeal to the Coloured Citizens of the World*, a pamphlet that came out in three editions and circulated across the North, as well as among enslaved people who obtained copies smuggled into Southern ports by sailors and other agents.[26] A black millennialist tract that sets out to establish the wretched condition of black people under the domination of hypocritical whites in America who call themselves Christians, Walker's *Appeal* insists that the mistreatment of Africans in the Americas far exceeds anything the world has ever seen before. Contrasting contemporary slavery with ancient systems of bondage, Walker was already anticipating twentieth-century scholarship that argued New World slavery ushered in modernity through its sheer scale, brutality, and race-based system of enslavement.[27] The *Appeal* doubles as a warning to white Americans to abolish slavery or expect violent retribution from God and from the dispossessed people they hold in chains. Walker promotes black action throughout his pamphlet, but he also has a vested interest in the slower revolutionary activities of reading, thinking, and writing, arguing that the political liberation of black people, both enslaved and nominally free, will ultimately hinge on their intellectual emancipation.

Drawing from the Bible as well as both classical and contemporary histories, Walker's part-history, part-ethnology, part-jeremiad also directly takes up Thomas Jefferson's arguments about the African race in *Notes*. Walker considered *Notes* a sacrilegious work that defied the Word of God by excluding the African race from the "human family," a formulation that anticipates Douglass's condemnation of Samuel George Morton and his followers on similar grounds in his "Claims of the Negro" speech in 1854.[28] To Walker's mind, *Notes* was an extremely dangerous text: far from seeing it as a rarified Enlightenment vanity project with little to no popular effect, Walker argued that Jefferson's words were "swallowed by millions of the whites" and were as "great a barrier to our emancipation as any thing that has ever been advanced against us."[29]

Although Walker vehemently rejects Jefferson's arguments on scientific, historical, and religious grounds, he nonetheless insists that it remains an important object for freed and enslaved peoples to wrestle with in their struggles against white supremacy. Again and again, Walker tells his readers that they ignore Jefferson's *Notes* at their own peril. This was a text that deserved a black response in action as well as writing: "For my own part, I am glad Mr. Jefferson has advanced his positions for your sake; for you will either have to contradict or confirm him by your own actions, and not by what our [white] friends have said or done for us."[30] In one of the most striking moments in a text filled with surprises, Walker notes that every black man in the United States should "buy a copy of Mr. Jefferson's 'Notes on Virginia,' and put it in the hand[s] of his son." Walker argues that while a number of sympathetic whites had ably refuted Jefferson's claims about race, this was not enough: a full-scale critique of Jeffersonian science must, in his terms, "emanate from the blacks."[31] This treatment of Notes not just as object of critique, but as fodder for black thought is part of Walker's larger focus on research and black history throughout the text. The Appeal is a zealous and impassioned call for action, but it is also a call for careful and sustained study. Just as Walker secretly disseminated the Appeal throughout the South to be used as a tool, and a weapon, by enslaved people, so did he see Notes, that most influential text of scientific racism and ongoing impediment to emancipation, as a tool to be mobilized in both the thought and practice of emancipation. Here, Walker's text serves as a reminder that early African American freedom struggles were waged on the terrain of black thought. More than merely serving as a "proof" of black intelligence for white readers, the Appeal records an ongoing struggle to be allowed to read, reflect, and write—to engage in the revolutionary act of study.[32]

References to Jefferson's Notes abound in Walker's Appeal, both in extended exegeses of excerpted quotations and in quick asides. Threaded into the very structure of the text, Notes was, next to the Bible, Walker's most important source-text for his Appeal. Jefferson also penned another key source-text for Walker: the Declaration of Independence.[33] In Article III, Walker discusses the sad state of education among young black men in the country, insisting that superficial forms of schooling that privileged fancy penmanship over a solid knowledge of grammar needed to be replaced by an intellectually robust curriculum. If Walker occupies the roles of historian and preacher, as well as of teacher, the Appeal itself doubles as a primer that models the kind of reading and analysis that Walker expected his "brethren" to bring to Jefferson's Notes and other works. While the section on education focuses on the education of young men, other moments in the text hail an audience of black women as well as children. Throughout, Walker's sermonic text makes its oratorical roots visible while indicating an awareness that some of his audience—including slaves in the South—would hear rather than read the Appeal. For example, one bracketed sentence introduces a passage from Notes with this performatively sermonic and pedagogical direction from the author: "[Here, my brethren, listen to him]."³⁴ His opening note recommends that all black people should either read the *Appeal* or find someone to read it to them. In preacherly, and admittedly preachy, moments such as these, Walker suggests that Jefferson's black critics might also include slaves and working people in the North. It is also likely that Walker thought his own *Appeal* would serve, for some readers and listeners, as their first and only introduction to *Notes* itself. Thus, Walker's inclusion of relevant passages from *Notes* also helped to circulate Jefferson's *Notes* among black communities in the North and South.

Walker's "gladness" at the existence of *Notes*, insofar as that nasty work provided a motivation for black people to raise themselves up and prove Jefferson wrong, also suggests something of the complexity of Walker's own relationship to *Notes*. Despite his outrage at Jefferson's theories, it is clear that *Notes* heavily influenced Walker's thinking and shaped his writing. Walker also signifies on Jefferson's language and rhetoric throughout the *Appeal*, in an echoing of Query XIV that registers Walker's careful study of Jefferson's text. At the same time as Walker absorbs Jefferson's rhetoric and style into the *Appeal*, he establishes a critical distance from Jefferson through his own rhetorical style, rooted in satire and wit. Indeed, in the moments when Walker directly signifies on Jefferson's language, he often does so to mock the founding father. For example, riffing on Jefferson's statement in Query XIV that he advances the idea of black inferiority "as a suspicion only," Walker, ventriloquizing and reversing Jefferson's rhetoric, writes: "I advance my suspicion of them [white people], whether they are *as good by nature as we are* or not."³⁵ Satirizing Jefferson's advancement of a racist position while claiming that such a view is simply an innocent "suspicion," Walker's reversal indicates that, suspicion or not, Jefferson's speculations had real and damaging effects on black people in the world.

Satirical and irreverent attitudes toward Jefferson were a powerful tool in the ongoing fight against *Notes* in the antebellum period. Such irreverence also characterized James W. C. Pennington's writings on Jefferson, discussed in more detail below. An 1852 critic of *Notes* in *Frederick Douglass' Paper* prefaced a reproduction of Banneker's letter to Jefferson with a wry note that the "colonizationists have recently dug up Jefferson, for the two-fold purpose of helping them berate African intellect" and "to aid [c]olonization."³⁶ This irreverent image of digging up a founding father who had encouraged comparative anatomists to take their knives to black bodies took on a particular force in an age when the bodies of African Americans were pillaged from cemeteries and plantations for scientific experimentation and medical training.[37] Across the antebellum period, black writers effectively turned Jefferson into an anatomical specimen of their own.

Throughout the *Appeal*, Walker resurrects Jefferson in order to mock and shame him, noting, at one point, "Here let me ask Mr. Jefferson, (but he is gone to answer at the bar of God, for the deeds done in his body while living)."[38] And yet, as much as Walker brings a sardonic wit to his treatment of Jefferson, there are moments when his signifying on *Notes* seems to be in earnest, serving as a way to legitimate and forward his own racial theories. For example, Walker's "suspicion" about the natural inferiority of white people appears again and again in the text. And ultimately, it is difficult to shed the sense that Walker may be sincere about the inherent badness of white people, as well as the possibility that Africans are actually God's only chosen people. Here, Walker's racial theories start to take on the form of Jefferson's theories on blackness and whiteness, just in reverse.

Another subtle and surprising bond is forged between Walker and Jefferson in the text through the authority granted through publication itself: Walker thought of his *Appeal* as an important work of philosophy that was worthy of the same recognition and circulation that *Notes* received. While he writes in Article II that all "men of sense" should purchase a copy of *Notes* and put it in the hands of their sons, Walker had already opened his tract with a parallel suggestion: that "all coloured men, women, and children, of every nation, language and tongue under heaven, will try to procure a copy of this Appeal and read it, or get some one to read it for them."[39] As much as Walker despised *Notes*, he hoped that the *Appeal* could stand next to it as a learned publication of broad circulation.

Pennington Takes on the "Jefferson School"

In the 1830s and 1840s, black writers continued to see *Notes on the State of Virginia* not only as an object of critique, but also as an impetus to study. The ongoing presence of *Notes* in antebellum black texts suggests that many people—and not just fathers and sons—purchased, borrowed, and circulated copies of Jefferson's book or read sections of it reprinted in the print sphere. James W. C. Pennington, who published both an ethnology and a slave narrative during the 1840s, levied his own critique against Jefferson while also pointing to a series of black voices surrounding Jefferson's text, a critical chorus that was not anticipated by Jefferson when he penned *Notes*. In this way, antebellum black responses to *Notes* reproduced and amplified the first surprise, and from Jefferson's perspective, shock, of Banneker's letter. Banneker was one of Jefferson's first black readers, but Pennington reminds us that he was far from Jefferson's last.

Pennington was a Congregational minister who later served as a minister of Presbyterian and African Methodist Episcopal Zion (AMEZ) congregations. He served ministries in Connecticut, New York, and late in his life, in Maine, Mississippi, and even Jacksonville, Florida. An antislavery activist, preacher, and lifelong advocate of African American missionary work in Africa, he was born a slave in eastern Maryland, where he worked as a blacksmith and at other forms of skilled labor before running away in 1827 at the age of nineteen. Pennington fled his master's plantation without telling his family, a choice he appears to have questioned for the rest of his life. Perhaps most spectacularly, Pennington's own congregation did not know he was a fugitive who escaped from the South until he disclosed this information in a letter to the church in 1845. In 1849, Pennington turned to the slave narrative form, publishing his autobiography under the title *The Fugitive Blacksmith* while traveling and lecturing in Great Britain.

Pennington published his critique of what he called the "Jefferson School" in his 1841 ethnological account of the African race, *A Text Book of the Origin and History, &c. &c. of the Colored People*. In being denoted as an entire "school" in Pennington's text, Jefferson's theories on blackness and reason in *Notes* come to stand in for a larger body of racist thought that stretches from Jefferson's time to Pennington's own in the 1840s. In other words, Pennington recognizes that Jefferson's ideas about African inferiority were being mobilized by a new generation of antiblack scientists and politicians. Writing in 1841, just two years after the 1839 publication of Samuel George Morton's *Crania Americana*, and during the rise of the American school of ethnology, Pennington's Jefferson comes to the antebellum period filtered through the vitriol and biases of American polygenesis. It may be true that Jefferson advanced his ideas about blackness as a hypothesis only, but this did not stop American ethnologists from transforming Jeffersonian speculations into polygenetic theorems.

In a stunning moment in his *Text Book*, Pennington faults Jefferson for the shortsightedness of his views on the mental capabilities of Africans and their lack of capacity for mental improvement. Writing as a former slave turned educated freeman and clergy member in 1841, Pennington speaks back to Jefferson in 1781: "O that he had reflected for a moment that his opinions were destined to undergo a rigid scrutiny by an improved state of intellect, assisted by the rising power of an unbiased spirit of benevolence."[40] Pennington points out that Jefferson did not expect black interlocutors; had he done so, he most certainly would have "modified that ill judged part of his work which relates to the colored people."[41] Here, Pennington conjures up an alternative "school" to Jefferson's, one that consisted of a cadre of black intellectuals, preachers, performers, and writers who had both the education and the motivation to scrutinize and deconstruct racist thought. In fact, Pennington goes on to juxtapose a rising intellectual class of free African Americans in the North with the degeneration of thought among white slaveholders. Suggesting the corrupting influence of slavery on Jefferson's mind, Pennington reveals *Notes* to be the product of a degenerated intellect. This is a particularly sly critique since Jefferson's goal in the natural history sections of *Notes* was to counter Comte de Buffon's claims about the degenerating effects of the American environment on New World species: in Pennington's view, it is an unnatural cause—slavery, rather than the environment—that is producing American degeneration. While both Walker and James McCune Smith establish some lines of filiation with Jefferson, Pennington refuses any connection with the contemptible founding father.

In the tradition of other black ethnologies, Pennington's *Text Book* sets out to offer a history of the origin and descent of the African race that runs counter to the polygenetic arguments of the 1830s, as well as arguments about black evolutionary degeneracy that had a much longer history in the United States, stretching back to the colonial period. The *Text Book* is a bold and vitriolic text, laced with irony, outrage, and a hefty dose of sarcasm aimed at those, in Pennington's terms, "stupid" advocates of black inferiority who provide dubious readings of scripture and science. In one such moment in the text, Pennington bluntly states, "We are not the seed of Cain as the stupid say."[42] Indeed, Pennington's text is startlingly bold in both its readings of scripture and its political polemic. Throughout the text, slaveholders and pro-slavery agents become the objects of derision and mockery for their attempts to justify slavery through blatant misreadings and gross manipulations of scripture. For example, Pennington argues that since blacks are not Canaanites, as he has proven in his treatise, Southern slaveholders must immediately "discharge the Africans, compensate them for false enslavement, and go and get *Canaanites* [to replace wrongly enslaved Africans]."[43] He is especially critical of comparative anatomy's violent—and fruitless—search for the origins of racial difference in black bodies: recalling the language of Jefferson's call for invasive experimentation in *Notes*, Pennington observes that "anatomists have diven with their fists full of sharp instruments, into the recesses of the human frame to search for the foundation of this curious stream [of thought]."[44] This sentence, which echoes Jefferson's language almost exactly, also serves as a record of Pennington's own reading of *Notes*. Throughout their treatises, both Walker and Pennington used their exegetical skills to carefully read—and dissect—*Notes*, rather than simply criticize or dismiss it in general terms.

Countering the professional and amateur comparative anatomists who wanted to prove the truth of black degeneracy through dissection, the *Text Book* performs a kind of reconstructive work: in the attempt to piece together the long, illustrious history of Africa across the divide of slavery and the slave trade, Pennington builds an archive of the past that could help to mobilize a coherent African American community in the present. In the preface to the *Text Book*, Pennington notes that the book is directed to "families, and to students and lecturers in history" and that its principal aim is to "unembarrass the origin, and to show the relative position of the colored people in the different periods among the different nations."[45] At the beginning of the first chapter, titled "The Vexed and Vexing Question," Pennington laments the absence of a proper historical record for the "colored people": "Every close observer must have seen that we suffer much from the want of a collocation of historical facts so arranged as to present a just view of our origin."[46] The *Text Book* thus sets out to serve as such a record of black origin. Where comparative anatomists and amateur planter scientists dissect blackness, the *Text Book* seeks a path to black re-construction.

This impulse to reconstruct the lines of black kinship back across the Middle Passage may have had something to do with Pennington's own family traumas forged out of the conditions of enslavement—the traumas of being separated from his father upon the sale of his mother and siblings and then reconnected on a whim after the purchase of his father by Pennington's owner, and later, of leaving his own family behind in slavery when he ran away. For Pennington, ethnology thus serves a reparative function of suturing kin in the midst of the displacements of enslavement *and* escape. But it is a highly imaginative and speculative act of reconstructing kinship: separated from his family, and from so many details about his own ancestry, Pennington turns from family genealogy to racial genealogy. Tracing the kinship between African Americans and an illustrious African ancestry, he finds in ethnology and biblical genealogy a language through which to reconstruct speculative lines of African American kinship, alliance, and community.

While much of Pennington's 1849 autobiography, *The Fugitive Blacksmith*, focuses on the details of his escape from Maryland to Pennsylvania, the text is also an extension of the reparative genealogical work he began in his 1841 ethnology. Just as he had opened the *Text Book* with comments on the need for a record of black history, he opens his slave narrative with an extended commentary on the frustrating absence of family records and documentation for the enslaved. In a polemical preface, Pennington rails against the chattel principle of slavery, which he refers to as the "soul and body" of the system. He blames this act of the "transfer of his ownership in himself to another" for destroying the family relation among enslaved people. But the chattel relation does not just destroy families through their separation; it also, crucially, throws "family history into utter confusion."[47] In other words, the chattel principle separates the enslaved not only from their kin, but also from the *records* of their kin. And this absence of family record and documentation is absolutely destructive for one's sense of identity, status, and social worth, leaving "him without a single record to which he may appeal in vindication of his character, or honour. And has a man no sense of honour because he was born a slave? Has he no need of character?"[48] According to Pennington, the slave can locate himself only in the records of the master:

> Suppose insult, reproach, or slander, should render it necessary for him to appeal to the history of his family in vindication of his character, where will he find that history? He goes to his native state, to his native country, to his native town; but nowhere does he find any record of himself *as a man*. On looking at the family record of his old, kind, Christian, master, there he finds his name on a catalogue with the horses, cows, hogs, and dogs. However humiliating and degrading it may be to his feelings to find his name written down among the beasts of the field, *that* is just the place, and the *only* place assigned to it by the chattel relation.[49]

Pennington outlines a series of practical reasons why slaves should be able to locate themselves in their family histories, including being able to defend themselves and vindicate their character in cases of "insult, reproach, or slander." But this longing for the family record is also about a more existential search and confirmation of one's own being: "but nowhere does he find any record of himself *as a man*." Separated from both his kin and the record of his kin, Pennington can find himself only in a record in which he is reduced to kinship with lowly "beasts of the field." Pennington's first chapter tracks the various separations and displacements of his family under the precarious conditions of enslavement. Near the end of his slave narrative, he once again returns to the master's severing of the slave from both his family and his family record, sketching a scene in which the enslaved child's natal alienation is marked by the master's recording of the infant's name in his "barbarous list of chattels personal." Pennington writes, "When I was laid in the cradle, he [the master] came and looked on my face, and wrote down my name upon his barbarous list of chattels personal, on the same list where he registered his horses, hogs, cows, sheep, and even his *dogs!*"[50]

While Pennington's narrative, like most antebellum slave narratives, illuminates the systematic destruction of social relations under slavery, the closing chapters of *The Fugitive Blacksmith*, as well as the Appendix, attempt to put back together his family. He attempts to transform his personal history into a family history, forged out of memories, scraps of evidence, and news learned about his family since his escape in 1827. In this way, Pennington's narrative seeks to reconstruct the familial and historical record destroyed by slavery: it *becomes* that record of family history he seeks at the start of his narrative, and perhaps also sought while crafting his 1841 *Text Book*. Both black ethnology and the slave narrative emerged out of the destruction of black genealogy and kinship wrought by the transatlantic and domestic slave trades. But slave narratives also extended the reparative, and speculative, genealogical work of black ethnology. While ethnologies attempted to reconnect African Americans to their African ancestry back across the Middle Passage, the slave narrative sought more often to repair lines of kinship fractured within the United States. While Pennington's family history includes information about how his father, brothers, and several sisters have found freedom in the years since his own escape, it remains incomplete because of "those members who are yet south of Mason and Dixon's line."[51] The supplemental status of Pennington's Appendix, which includes an 1844 letter addressed to his family, as well as a late chapter that gives "Some Account of the Family I Left in Slavery" and his "Proposal to Purchase Myself and Parents," suggests that Pennington's enslaved family haunts the narrative of his own escape from slavery.

Pennington closes one of the final chapters of his slave narrative with a statement of his "faith" that "all of our remaining members [of the family] will in time be brought together." He looks forward to recording that history in a "reviewed and enlarged edition of this tract."[52] In other words, Pennington imagines that the slave narrative form will continue to serve both a genealogical and ethnological purpose as a record of sociality and kinship. And while seemingly unrelated to Pennington's critique of *Notes on the State of Virginia*, the very concept of a record of black sociality cuts against the grain of Jefferson's theories. One of the most pernicious aspects of Jefferson's *Notes* is his separation of the African race from the social itself.[53] Pennington responds by using both ethnology and the slave narrative to reconstruct black kinship and its connection to the rest of humanity.

Another Unanticipated Critic

Into the 1850s, black intellectuals continued to write back to Jefferson. James McCune Smith's responses to Jefferson in his published essays are both sustained and artful. If Jefferson had anticipated that his *Notes* would have been subjected to the "rigid scrutiny" of someone like McCune Smith, then Pennington is likely right that he would have "modified that ill judged part of his work which relates to the colored people." McCune Smith was indeed an intellect with whom to be reckoned. Even though John Stauffer's 2001 study, *The Black Hearts of Men: Radical Abolitionists and the Transformation of Race*, made an impassioned argument for the recovery of McCune Smith's life and role in the abolitionist movement, in which he was a founding member of the Radical Abolition Party, he continues to be neglected by literary scholars. This neglect is particularly unfortunate given McCune Smith's prominence in the nineteenth century: Douglass said that McCune Smith had more influence on his thinking than anyone else, and he was widely celebrated as the most highly educated African American of the nineteenth century before Du Bois. After being rejected at both Columbia College and the medical school in Geneva, New York, because of his race, he was accepted at the University of Glasgow in Scotland, where he began his course of study in 1832. He received three degrees from there, including his BA, MA, and medical degree. Upon returning to the United States, he became the first university-trained black physician to establish his own practice in the country.[54] Among literary scholars, McCune Smith is best known as the author of the introduction to Douglass's second autobiography, *My Bondage and My Freedom* (1855), the text that cemented Douglass's break from the Garrisonians and turn toward radical abolitionism. But McCune Smith deserves credit as a writer in his own right, especially given the wide-ranging nature of his writing and the rich cross-fertilization of art, science, literature, and social commentary displayed across his essays.

References to Jefferson appear throughout McCune Smith's oeuvre, revealing *Notes* to be a touchstone for his thinking and writing across a career as a New York physician, pharmacist, abolitionist, and essayist. McCune Smith's most direct engagement with Query XIV appeared in a two-part series featured in the *Anglo-African Magazine*. The first essay, "Civilization: Its Dependence on Physical Circumstances," was published in January 1859, in the same issue as the first installment of Martin Delany's *Blake; or, The Huts of America* as well as Delany's essay on astronomy, "The Attraction of Planets." McCune Smith's second essay in the series, "On the Fourteenth Query of Thomas Jefferson's Notes on Virginia," appeared in the *Anglo-African* in August of that same year. In these two essays McCune Smith supports the monogenetic theory of descent, the theory that God created the human race in one unified act. According to McCune Smith, the races look different because of superficial differences produced by the environment, not because of innate, intractable differences produced at the moment of creation. More precisely, following Charles Lyell's *Principles of Geology* (1833), McCune Smith argues that such phenotypical and anatomical differences are produced by geological influences.[55] Here, McCune Smith's climate theory starts to look closer to Darwin's evolutionary theory of natural selection than to the climatism of natural history: through his insistence on the importance of geographical variety and microclimates on the development of a people, he gets surprisingly close to the theory that ecological niches affect the descent and differentiation of a species.[56] As Darwin hypothesized in *Voyage of the Beagle* (1839), further elaborated in *On the Origin of Species* (1859), and finally committed to in *The Descent of Man* (1871), so McCune Smith insists that the "so-called 'races' of mankind" are really only varieties of one species, the "human family."[57] Moreover, McCune Smith argues that there is as much variability within the races as there is between the races (a prophetic argument that has been confirmed by modern genetics).[58] Inferior qualities in the black race are exceptions, not rules among the population: "Hence it appears that the black comprises no special variety of the human race, no distinctive species of mankind, but is part and parcel of the great original stock of humanity—of the rule, and not of the exception."[59]

Across these two essays, McCune Smith further emphasizes the tangled lines of descent among the races, refusing the existence of five pure races on earth, while exposing the fiction of whiteness: since the only true white people are albinos, "the pure white," he observes, "is a deformed variety of the human species."[60] Ultimately, McCune Smith counters Jefferson's "mixed and confused" speculations on ethnology with the thick empiricisms of physiology: looking to the blood and bones, the physician-writer refutes Jefferson's suspicions about the insurmountable physical differences between European and African peoples.[61] Moreover, supported by a creative etymology, he argues that progress in the United States depends on the mixing of the races since the essential condition of civilization, derived from the Latin *civis*, is "co-ivis," a "coming together," which requires the assemblage and commingling of diverse peoples.[62] Whereas Walker and Pennington refuted Jefferson largely on scriptural and rhetorical grounds, McCune Smith's critique is deeply rooted in his medical expertise.

In addition to the sustained treatment of *Notes* in McCune Smith's scientific articles, Jefferson also appears in the writer's more occasional essays in the black press. From 1852 to 1854, McCune Smith published a series of sketches titled the "Heads of the Colored People, Done with a Whitewash Brush," under the pseudonym "Communipaw" in *Frederick Douglass' Paper*. In 1851, Douglass had asked McCune Smith to become the New York correspondent for his new newspaper. Highly erudite and a bit esoteric, his prose peppered with foreign languages and allusions to classical and modern literature, McCune Smith's essays likely presented challenges for black and non-black readers of all literacy levels and educational backgrounds. A highly experimental, beautifully written series that incorporates satire, ethnography, and even black dialect decades before it would become a standard feature of African American writing, McCune Smith's "Heads of the Colored People" sketches also draw on phrenology and physiognomy to represent the black working class of New York.

In the March 25, 1852, installment of the "Heads of the Colored People," the first essay in the series, McCune Smith gives a detailed, physiognomic portrait of a "black news-vender" and fugitive slave whose legs were amputated. McCune Smith comments on the man's "broad and swelling chest, whose symmetry proclaims Virginia birth, fine long hooked nose, evidently from the first families, sharpish face, clean cut hazel eyes, buried beneath luxuriously folded lids, and prominent perceptive faculties."[63] Suggesting that the newsvendor shares ancestry with the well-bred, aristocratic families of colonial Virginia, McCune Smith goes even further, stating, "I did not ask him to pull off [his] cloth cap [covering] long greasy ears, lest his brow should prove him the incontestable descendent of Thomas Jefferson and Black Sal."[64] Rather than serving as a mere jab at Jefferson's character, McCune Smith's turn to the Hemings-Jefferson gossip performs a more critical function. He immediately moves from the physiognomy of the newsvendor to note that "it is well known that Jefferson contradicted his philosophy of negro hate, by seeking the dalliance of black women as often as he could, and by leaving so many descendants of mixed blood, that they are to be found as widely scattered as his own writings throughout the world." It turns out that McCune Smith does not need extensive scientific evidence to challenge *Notes*: Jefferson's own desire—his "unphilosophical lust"—reveals the absurdity of "all the stale anti-negroisms" of his text.[65] Moreover, the existence of Jefferson's "mixed blood" descendants "scattered" around the world counters and contradicts the statesman's widely circulating writings on "negro hate." McCune Smith's forceful hyperbole spectacularly implies that Jefferson's mixed-race descendants are just as numerous across the world as his transnationally circulating writing (a fantasy of circulation that also resonates with Walker's ambitions for his *Appeal*). He further suggests that the descendants of Jefferson, and Jeffersonian America more broadly, stand as embodied proof of the interracial desire and the specter of miscegenation disavowed in *Notes*. These people are figured in the text as global, even cosmopolitan subjects, widely "scattered" around the world and circulating alongside Jefferson's *Notes*—and McCune Smith figures them in such a way as to materialize the ghostly presence of what David Kazanjian calls the "critical, black globality" of "black Enlightenment discourse."[66] McCune Smith's mixed-race global multitude thus stakes their claim not only to a biological inheritance from Jefferson, but also to the Enlightenment itself.

While McCune Smith's exposure of Jefferson's "unphilosophical lust" serves as an unabashed critique of *Notes*, the writer-physician's naturalistic method in the sketches challenges *Notes* in a more subtle way. In opposition to Jefferson's description of the "immoveable veil" of blackness that "covers all the emotions" and refuses access to interiority, McCune Smith uses physiognomy to read black faces as visual archives that reveal robust, complicated interior lives.[67] Such careful delineations of black interior life through physical representation anticipate William J. Wilson's 1859 "Afric-American Picture Gallery," published serially in the *Anglo-African Magazine*, in which Wilson uses his pen to "paint" and "sculpt" a series of noble busts of black subjects—including eighteenth-century ancestors Phillis Wheatley, Toussaint L'Ouverture, and Benjamin Banneker. McCune Smith similarly referred to his "Heads of the Colored People" sketches as "word paintings," and his pen mimics the paintbrush of an artist seeking to depict the inner life of his or her subject through cues represented visually on the face and body.

In addition to lifting Jefferson's "immoveable veil" of blackness to depict the diversity of life, intellect, and emotion that resided underneath, "The Heads of the Colored People" also turns Jefferson's racist discourse of African lust into a sophisticated argument about black desire. Rather than countering Jefferson's argument by insisting on the proper desires and normative relationships among the race, McCune Smith offers a surprisingly frank depiction of human sexuality and the many desires, among both blacks and whites, which did not adhere to the heteropatriachal norms of bourgeois society. McCune Smith's openness about sexuality—especially black women's sexuality—is startling given the politics of respectability that surrounded and often censored black writing in the public sphere. Indeed, it is this aspect of the "Heads" sketches that likely disturbed the readers of *Frederick Douglass' Paper*. The series even upset Douglass, who printed an editorial on May 27, 1853, in which he observed that "in respect to talents and real ability, I believe there is enough among the colored citizens of New York, to give wise and wholesome laws to an empire. Why will not my able New York correspondent bring some of the real '*heads of the colored people*' before our readers?"[68] The "real" people, according to Douglass, are to be found "in the way of churches, Sunday Schools, Literary Societies, intelligent ministers and *respectable* congregations among our people in New York."[69] Douglass was clearly uncomfortable with McCune Smith's valorization of the working class and his rejection of bourgeois values: Why, Douglass wondered, would McCune Smith offer portraits of the city's poor black laborers rather than members of the black professional class (including McCune Smith himself)? But Douglass's unstated critique here, a critique that sits just below the surface of his editorial, has to do with McCune Smith's depiction of desire in his treatment of the working peoples of New York. McCune Smith's straightforward articulation of black desire and (feminine) sexuality at once challenges the racist discourse of desire in *Notes* and the emphasis placed on bourgeois respectability in the African American print sphere.

I want to suggest that the radical nature of McCune Smith's intervention here, and the intervention that likely disturbed Douglass, lies in his introduction of sexual desire into his sketches. Sexual desire similarly threatened to disrupt the dominant discourses of ethnology. Ethnological treatises from the period, including Jefferson's Query XIV, focused on the origin and descent of the races, but in a telling elision, they also frequently absented reproduction. In other words, the bodies of women, through which the races are reproduced, are regularly expunged from these texts. Evacuating sex and desire, these scientific discourses attempt to abstract race from reproduction, while disavowing the realities of interracial relations, both coercive and consensual. In other words, ethnology is structured on a myth: the descent of pure, unmixed races that reproduce themselves without women.[70] In the "The Black News-Vender," however, as well as in many other sketches from the "Heads of the Colored People" series, McCune Smith continues to remind his readers of the wayward workings of sexual attraction and the activity and labor of black women. Indeed, he remarks on the pervasiveness of interracial relationships over and over again in his essays, both in the "Heads of the Colored People" as well as in his scientific writings.

In this way, McCune Smith anticipates some of the arguments that Sharon Patricia Holland advocates in her 2012 book, *The Erotic Life of Racism.* These include the importance of returning to the white/black binary that has so fundamentally structured the psychic life of race and racism in America, of excavating and animating the black body upon which Anglo-American science and philosophy has been built (and then disavowed), and of revealing the quotidian acts of desire and racism that lie behind abstract theorizations of race.[71] In short, by returning us to the body of Sally Hemings, McCune Smith unearths the unspoken anxieties of ethnology, including the specter of miscegenation and the rape of black women by white men. But in addition to glimpsing histories of rape and coerced reproduction under the conditions of slavery, McCune Smith also reminds readers of the unruly, unscientific workings of consensual desire across the color line. We might, then, finally return to Jefferson's comment in *Notes* that "love seems with them [Africans] to be more an eager desire, than a tender delicate mixture of sentiment and sensation"[72] Countering Jefferson's crude account of "brute lust," Mc-Cune Smith crafts a complex and nuanced approach to black desire. He excavates the gendered, racialized bodies of American ethnology while forwarding a theory of social change that is powered by filiation, desire, and, even, love, a "tender mixture of sentiment and sensation."

McCune Smith's essays illuminate the creativity with which early black interlocutors approached *Notes*, and the passion and interest with which they adapted and expanded early national racial science. The "Heads of the Colored People" sketches and McCune Smith's essays on *Notes* in the *Anglo-African Magazine* not only excavate Jefferson's mixed-race descendants, but also announce themselves as the experimental literary descendants of the Enlightenment. Stauffer notes that in the midst of the rampant racism and setbacks for the abolition movement in the early 1850s, McCune Smith turned from sentimentalism and a naïve empiricism to a more speculative and experimental writing style: "McCune Smith's writing evolved from using words (and numbers) as tools for fighting oppression, to treating language as an open-ended symbolic process. . . . McCune Smith's scientific and positivistic methods could no longer adequately capture what he perceived or felt. In the face of personal and national tragedy, he found solace in the pleasure of words; in the midst of state-sanctioned outrages, he experienced release in sarcasm. He could write playfully and ironically without losing his abiding faith in the possibility of 'human brotherhood.'"[73] In other words, Mc-Cune Smith stretched the narrow empiricism of natural history toward a more radical empiricism. Clearly influenced by his daily medical practice, McCune Smith's writing is meticulously descriptive—almost clinically diagnostic—as he attempts to capture the thick and varied richness of experience, both happy and tragic, in black life in America. Drawing from the methods of clinical diagnosis and careful observation in his medical practice, McCune Smith produces an experimental, almost modernist aesthetic through the essay form.

McCune Smith's experimental writing style also shaped the creativity of his scientific theories. Drawing on the monogenetic and climatic theories of James Cowles Prichard, as well as earlier, eighteenth-century environmentalist ideas about the climatic production of racial difference, McCune Smith's critiques of Jefferson also include his own theories on the geographic production of race and civilization.[74] Just as we saw with David Walker in the 1820s, so in the 1850s, Jefferson's racist theories prompted black intellectuals to develop their own theories of race. Rather than reproducing arguments about the superiority of people in "temperate" zones over those from "torrid" zones, McCune Smith re-maps the entirety of the "temperate zone" to include all areas around the world that are in contact with water. For McCune Smith, the ocean naturally "tempers" the land it touches, and thus, vigorous, civilized people are produced wherever the land meets the sea.[75] McCune Smith's sea-faring ethnology is also an Atlantic ethnology, which locates the progress of civilization not in a static geographic zone, but in all of those liminal, coastal places that foster the intermingling of people from different areas around the world, through both "free" (trade) and unfree (slave trade) forms of exchange. Here, McCune Smith also harnesses the Atlantic dimensions of racial science in order to challenge the racist provincialisms of US ethnology.

McCune Smith's theories on the origin and descent of the human races—as well their connection to the descent of nonhuman species—also appear in his preface to Frederick Douglass's *My Bondage and My Freedom* (1855). In the middle of his introduction, McCune Smith turns to the emerging languages of embryology and evolution to construct a powerful metaphor about Frederick Douglass's manhood, but in so doing, he also swiftly reveals the anthropomorphism and heteronormativity of white as well as black ethnology. Indeed, for all of the fascinating and progressive arguments made by black ethnologies, these texts, like the tracts of the American school of ethnology, often perpetuated sexist ideas and norms in their accounts of human reproduction and the progress of civilization. Like their white-authored counterparts, black-authored ethnologies understood the progress of civilization in distinctly reproductive terms—through the reproduction of the races—all the while mysteriously erasing, or underplaying, women's fundamental role in the process. In most black ethnologies, moreover, human sexuality is completely erased. The equation of civilization with reproduction proved highly problematic for the representation of black womanhood and sexuality in ethnological texts, as we will continue to see in Chapter 2.

By the 1850s, and with the coming of the Darwinian Revolution, new evolutionary theories and ideas began to circulate among black intellectual communities. Darwinian and proto-Darwinian theories helped to spawn new imaginaries about the origin and descent of the races, as well as new understandings of human and animal sexuality.[76] They also opened up new possibilities for thinking about the relationship not just among kin but also among different species (kind). In his 1849 autobiography, Pennington expressed horror at the cataloguing of men with mere beasts in evolutionary taxonomies as well as in planters' records and daybooks, where enslaved people and livestock were routinely catalogued together. But McCune Smith seems, rather, to revel in the cross-species identifications that were being suggested by new evolutionary theories, as well as in the emerging field of developmental embryology, which argued that human embryos progressed through the evolutionary stages of "lower" species before "becoming human." In his introduction to the 1855 narrative, McCune Smith dramatizes Douglass as an exemplary "specimen" of the American "type" with an embryological metaphor:

> Naturalists tell us that a full grown man is a resultant or representative of all animated nature on this globe; beginning with the early embryo state, then representing the lowest forms of organic life, and passing through every subordinate grade or type, until he reaches the last and highest—manhood. In like manner, and to the fullest extent, has Frederick Douglass passed through every gradation of rank comprised in our national make-up, and bears upon his person and upon his soul every thing that is American. And he has not only full sympathy with everything American; his proclivity or bent, to active toil and visible progress, are in the strictly national direction, delighting to outstrip "all creation."[77]

Here, the embryo, moving from the lowest to highest stage of development, becomes a figure for Douglass's own incredible transformation from degraded slave to ennobled freeman. More than simply dramatizing Douglass's status as a "representative" American, McCune Smith's metaphor also suggests something about Douglass's place in the larger animal kingdom: according to McCune Smith, every "full grown man" is a culmination of all forms of "animated nature on this globe," but Douglass is elevated to an even higher level of evolution, as he is poised to outstrip "all creation." While we might read this passage as anthropocentric, with the human—and man, more specifically—being figured as the apex of creation, the language of evolution and embryology exposes humanity's kinship with the rest of the animal and plant kingdom. Humanity's inextricable connection to nonhuman species is further solidified with a footnote. Not being able to resist an opportunity for scientific explication, McCune Smith offers this note in the middle of his remark about the early embryo's presentation of the "lowest forms of organic life": "The German physiologists have even discovered vegetable matter—starch—in the human body. See Med. Chirurgical Rev., Oct. 1854, p. 339."[78] Indeed, McCune Smith's evolutionary account of humanity's kinship with and incorporation of plants, animals, and microorganisms actually undermines the slave-becomes-man archetype of Douglass's 1845 and 1855 narratives. At the same time as he challenges the slave narrative's dependence on certain ideals about manhood through the language of embryology, McCune Smith's focus on the queer human-animal-vegetable alliances of evolution also exposes the problematic anthropocentric underpinnings of antebellum ethnology by both black and white authors. Again and again in McCune Smith's writings, scientific treatises, and nonfiction essays alike, evolution displaces and decenters "man." In moving from the evangelical, somewhat Victorian ethnology of Pennington to the non-prudish, secular science of McCune Smith, we find McCune Smith providing a decidedly queer correction to the situation of heterosexual and even human reproduction at the center of ethnology. The next chapter will continue to explore how black male writers reproduced, challenged, and otherwise negotiated the gendered blind spots of ethnology.

The Banneker Age from Science to Fiction

Ranging from Walker's direct attack on Jefferson's anti-blackness in 1829 to McCune Smith's experiments with queer evolution in the 1850s, this chapter has come quite far from Banneker's original contributions to the Jefferson debate. But in continuing to respond to Jefferson's *Notes*, and in producing their own forms of defiant, engaged scientific writing, these antebellum interlocutors supplemented the limited documentation of Banneker's life and work in the eighteenth century. In so doing, Walker, Pennington, and McCune Smith also placed themselves in a scientific genealogy that owes as much to Banneker as to Jefferson himself, thereby replacing the "Jefferson Age" with the "Banneker Age."

In addition to being manifest in the many black responses to *Notes* that were published across the decades of the early nineteenth century, "The Banneker Age" was also imagined and enacted in the memorialization of Banneker himself in antebellum print, politics, and performance. The Banneker letter was, for example, recirculated in many forms: it appeared regularly in black newspapers and periodicals, it was reprinted in books, and Frederick Douglass even performed it publicly. Mini-biographies of Banneker also appeared in the black press and in book form.[79] A group of young African American men in Philadelphia memorialized Banneker by naming their learned society "The Banneker Institute." In addition to providing lectures on scientific and other intellectual topics, meeting to discuss books and current events, and promoting forms of collaborative study among group members, the Banneker Institute hosted community birthday celebrations in memory of Banneker.[80] Providing updates on the society as well as black intellectual life in Philadelphia, the secretary of the Banneker Institute also contributed to the presence of Banneker in the black press by signing his columns in the *Weekly Anglo-African* as "Banneker."[81] The act of taking Banneker's name as a pseudonym is yet another example of antebellum supplements to the Banneker archive, and in this case, an important act of surrogation as well.[82] The Banneker Institute's records also include original correspondence from Banneker, George and Andrew Ellicott, and James Pemberton on arrangements to publish Banneker's almanacs. More than just memorializing and extending Banneker's legacy, then, the Banneker Institute itself served as a repository for Banneker's papers.[83]

Other groups and individuals memorialized Banneker's legacy in stone, from planned statues to monuments sited in black cemeteries, gardens, and other community spaces.[84] When actual monuments were not financially feasible, the print sphere stood in as a more ephemeral, though still important, form of memorial building. Indeed, memorialization was one of the most important functions of the antebellum black print sphere. Interestingly, such memorials rarely used the language of "black genius" to talk about Banneker. Rather, Banneker stood as a symbol for collective black intellect. The language of the "black genius" has, indeed, sometimes been used as a tool of surveillance and control by white Americans, not only by separating out supposed "exceptions" to the rule, but also by containing and ignoring the specific interventions made by thinkers like Banneker. William Andrews's reading of Jefferson's reply to Banneker's letter suggests the dismissiveness at the heart of some white ascriptions of black genius: "Instead of joining Banneker in a common effort to articulate a morally and socially viable ideal of human liberty and equality, Jefferson opted instead to act as a freeman's intellectual patron, offering him what he never asked for—the promotion of his personal reputation as a black scientist."[85] Through its memorializing of Banneker, Wheatley, Alexander Dumas, and Crispus Attucks, among others, the nineteenth-century black print sphere served an important compensatory function for the elision of black voices in eighteenth-century texts and archives, a silencing often performed *through* the recognition of "genius," as in the case of Jefferson's dismissal of Banneker in which he recognizes Banneker's intelligence rather than addressing the actual content of his thinking.

The many calls to memorialize Banneker in the antebellum period are particularly striking given the declining reputation of Jefferson in this same moment. And while Banneker's archive was only growing in reputation and in size, Jefferson's archive was being dismantled: Monticello fell into the hands of a number of different owners in the nineteenth century, and his natural history collection, the artifacts that stood behind the text of *Notes*, was sold off at auction and dispersed after Jefferson's death in 1826, along with Jefferson's slaves. Burdened by accumulating debts, the plantation estate was already beginning to fall into disrepair in Jefferson's final years. Despite uneven efforts to restore the mansion in the nineteenth century, it was not until the early twentieth century that the Jefferson memorialization industry took off, when the newly formed Thomas Jefferson Foundation bought and rehabilitated the plantation into a historic site and tourist destination.

Although he could no longer be called a standard reference point in black scientific writing by the end of the nineteenth century, a period witnessing the rapid professionalization of science and medicine and a distancing from various forms of vernacular science, Banneker did begin popping up in new places at the turn of the twentieth century. Riffing on a type of science-fiction adventure-invention story called the "Edisonade," Lisa Yaszek has coined the term "Bannekerade" to describe black science-fiction narratives featuring black genius-inventors.[86] The Bannekerade also include fictionalizations of Banneker himself, as in Sutton Griggs's 1899 *Imperium in Imperio*, an uplift novel that becomes increasingly speculative across its chapters and concludes with the revelation of a black shadow government headquartered in Waco, Texas. A temporary government that still holds out hope for reunion with the United States and the coming equality between the races, the Imperium's secret empire closely monitors and parallels the debates, discussions, and decisions of the US government within its own legislature and leadership. Throughout the novel, the imperial history of Texan annexation is used to debate the possibilities and pitfalls of founding an all-black state in the South(west).[87] The Imperium's president, Bernard Belgrave, convinces the group that a violent uprising and usurpation of the entire state of Texas is the only hope for the future of the race, a plan that is, at the novel's end, thwarted by a society member who cannot stand the thought of such violence being brought down upon the United States. While the narrative flirts with separatism throughout, readers are ultimately meant to understand that the right way forward is to wage the fight against Jim Crow with "the ballot box" rather than "the sword."[88]

Griggs's secret society-turned-government is given a specific and significant origin story, having been created by none other than a "negro scientist" from the "early days of the American Republic."[89] Clearly modeling this character after Benjamin Banneker, Griggs thereby transforms Banneker into a "black founding father" of a secret black government within the United States.[90] He also imagines a speculative history in which Banneker receives wealth and recognition for his scientific work and goes on to become a freedom fighter who provides the initial funds and financial wealth that continue to sustain the Imperium. This part of the novel contains a fascinating alternative history, which takes the hints and suggestions of Banneker's political activity in the eighteenth-century archive and uses them to fashion him into a true "race leader" in the style of late nineteenth-century racial uplift. The protagonist's comment that "in our school days, we spoke of him often," also represents Banneker as an important figure in black classrooms across the long nineteenth century.[91] And finally, this speculative history retroactively gives Banneker the financial security and professional identity denied him during his life.

At this point, it should not come as a surprise that if Banneker is referenced, then Thomas Jefferson cannot be too far behind: like the antebellum practice of critiquing the racism of Thomas Jefferson's *Notes* while simultaneously upholding Jefferson's own statements on the equality owed to all men by nature, the Imperium follows the "teachings of Thomas Jefferson," especially his theory of absolute equality enshrined in the Declaration of Independence. Indeed, the Imperium is even headquartered in a complex called "Thomas Jefferson College," a reference to the University of Virginia and possibly Jefferson's Monticello as well.[92]

Ultimately, the Bannekerade extends the creative memory-work surrounding Banneker in nineteenth-century black science and culture, as well as the black afterlives of Jeffersonian science that continued to proliferate long after the publication of *Notes*. Interestingly, when detailing the Imperium's origin story, protagonist Belton Piedmont is sure to note that Banneker's important "book of science" is "now obsolete, science having made such great strides since his day."[93] And yet, this does not mean that Banneker had ceased to be useful in black culture. Griggs's fictionalization of Banneker is yet another retrospective addition to the Banneker archive, and an indication that by the turn of the twentieth century, the Banneker Age had migrated from science to (science) fiction.

2

Comparative Anatomies

Re-Visions of Racial Science

In 1900, W. E. B. Du Bois compiled three photograph albums for display at the Paris Exhibition. Echoing the title of Josiah Nott and George Gliddon's 1854 ethnology, *Types of Mankind*, one of Du Bois's albums was titled *Types of American Negroes*. These albums register the long afterlives of nineteenth-century racial science into the following century. But more than just referencing the title of Nott and Gliddon's notorious text, Du Bois's photo albums also recall the "scopic regime" that "subtends scientific racism in the modern West."[1] As Shawn Michelle Smith has argued, Du Bois's photographs specifically signify on the "photographic archives of early race scientists," through the positioning of subjects in rigid poses and the pairing of hard frontal headshots with profiles.[2] These photographs also cite late nineteenth-century uses of composite photography in criminology and eugenics. But Du Bois goes on to challenge the scientific/criminologist frame-up of black subjects by including a series of sentimental photographs that look as if they belong in an African American family album. In this way, Smith argues, *Types of American Negroes* challenges the racial typologies of turn-of-the-century science by producing a "counterarchive" that offers "competing visual evidence."[3] Troping on the narrow, crude "types" of racial science, Du Bois reveals instead the broad variation of African American bodies, physiognomies, and colors in the Deep South.

Such challenges to the visual dimensions of racial science have even earlier precedents. Beginning in the 1830s, black ethnologies showed a profound sensitivity to the visual dimensions of racial science: they built evidence of black physiological and intellectual fitness, shifted the burden of black degradation onto white actors, and connected Black and Native peoples to one another where polygenesis sought to rip them apart. The ground of the visual became a key site upon which African

Americans waged their battle against racist science, print, and popular culture in the 1830s and 1840s.[4] Taking direct aim at the damaging images produced by the American school of ethnology, these writers also challenged the ascendency of racist imagery in visual culture. African Americans were highly aware that a growing culture industry of anti-black imagery both fed off of racial science's anti-black theories and further amplified those claims.

Without the same access to the technologies of image production as writers for commercial publications, African American writers answered this racist archive with an alternative one that made use of ekphrasis, the dramatic description of visual objects in texts. Emerging visual technologies, including the camera, the microscope, and the telescope, further inspired new ways of visualizing the racialized body through ekphrasis. I follow Jasmine Nichole Cobb's helpful notion of "black visuality," which includes a broad array of visual practices and representations, from everyday encounters on the street to the act of sitting for a daguerreotype. Black visuality emerges out of "a complicated interplay between subjectivity, social context, and cultural representations as circumscribed by the trauma of slavery"; it also recognizes the dynamics of opacity and invisibility that structured the visual archive of slavery and against which African Americans, especially black women, attempted to "picture freedom" before the legal end to slavery.[5]

Given the centrality of scientific images that separated black people from humanity and from the social itself, black ethnologies were especially interested in using the visual—in both text and in image—to reconstruct the forms of relation denied and destroyed by polygenesis, which uncannily doubled a history of detachment and alienation that began centuries earlier with the slave trade. Black ethnology's efforts thus paralleled those of men and women who sought to reconstitute their own families and social networks in the New World, as registered in Black Atlantic slave narratives from Olaudah Equiano to Harriet Jacobs. Because of the work performed by the Middle Passage and regimes of enslavement to detach peoples of African descent from their biological and chosen kin, and indeed, from their own names and identities, the process of repairing lines of ancestry among African American communities has always been a highly complex and tentative endeavor. Today, even the science of genetic ancestry testing must be supplemented by historical documentation, oral family histories, and the imaginative work of connecting oneself to the diaspora in a creative act this chapter theorizes as *speculative kinship*. Among black intellectuals in the antebellum North, ethnology became a privileged site for conducting such speculative forms of genealogy, allowing writers to boldly imagine and recover lines of kinship that had been destroyed by the slave trade and domestic institutions of slavery and reinforced by racial science. Like the use of contemporary genetics by African-descended populations for what Alondra Nelson calls "reconciliation projects," those "endeavors aimed at ameliorating the injurious repercussions of the past," antebellum black ethnology performed an important reparative work: these texts constructed genealogies of speculative kinship that included, but were in no way reducible to, the biological family.[6]

This chapter chronicles the important reparative work of black ethnology in the 1830s and 1840s, focusing on how Robert Benjamin Lewis and Hosea Easton imagined and imaged speculative genealogies of kinship. In this way, my analysis takes shape around genealogy and visuality, but more specifically, it considers the visualization of genealogy in both black images and textual production. Chapter 1's account of the reparative genealogical work of James Pennington's ethnology and slave narrative is extended in this chapter's account of how black ethnologists used the visual, in text and occasionally in actual images, to produce visions and revisions of black kinship, a broad determination that included biological forms of connection, but also political, social, and religious forms of alliance. Following from Nancy Bentley's understanding of the expansive kinship work performed in African American narrative, this chapter argues that black ethnological writing—works that explicitly imagined new conceptions of "families, social spaces, and histories" from the position of "social dispossession"—should be also taken seriously as an important site for the theorizing of black kinship, especially in its more speculative forms.[7]

More often rooted in contesting racist cultural theories drawn from biblical sources than in contradicting comparative anatomists, early black ethnologies nonetheless established an important context for fugitive science. And as race science became increasingly secular, so did black ethnology: works like Robert Benjamin Lewis's 1836 *Light and Truth*, published even before Samuel George Morton's *Crania Americana* in 1839, were transformed from their original exegetical and religious contexts when they were reprinted throughout the 1840s and 1850s. When Lewis's *Light and Truth* was published in a reprint edition in 1855, it was immediately recognized as a powerful rejoinder to the racist science being produced in the 1850s. In this way, early nineteenth-century black ethnology both anticipated and challenged the mid-century ascendency of polygenesis.

Black Ethnology: Beginnings

As Chapter 1 traced, Thomas Jefferson's *Notes on the State of Virginia* had a formative influence on the emergence and shape of black writings on ethnology, beginning as early as Banneker's brief account of the monogenetic origin of humans in his letter to Jefferson. Into the 1820s and 1830s, Black and Native American bodies became objects of study within a growing body of ethnological writing in the United States. African Americans were subjected to the decentralized investigations of pro-slavery scientists and doctors in the South, academics in the North, and curious gentlemen scientists in both the North and the South, while Native Americans were largely subject to a more centralized, federal ethnology, produced at the hands of agents working for the US government.[8] The increasing subjection of Black and Native bodies in ethnology led both Black and Native writers to begin challenging ethnological discourse from within its own terms, which, in turn, produced a vibrant counterarchive of ethnological writings.

In Jacksonian America, US ethnology grew under the influence of a number of concomitant developments. The market revolution in the years following the War of 1812 helped to instantiate a new age of US expansionism as an economy increasingly rooted in capitalist production required more land, more labor, and more capital.[9] The imperialist designs of the US government were also rooted in a desire to increase the territorial domain of the country across the West, to establish the nation as a strong, unified world power, and to squelch competing land claims by the British, French, and Spanish, as well as Native nations across North America.[10] This period witnessed the transition from an artisanal and cottage-factory system to an industrial factory system run on urban and immigrant labor. The South became further dependent on slavery as it shifted from sugar, wheat, and other planation crops to mass cotton production. The plantation complex of the antebellum South was, of course, intimately connected to industrialization and capitalization in the North, where anti-black violence and mob activity grew in the early 1830s, as anxieties proliferated about competition from free black labor, the "promiscuous" mixing of blacks and whites in urban neighborhoods, which raised the specter of miscegenation, and the mobilization of black political power and abolitionism in the Northeast.

At the same time, the expansionist imperatives of the US government produced tensions between the North and South over the status of slavery in newly acquired territories and potential territorial acquisitions in the future. Indeed, the 1830s mark the beginnings of US sectionalism, characterized by divisive debates between Southern agricultural interests and Northern manufacturing interests in Congress. The increasing division between the Northern and Southern states came to a head with the Nullification Crisis of 1832, in which South Carolina's rejection of a high tariff for raw materials nearly led to the state's secession from the Union. Signs of disunion were also apparent in the Northeast, especially with the rise of the abolitionist movement under the leadership of William Lloyd Garrison and the American Anti-Slavery Society, as well as the proliferation of evangelical Protestant sects that thoroughly disrupted fantasies about a coherent, unified nation. Throughout the 1830s, anxieties about Southern, Western, and even New England secessionism percolated across an imperially expanding nation.

During this period characterized by both territorial incorporation and political division, science began to be marshaled in the project of solidifying the racial differences and hierarchies that were needed to justify regimes of forced displacement, enslavement, and dispossession by the state. Andrew Jackson insisted that the separation of Indians from whites was the only way to avoid outbreaks of violence between the groups.[11] But the removal of Native Americans, as well as the continued enslavement of African Americans, also required an ideological justification beyond political necessity. Ethnological theories of inalienable racial difference were thus mobilized within a white imperial project that was transitioning from a model of racial assimilation to one of exclusion from the national body politic. The Indian Removal Act of 1830 concretized this shift from ideas of Native assimilation, built on theories of white and Native similarity, to doctrines of Native displacement, which were increasingly undergirded by theories of Indian difference.[12] The Indian Removal Act and the subsequent removal of approximately 50,000 people from their lands to the Indian Territories in the West were in many ways an extension of US Indian policy from the turn of the nineteenth century. Thousands of Native deaths on the Trail of Tears, the Second Seminole War of 1832, and related events in the 1830s were a continuation but also an intensification of a long history of violence associated with the suppression of Native American sovereignty and displacement of tribes from their lands in the East and South.[13]

The transition from dealing with Native Americans through treaties and negotiation to forced removal paralleled the movement to remove free African Americans from the United States. Just as models of Native assimilation were replaced by policies and practices of Native removal, eighteenth-century ideas about the possible peaceful incorporation of African Americans into American society gave way in the 1820s and 1830s to colonization schemes that sought to remove and resettle black people, including both recently freed slaves and established free black communities, in West Africa. The American Colonization Society (ACS), founded in 1816, was the major arm of this movement. As the ACS gained strength and political power, black activists, including some of the writers considered in this chapter, threw their weight behind fighting the colonization movement.[14]

While the American school of ethnology did not contribute significantly to pro-slavery ideology until the late 1840s, Samuel George Morton and his followers, especially George Gliddon in his popular lectures, contributed to a larger national project of reifying racial difference: separating the races into a series of "types" did much to justify the dispossession of peoples of color and their containment from the white population. US ethnology in the 1830s did not establish an absolute biological difference between the races as much as it suggested an inflexibility of racial categories. The perceived intractability of race would become increasingly important for anti-Black and anti-Native policies of racial separation and removal. In addition to the early works of Morton and his followers, US ethnology was also constituted by a number of pro-slavery political tracts and sermons that rooted theories of racial inferiority in biblical exegesis, especially the Curse of Ham and the Curse of Cain. Federal agents of US Native policy produced another substantial body of ethnological discourse, delineating the origins and history of Native American languages in such a way that, as Sean Harvey argues, theories of Native linguistic difference, rather than theories of biological and bodily difference, largely undergirded Indian Removal policies.[15]

Like all antebellum scientific writing, ethnology was an eclectic discourse, drawing from multiple literatures and fields, including natural history, philology, the Bible, universal history, classical history, modern history, ethnography, phrenology, American antiquarianism, and "Holy Land mania," or the enthusiasm among Anglo-Americans surrounding pilgrimages to Palestine. Universal history, the eighteenth- and nineteenth-century term for world history, traced the history of mankind from its beginning to the present through the use of both sacred (biblical) and secular (ancient Greek and Roman) history. Black ethnologies drew from an even more diverse range of sources, including abolitionist tracts, African American intellectual writing, the black press, the work of literary and historical societies, and the teachings of the black church.[16] As Stephen Hall notes, universal histories from the eighteenth century proved to be particularly valuable resources for these writers, as they allowed African Americans to draw on positive depictions of Africa and its peoples, unlike the racist depictions that filled imperialist US history in the nineteenth century. Knowledge of classical authors allowed black writers to affirm the "authority of eighteenth-century (rather than nineteenth-century) historical conceptions of blackness and the place of Africans in the ancient world."[17] These writers mobilized "eighteenth-century historical conceptualizations of universal history that put the Mediterranean world, which included Egypt (Africa very broadly defined), Greece, and Rome, at the center of the construction of the West's intellectual foundations."[18]

Just as David Walker's *Appeal to the Coloured Citizens of the World* expanded on a tradition of critiquing Jefferson that was founded by Benjamin Banneker, the *Appeal* itself helped to found a rich ethnological tradition by writers of color in the nineteenth century. Walker's 1829 *Appeal* looms large in the history of black ethnology as a major reference point for all subsequent texts in the tradition, as well as in some Native-authored ethnologies in the period. Like later ethnological texts, the *Appeal* is an eclectic work, combining classical history, universal history, and biblical genealogy with a political discourse on the oppressed, degraded condition of black subjects—nominally free and enslaved—in the United States. The *Appeal* itself was influenced by and indebted to a series of articles on Africa and the history of humankind in *Freedom's Journal*. The *Appeal's* fiery biblical rhetoric was also influenced by sermons in the black church that challenged the Curse of Ham/Mark of Cain justification of slavery and provided alternative biblical genealogies that ennobled, rather than degraded, the African race.

Walker's text was perhaps the most important factor leading to the rise of African American and some Afro-Native ethnological writings in New England in the 1830s and 1840s. James W. C. Pennington, Hosea Easton, and Robert Benjamin Lewis all reference Walker in their works, and the notoriety related to its publication and circulation made the *Appeal* an attractive template for subsequent ethnological investigations.[19] Although Maria Stewart never published a book-length ethnology, her speeches also addressed the origins and descent of the African race and bear traces of her intellectual exchanges with Walker.[20] Walker's *Appeal* also shaped the ethnological writing of William Apess, the Pequot Methodist preacher, activist, and writer who appended an ethnological treatise on the origin and history of the "red race" to the second edition of his autobiography, *A Son of the Forest*, in 1830.[21]

All black ethnologies from this period forwarded a monogenetic theory of the origin and descent of the races, affirming that all men had been made "of one blood" by God. These writers, who were all preachers or had strong ties to the church, also set out to demolish the justification of slavery through the Curse of Ham story as forwarded by pro-slavery advocates and preachers. The "assumed biblical justification for a curse of eternal slavery imposed on Black people, and Black people alone," the Curse of Ham more specially refers to Noah's cursing of his son Ham's descendants with eternal slavery as punishment for Ham looking upon Noah naked.[22] But as David Goldenberg notes, the biblical "curse" refers only to slavery, not to blackness. The Curse of Ham as a "dual curse" that linked blackness and slavery emerged over time through creative mixings of biblical and nonbiblical writings, as well as through the conflation of the Curse of Ham and Mark of Cain stories, whereby Ham married a descendent of Cain, making all of their descendants black and enslaved. The "dual curse" of blackness and slavery was picked up and disseminated by Europeans from the beginnings of the African slave trade and became a standard justification for slavery in the antebellum United States.[23] Antebellum writers also referenced the Mark of Cain story in which Cain was "marked" by God as punishment for killing his brother Abel. Accordingly, peoples of African descent were presumed to be the "marked" descendants of Cain.[24] In the *Appeal*, Walker provides a vicious attack on proponents of this story. He not only disputes the idea that blacks are the descendants of the murderous Cain, but also challenges and mocks the poor research skills of the "ignorant and avaricious wretches" who circulated this story.[25] Pennington amplified Walker's outrage over the heresy of the "Mark of Cain" when he bluntly informed his readers that blacks were not the seed of Cain, "as the stupid say."[26]

Walker, Lewis, Easton, and Pennington all turned to biblical history to combat emerging forms of racist science and racist Christian doctrine in the United States. Their ethnological writings were in many ways what Mia Bay calls "messianic ethnologies," a conceptualization that captures the blending of science and scripture in these texts, as well as their relationship to the evangelism and millenarian beliefs that were a major part of the Second Great Awakening.[27] As messianic texts, black ethnologies placed people of African descent at the center of providential history, suggesting that African Americans—courageous and faithful members of God's army fighting for the rights of the oppressed and degraded on earth—would take a central role in the coming of God's reign of peace on Earth.[28]

Like their use of classical and universal history to establish the centrality of Africa in the history of the West, African Americans also used the Bible to establish counter-histories of the origin and descent of the races. Biblical genealogy allowed black writers to imagine a long, rich history of the African race that was not reducible to the history of slavery in the Americas. As Stephen Hall notes, these writers were thus able to "construct a longer genealogy of human existence that extended and expanded the narrow timeline of popular nineteenth-century romantic histories."[29] By delineating a biblical and ancient black history that was anterior to the history of the modern world, these writers offered a vision of the past—and a glimpse of a future—that was not overdetermined by the history of enslavement and disenfranchisement in the New World. Thus, biblical genealogy provided powerful fodder for meditations on speculative kinship, an imaginative project of mapping descent and genealogy across the African diaspora that did not hinge upon the Atlantic slave trade and slavery in the United States.

Taken together, black ethnologies set out to recuperate the status of Africa and its descendants in world history. As Hall notes, these writings replaced the nationalist, "manifest destiny" histories of white historians with global, diasporic histories.[30] Placing African and other peoples of color at the center of world history, these diasporic histories offered detailed visions of a majestic, precolonial Africa that was the world's leading civilization before its destruction at the hands of imperialist, greedy Europeans.[31] Displacing the history of slavery and the Middle Passage with a rich vision of precolonial Africa, ethnology allowed African Americans to draw and imagine their direct ancestral connections to the grand civilizations of ancient Africa, sometimes wildly compressing time and space in the process.[32] In so doing, ethnology could be used to repair the lines of kinship destroyed by the Middle Passage and slavery in the Atlantic World. Moreover, biblical genealogy opened a space from which African Americans could imagine and speculate on forms of kinship that were not linked to systems of rape and coerced reproduction under slavery. Black ethnologies thus read like speculative fictions, anticipating the bold thought experiments of Martin Delany's 1859 serial novel, *Blake; or, The Huts of America*, as well as much more recent works of Afro-diasporic speculative fiction.

Beyond their investments in monogenesis, their portrayal of a rich African past, and a kind of racial messianism, black ethnologies take up diverse lines of inquiry and differ from each other in key ways. Rather than just producing a master narrative about black ethnology, and about monogenesis more specifically, the individual texts that constitute this genre are characterized by rich particularities and unique interventions. Each black ethnology of the period tells a different story, even as they all are deeply sensitized to similar intellectual movements and questions. In other words, these texts are not doctrinal, which suggests that the black church provided rich resources for the growth and development of diverse avenues of black thought in the period. Rather than regurgitating scriptural teachings, black ethnologies are creative and flexible documents that reflect a range of different viewpoints and arguments.

Although white abolitionists were largely indifferent to the ascendency of racial science in the 1830s, some engagements with ethnology did appear in white abolitionist tracts and newspaper publications. For example, in *An Appeal in Favor of That Class of Americans Called Africans* (1833), Lydia Maria Child turns to the resources of ethnology in order to answer abolition's rhetorical question, "Am I Not a Man or a Brother?," with a resounding "yes." At the beginning of the chapter entitled "The Intellect of Negroes," Child writes, "In order to decide what is our duty concerning the Africans and their descendants, we must first clearly make up our minds whether they are, or are not, human beings—whether they have, or have not, the same capacities for improvement as other men."[33] The rest of the chapter draws on ethnology, natural history, and the biographies of distinguished people of African descent to demonstrate that Africans are, indeed, human beings: "The negro's claim to be ranked as a *man*, is universally allowed by the learned."[34] From the very beginning of the movement in the early 1830s, white abolitionists rooted their rhetorical war on slavery in a series of "proofs" of the humanness of the African race. Thus, even when white abolitionists did not explicitly address ethnology, the theory of monogenesis as well as ethnology's discourse on race and the human routinely found their way into abolitionist rhetoric and polemic. But while white abolitionists like Child used ethnology to establish the humanness of the African race, black ethnologists use this basic tenet—the humanity of African descended peoples—as a jumping off point for a complex set of discussions of political filiation, race relations in America, and sin and salvation, as well as speculations on kinship, affinities, and alliances between and among populations of color in the United States and across the diaspora.

Visualizing Kinship

Robyn Wiegman notes that the shift in focus from the climate to the body in late eighteenth-century natural history anticipated the rise of the human sciences, especially biology, in which the tethering of race to skin, or the epidermalization of racial difference, unequivocally tied race to economies of the visible and visual in modernity.[35] In such a context, the popularization of image production, including the commercial development of engravings, lithography, and other forms of visual representation, aligned neatly with racial science's visual imperatives. In the transition from natural history to comparative anatomy and eventually biology, the terrain of the visual became an important field of evidence for comparative anatomy's interest in making internal structures visible and readable to both the trained and untrained observer. [36]

Visual evidence buttressed the claims of racial science, but the images of ethnology also traveled far beyond the bindings of ethnological texts. Widely reproduced and reprinted, these images contributed to the popular dissemination of polygenesis in American culture, as well as in transatlantic spaces. For example, *Types of Mankind*'s images of human-animal physiognomies and polygenetic taxonomies, linking the human races to flora and fauna rather than to each other, achieved an almost iconographic status. The columnar illustration of Apollo, an African man, and a chimpanzee in *Types of Mankind*, which was taken from Julien-Joseph Virey's *Histoire naturelle du genre humain* (1801), highlighted the hierarchy of the races by its vertical organization, and represented the facial angles in profiles in such a way as to position Africans closer to apes than white people.[37] These and other illustrations drawn from European ethnology and Egyptology were key sources for the American school of ethnology, and the Atlantic dimensions of racial science were solidified through the transatlantic exchange of images as well as texts. For example, the French Egyptologist, writer, and artist, Émile Prisse d'Avennes, sent Samuel George Morton portraits of Abyssinian (Habesha) men and women, which he produced in Luxor, Egypt. One of the portraits, a painting of a Bishari man, was turned into an illustration that appeared in Nott and Gliddon's *Types of Mankind*.[38]

Just as the iconography of ethnology was produced in transatlantic networks of scientific exchange and dissemination, the circulation of racist prints and other forms of visual ephemera also crisscrossed the Atlantic.[39] In the United States and abroad, visual illustrations in racial science and anti-black imagery in popular culture did much to popularize the theories of the American school of ethnology beyond the reading and circulation of actual ethnological texts. Even today, the images in *Types of Mankind* are often used to stand in for the whole history of racial science. But *Types of Mankind* was not published until 1854, and the visual history of racial science before the 1850s is much more oblique and complex. For example, Samuel George Morton's 1839 *Crania Americana* was perhaps more notable as an art object than as a scientific work: the book's ethnological text at times feels like an accessory to the moribund, yet technically gorgeous lithographs of indigenous skulls from North and South America that fill the book. But despite the importance of the visual archive in *Crania Americana*, the images in this founding text of American race science made it too expensive to circulate widely.[40] Thus, more than simply serving as a popularization of Morton's text, *Types of Mankind* was also central to extending the visual evidence and visual impact of American ethnology. Gliddon and Nott's 1854 book also deemphasized the centrality of Native Americans to the visual and intellectual project of *Crania Americana*. Embracing the myth of the "vanishing Indian," Nott and Gliddon instead focused on the anti-black implications of Morton's project to mobilize polygenesis within anti-abolition and anti-black debates of the 1850s.

During the 1830s and 1840s, the visual archive that supported American racial science was largely found in popular culture, rather than in scientific texts themselves. The typologies of American race science infiltrated periodicals, caricatures, broadsides, and other illustrated forms of print, including joke books, almanacs, and ephemera emerging from the culture industry of blackface minstrelsy.[41] By the 1850s, those racial typologies circulated back from popular culture to racial science: some of Nott and Gliddon's own visual depictions of Africans were racist caricatures drawn from newspapers rather than from scientific works.[42]

Throughout the antebellum period, it was indeed increasingly difficult to parse scientific images of blackness from their popular siblings, and the influence between race science and popular culture ran both ways. In his *Treatise on the Intellectual Character, and Civil and Political Condition of the Colored People of the United States* (1837), which I discuss at greater length below, Hosea Easton links the rise of anti-black violence in the 1830s in the Northeast to the proliferation in public spaces of racist images that both reflected and produced prejudice. His comments indicate that in urban environments like Boston, African Americans daily encountered images of their own subjection and abjection: "Cuts and placards descriptive of the negroe's deformity, are every where displayed to the observation of the young, with corresponding broken lingo, the very character of which is marked with design. Many of the popular book stores, in commercial towns and cities, have their show-windows lined with them." Moreover, the "barrooms of the most popular public houses in the country, sometimes have their ceiling literally covered with them. This display of American civility is under the daily observation of every class of society, even in New England. But this kind of education is not only systematized, but legalized."[43] This startling image of the ceilings of taverns "literally covered" with degrading images of black "deformity" illuminates the fact that practices and institutions of Northern racism were sustained by a visual archive of racial difference and physical inferiority, an archive that both fed off of and contributed to racial science.

It was against the interanimating, even synergistic, power of ethnology and racist visual culture that African Americans constructed speculative genealogies of kinship and belonging. Robert Benjamin Lewis was one such critic of the popular and scientific degradation of the Black image. Through his ethnology he sought to establish the learnedness and dignity of the Black subject in the United States and to connect African Americans both to Africans across the diaspora and to a biblical and ancient history in which African people were central actors. In addition to using ethnology—as well as portraiture—to draw lines of kinship among Black people across the diaspora, he also articulated biological, social, and political forms of kinship between Black and Native peoples in 1830s New England.

The first edition of Lewis's *Light and Truth*, the earliest known book-length black ethnology, was published in 1836 in Portland, Maine.[44] Lewis was born in what is now Gardiner, Maine and lived, worked, and raised his family in the area until he moved with his wife and many children to Bath in the late 1840s, where he built a house.[45] It is possible that Lewis's interest in the globally oriented discourse of ethnology was first ignited not through book reading (though that would become important later on), but through travel, which brought him in contact with people of color both within and outside the United States. Early in his life, Lewis took to the sea, where he worked on ships that sailed along the Eastern seaboard and in the Caribbean. Maine, in this context, emerges not as a provincial, isolated, northernmost state of New England, but rather as a seaport state that was deeply connected to both the rest of the coastal United States and the Caribbean through travel and trade. Lewis's early travels on the Atlantic could have very well sparked his interest in the history of Africa and the African diaspora, and it may even have been during those travels that he hatched his idea to research and write a text that would connect populations of peoples of African descent dispersed across the world.

Despite the fact that Lewis spent the majority of his life in southern Maine, his eyes remained fixed on Africa, as well as the Afro-Caribbean. Reginald Pitts notes that Lewis had connections to local, white Congregationalists through their organization, the Maine Missionary Society; after Lewis's death, the society noted that they had supported Lewis's education "with a view to his becoming a missionary in Africa."[46] Lewis's connections to the Maine Missionary Society likely afforded him the textual resources in biblical and ancient history that allowed him to research and write his ethnology. While Lewis's engagement with the diaspora was primarily textual and speculative during this part of his life, culminating in his publication of *Light and Truth*, travel connected him physically to the diaspora at the end of his life. In late 1857, Lewis sailed for Port-au-Prince, Haiti, on a Bath merchant ship, where he served as a cook and steward. Lewis's daughter Mary reported that he had been using this work opportunity to scout out a spot for his family to ultimately resettle in Haiti and was particularly interested in "securing a position" for Mary so that she might escape the conditions of prejudice in the United States. However, Lewis came down with yellow fever and passed away in Haiti in 1858. Mary noted that a large funeral was held for her father and that many people in Port-au-Prince knew of his *Light and Truth*.[47]

Light and Truth was Lewis's life work, a sustained intellectual project intended to delineate the regal origins and history of the African and Indian race, which would occupy him, in various ways, for nearly two decades. The first edition of *Light and Truth* was a small book, in dimensions, and was also relatively short, running to only 176 pages. Soon after its publication, Lewis began preparing a revised and much expanded edition. The complete expanded edition, which appeared in 1844, holds an important place in book history as the first known book to be produced entirely by African Americans, from its author and editors to its printer and subscription agents.[48] Published by a "committee of colored gentleman" in Boston, the 1844 edition was printed by Benjamin Frank-lin Roberts, a radical shoemaker, activist, lecturer, and one of the first black printers in the United States[49] Roberts reprinted the expanded, 1844 version of *Light and Truth* again in 1849.[50] Mia Bay suggests that because of Lewis's regular book tours throughout New England, *Light and Truth* may have been the most widely circulated black ethnology in the nineteenth century.[51]

Subsequent editions of *Light and Truth*, which further expanded the readership of the work into the 1850s, put Lewis's text in circula-tion with *Types of Mankind* and other texts on polygenesis. Across the decades, Lewis's *Light and Truth* would be increasingly brought into the orbit of a secularizing racial science. Commentary on Lewis's text among black intellectuals indicates that ethnological writing by writers of color entailed a certain risk—namely, the appearance of reproducing white ethnology by engaging with a highly compromised, and compro-mising, discourse. Referring to either Roberts's expanded 1844 edition or an 1851 edition printed by a Reverend Moses M. Taylor of Boston, Martin Delany's 1852 *Condition, Elevation, Emigration and Destiny of the Colored People of the United States* references "a book issued in Boston, purporting to be a history of ancient great men of African descent, by one Mr. Lewis, entitled 'Light and Truth.'"[52] Delany's scath-ing review of *Light and Truth* goes so far as to claim that the book is nothing more than a compilation of excerpts taken from well-known English histories, added to which is "a tissue of historical absurdities and literary blunders."[53] In one final blow, Delany makes a suggestion to booksellers: that *Light and Truth* be packaged and sold with George Gliddon's *Ancient Egypt*. For, if Gliddon's offensive history seeks to turn all ancient black men white, Lewis's history is just as offensive as it turns all "ancient great white men, *black*."[54] Despite his bold and scath-ing tone, Delany's inclusion of Lewis in his chapter on "Literary and Professional Colored Men and Women" also reveals that Lewis's book was being read by black intellectuals and activists in the 1850s. Delany's imaginative binding of Lewis with Gliddon further speaks to the dia-logism, and sometimes dangerous proximity, between black ethnology and the American school of ethnology it opposed, a dynamic that can be traced back to Walker's own flirtation with *Notes on the State of Vir-ginia* in his 1829 *Appeal*.

Light and Truth gained new printings as racial science gained currency within anti-black and anti-Native policy debates from the 1830s through the 1850s. The multiple editions of *Light and Truth* published in the 1840s and 1850s indicate that many different parties recognized the continued relevance of this text as a response to the texts and ideologies of US ethnology. Into the 1850s, Lewis continued to work on his ever-expanding ethnology and sought more publishing ventures that could accommodate the ambition and scope of his vision. In 1852 and 1853, nearly twenty years after the publication of the first edition of *Light and Truth*, he published a book prospectus in both *Frederick Douglass' Paper* and the *Liberator* in which he sought financial support for the publication of a "new history" that was "intended to remove the prejudices from Whites against the Colored and Indian people in the United States." Given Lewis's ongoing interest in further contributing to *Light and Truth* and including images in its publication, it is likely that this new history was a further expansion of his project in *Light and Truth*. Lewis states that the grandiose work, intended for families and schools, was composed of four volumes: two volumes on geography and two on history, complete with a corresponding atlas including charts and maps of "all the different nations and countries." In addition to a chart giving "figures of the ancient historians, with the prophets of Christ and his Apostles, who were colored," the work would have a map of the world that places the "men of all nations in their own countries, in which they were born—giving the true complexion and figure of the nations in the five Zones of the whole inhabited Globe."[55] In the advertisement, Lewis states that the volume is already completed, but it is more likely that he was seeking financial support so that he could begin this wildly ambitious undertaking. Despite the fact that this grand "new history" never appeared, the 1852–1853 prospectus highlights Lewis's desire to buttress his textual ethnological arguments with the visual evidence and proof supplied by maps and charts, as had become common in white-authored ethnologies by the 1850s.

While the book prospectus indicates that Lewis understood the power of images in responding to both the visual and textual evidence of US ethnology, the notice's appeal for funding support also indicates the financial prohibitions of image production for black writers in the period. An image did appear in one edition of *Light and Truth*: the frontispiece of the 1849 Boston edition is an engraving of a Native American with an elaborate headdress, holding a bow in one hand and a small plant in the other (see Figures 2.1a and 2.1b). The caption below the image, "Antiquity of America. See page 124," directs readers to a section of the text that collates references to an unknown continent in the

Antiquity of America. See page 124.

Figures 2.1a and 2.1b (facing page). Frontispiece and title page to the 1849 edition of Robert Benjamin Lewis's *Light and Truth*. Courtesy of Rare Books, Special Collections and Preservation, University of Rochester River Campus Libraries.

West (America) in classical texts and forwards a colonial-period argument that persisted into the nineteenth century that Native Americans were actually ancient Jews from one of the Ten Lost Tribes of Israel. The plant in the indigenous figure's hand further signals indigenous botanical knowledge of the Americas.

LIGHT AND TRUTH:

COLLECTED FROM

THE BIBLE AND ANCIENT AND MODERN HISTORY;

CONTAINING THE

UNIVERSAL HISTORY

OF THE

COLORED AND THE INDIAN RACE,

FROM THE CREATION OF THE WORLD
TO THE PRESENT TIME.

BY R. B. LEWIS,
A COLORED MAN.

Search this work with care and candor;
Every line and page you read
Will brighten all the truths of Scripture,
Proved by history — plain indeed.

BOSTON:
PUBLISHED BY A COMMITTEE OF COLORED MEN.
BENJAMIN F. ROBERTS, PRINTER.
1849.

It appears that Lewis had additional visual ambitions for his *Light and Truth*, beyond this single frontispiece. A surviving copy of a rare portrait of Lewis further indicates his interest in linking both Black and Native images to his ethnology and in using portraiture to challenge the racist visual culture that buttressed the claims of US ethnology (see Figure 2.2). Lewis's portrait must have been printed sometime in the late 1820s or early 1830s since it was produced by Pendleton's Lithography, an important yet short-lived firm in Boston owned by brothers William S. and John B. Pendleton. The Pendleton brothers were at the forefront of American use of lithography, a printing process that made it cheaper and quicker to reproduce graphic prints.[56] Lewis's portrait was done by Benjamin Franklin (B. F.) Nutting, a popular Boston artist and engraver who worked as an apprentice at Pendleton's from 1828 until about 1834.

Lewis took advantage of the revolution in lithography in the 1830s to intervene in the racist caricaturing of African Americans in both print and visual culture. Likely produced in anticipation of Lewis's forthcoming book publication, the handsome, large lithograph offers a visual supplement to the account of the regality and intelligence of the African race found in *Light and Truth*. Given Lewis's travels throughout New England and the circulation of his book throughout the region, it seems likely that the lithograph was produced to sell at Lewis's book tour stops, as many activists sold their portraits at public appearances. Although it did not appear in the 1836 edition, or in any subsequent editions, the lithograph may have been also intended for use as a frontispiece to an existing edition of *Light and Truth* or one planned by Lewis that never came to fruition. Many other portraits from the studio were used for this purpose.

In his foundational history of lithography in America, *America on Stone* (1931), Harry T. Peters notes that Pendleton's specialized in portraits for magazines and books. The question remains: After going to the trouble of having his portrait engraved on limestone, printed, and reproduced, why wasn't the lithograph of Lewis included in *Light and Truth*? Peters notes that artists working for Pendleton's received upward of sixty dollars for each portrait, and the studio charged additional printing fees for copies (a bill from Pendleton's, for example, lists a fifty-dollar charge for the cost of five hundred copies plus paper). While Lewis benefited from the democratization of image production and the rise of commer-

ROBERT BENJAMIN LEWIS,

Who will plead the rights of All.

Parentage Indian, Ethiopian, & European.

Born in Maine in 1802.

Figure 2.2. B. F. Nutting, "Robert Benjamin Lewis," Pendleton's Lithography, Boston, date unknown. Courtesy of the American Antiquarian Society.

cial lithography during the 1830s, printing costs may have made further reproduction of the lithograph unfeasible.

Light and Truth provided a textual archive of respectability, intelligence, and character, and Lewis's portrait performed a similar kind of work. African Americans understood that the visual field was a key site of struggle for representing the race. And the lithograph—the visual representation of Lewis himself—illuminates that *Light and Truth* was not just about challenging claims of degeneracy and inferiority in ethnology and popular culture; it was also about the politics of visibility and representation for people of color in the United States. Like ethnology, portraiture could serve as a powerful counterarchive to the crude typologies of racial science, typologies that also proliferated through racist cartoons in the antebellum print sphere. Black portraiture made important interventions into discourses of race and physiology throughout the antebellum period.[57] Crude illustrations were regularly used to delineate racial "types" by ethnologists and to establish racial inferiority through the field of the visual. In response, figures like Frederick Douglass, Martin Delany, William Wells Brown, and Lewis himself turned to the art of portraiture in order to establish counterarchives of black respectability, beauty, and intelligence.[58] Those looking at Lewis's portrait confronted an image of undoubtable masculinity and dignity, embodied in his straight posture, regal garb, slightly pursed lips, and a downward glance that seems to resist even as it receives the gaze of viewers.

Thus, *Light and Truth* was not Lewis's only intervention into the dominant discourses of antebellum ethnology: with his noble visage displayed and multiracial ancestry—"Indian, Ethiopian, & European"— prominently announced in the caption, the portrait itself served as a powerful challenge to the texts and visual representations of the American school of ethnology. Lewis's book tour stops and the lectures that may have accompanied them served as a similarly embodied intervention into the discourses of ethnology. In the portrait, Nutting portrays Lewis with a seven-pointed star on his head and a striking pendant around his neck bearing the famous Eye of Providence. These two Masonic symbols would have signified Lewis's relationship to black freemasonry for nineteenth-century viewers.[59] Lewis's racial background is deliberately ambiguous in the image, an ambiguity that positions him as an apt representative for all oppressed people, not only in New England and the broader nation, but also around the globe. The caption notes he "will plead the rights of All." This is not the image of a slave, or even a provincial Northern freeman. Through the image and its caption, Lewis is presented as a cosmopolitan man of color, combining and representing the noblest qualities of the global races of humankind ("Indian, Ethiopian, & European"). Representing Lewis donned in "Oriental Dress," which was popular in visual art of the period and connected to a broader Orientalism in European and American culture, the portrait specifically connects Lewis to the Afro-Arab world of Africa, especially to Egypt and Ethiopia, the birthplaces of learnedness in the arts and sciences celebrated by Lewis throughout the text of his *Light and Truth*.[60]

The highlighting of Lewis's mixed "parentage" as well as the portrait's representation of its subject as a cosmopolitan man of color suggest that categorizing *Light and Truth* as a black ethnology does not adequately capture the complexities and political aims of the text, nor the identity of its author. Lewis was a freeman of both African and Native American descent; his father was Mohegan or Pequot, and his mother was likely the daughter of slaves. In the 1844 edition of *Light and Truth*, the preface by the publishing committee notes that they have published the book so that a "correct knowledge of the Colored and Indian people, ancient and modern, may be extended freely." They proceed to package the volume as an Afro-Native ethnology by an Afro-Native writer: "The author of this compilation has been some years in gathering this information. He is a descendent of the two races he so ably vindicates."[61] Lewis's Black and Native ancestry is representative of the intermingling of many African Americans and Native peoples in New England in this period, as well as the residential, religious, and cultural spaces that increasingly brought together African Americans and Native Americans in cities across the Northeast, especially as members of dispossessed tribes and nations found their way into the "colored" sections of Northern cities. This was a moment when "colored" could refer to both Black and Native peoples, as well as to those with mixed ancestry—a fact that challenges the common separation of Black and Native life in academic subfields and even points to the limits of maintaining hard distinctions between Black and Native literature in the first decades of the nineteenth century.[62]

Given Lewis's ancestry as well as his political commitments to the solidarity of "colored" peoples in his region, *Light and Truth* might be more appropriately categorized as an Afro-Native ethnology. From this perspective, Lewis's portrait is also reframed as that of an Afro-Native subject, another important intervention into the presumed separation of the races in polygenetic discourses and images. The frontispiece of a Native American at the beginning of the 1849 edition of *Light and Truth*, referenced above, similarly reflects the Native-Black connections at the heart of Lewis's project. Even if Lewis did not himself select this image (his input into the Boston editions is unclear), Lewis's printer, B. F. Roberts, highlights Lewis's interest in Native American history and identity through the frontispiece. On the facing title page, Lewis is listed as the author and as a "colored man," a designation that included both Black and Native subjects in the 1840s. But importantly, Lewis does not conflate "Black" and "Indian" under the category "colored" in his text. Instead, he emphasizes the forms of political and cultural alliance among African Americans and Native Americans, while insisting on the specific, yet connected, histories of these groups, especially at the hands of colonial settlers in the New World.

In both the text and in its supporting visual evidence, ethnology provided Lewis with a powerful language with which to articulate the shared descent of African and Native peoples. But despite his own mixed-race ancestry, highlighted in the lithograph, the text of *Light and Truth* is more interested in forms of filiation that, like shared histories of oppression, did not depend on biology and reproduction. As a discourse used to justify the exploitation of enslaved black labor and dispossess Native Americans of their land, ethnology was deeply implicated in the subjection of both African American and Native American communities. In addition to challenging the American school of ethnology's pro-slavery arguments, Black and Afro-Native ethnologists like Lewis were also producing their texts in responses to the US government's production of ethnological knowledge to justify Native American removal and acts of anti-Native violence and dispossession. In *Light and Truth*, ethnology is ultimately transformed from a science of subjugation to a science of Afro-Native alliance. At one point, the author even hails a Native readership alongside its Black one, calling out to both "colored and Indian brethren" reading the text. In opposition to the various scientific "proofs" of black and Native inferiority that populated dominant ethnological discourses, Lewis imagines new forms of solidarity in America in and through ethnology.

Lewis's ethnological project is thus also a project of speculative kinship. *Light and Truth* is not just a history of the races; it is a complex work of Black and Native genealogy, a "patchwork" genealogy stitched together with multiple sources ranging from the Bible, dictionaries, and classical histories translated into English to works of Native ethnography and speeches by chiefs.[63] Throughout, Lewis's ethnology speculates on forms of kinship in the absence of reliable family records and in the face of the enormous losses and absences of the Middle Passage, the dispossession and dispersal of Native American populations, and the many gaps in the colonial archive.[64] Such acts of speculative kinship clearly held much cultural power for African American, Native American, and Afro-Native peoples.

While Lewis's lithograph represents a history of intermarriage and reproduction between African American and Native American communities, *Light and Truth* is more interested in forms of community that do not depend on blood. Much of the text does indeed hold to Delany's estimation of its interest in turning all ancient men "black" while, interestingly, the history of Native Americans is kept separate from the history of African descended people through most of the book. A discourse of mixed-race identity does finally show up in the "Scale of Complexion" that concludes the book and gives names for several common "amalgamations" of race: "Between Black and White is a Mulatto," "Between Mulatto and a Black is a Sambo," "The complexion of the Indian tribes:—Reddish, Copper, Brown, Black, and a white mixed hue."[65] The taxonomy of skin color in Lewis's "Scale of Complexion," as well as his use of the term "Sambo," is one of the moments that probably infuriated Delany, flirting as it does with the hierarchizing of racial difference and an obsession with miscegenation that also characterized the writings of the American school of ethnology. And yet, this biological categorization of race is only a fleeting moment in a book that tracks a more complicated network of kinship through biblical genealogy, American and ancient history, and Black and Native intellectual production. The very last line of the book, immediately following the "Scale of Complexion," shifts to a language of political alliance, forged through the conditions of oppression and the monogenetic creation of all races as "one blood" by God: "We are all one, and oppressed in this land of boasted Freedom and Liberty."[66] Thus, in *Light and Truth*, speculative kinship ultimately hinges not on consanguinity but on a shared plight between Black and North American indigenous peoples, a plight rooted in a history of state violence, removal, containment, and subjugation. In Lewis's words, "We are all one, and oppressed."

One important visual antecedent for Lewis's lithograph appeared in the second edition of William Apess's *A Son of the Forest: The Experience*

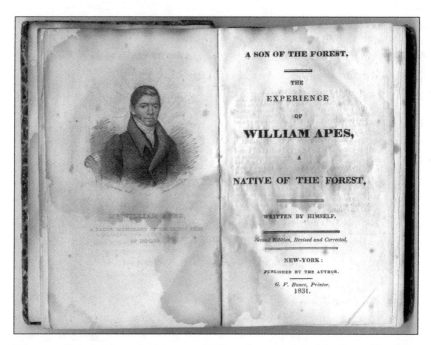

Figure 2.3. Frontispiece and title page to William Apess, *A Son of the Forest: The Experience of William Apes[s], A Native of the Forest* (New York, 1831). Courtesy of the American Antiquarian Society.

of William Apes[s], A Native of the Forest (1831), the first book-length autobiography authored by a Native American.[67] Apess himself turned to ethnology in order to discount theories of Native inferiority: his *Son of the Forest* was appended by an account of the "origins and character of the Indians."[68] Philip F. Gura notes that while the 1829 edition of Apess's book received no known public notices, sinking like a "stone" in the book marketplace, a second edition, "revised and corrected," appeared in 1831, complete with a handsome portrait of Apess serving as its frontispiece (see Figure 2.3).[69] With a caption stating, "Mr. William Apes[s], a Native Missionary of the Pequot Tribe of Indians," the image represents Apess as a dignified gentleman and like Lewis's portrait, serves as a visual supplement to the ethnological text included at the end of his autobiography.

Degraded and Degrading Visual Archives

In addition to working as images of racial fitness and physiognomy, lithographed portraits of writers of color were also appealing embellishments that could be used to sell books. The inclusion of Apess's portrait in the 1831 edition of *A Son of the Forest* helped to broaden its appeal and circulation. Evidence that Lewis's portrait did in fact circulate—either on its own or as a frontispiece to an edition of *Light and Truth* that has not been recovered—appears in a curious and remarkable citation of Lewis's image, which sought to debase Lewis, and his people, from their regal origins. Lewis, in turn, became a part of the anti-black visual archive that his *Light and Truth* and his portrait both challenged. This strange citation of Lewis appeared in *The Light and Truth of Slavery*, a narrative of a former slave named Aaron, which was published sometime between 1845 and 1847. The narrative was not bound as a book like Lewis's *Light and Truth*, but instead appeared in the cheaper form of a pamphlet. It was "printed at Worcester, Mass.," "for Aaron," nearly a decade after Lewis's first publication of *Light and Truth*, but just a couple of years after an 1843 edition was printed in Augusta, Maine, and only one year after Benjamin F. Robert's revised and expanded edition of Lewis's *Light and Truth* was printed in Boston in 1844.[70]

Given the 1843 and 1844 publications of *Light and Truth*, as well as the fact that *The Light and Truth of Slavery* was printed in such close proximity to Boston, it is clear that the title of this little known narrative cribs from the title of Lewis's book. John Blassingame counts Aaron's among the "unreliable narratives" of the slave narrative genre.[71] Ironically, the narrative itself refers to and even uses excerpts from other fraudulent slave narratives of the period, including James Williams's 1838 narrative. But more than simply displaying a heavy editorial hand that obscures Aaron's story, several aspects of the text suggest that Aaron was a fictional creation of the pamphlet's editor. Indeed, the narrative does not follow any of the archetypal conventions of the slave narrative and contains no reference to or apparent knowledge of the geographical coordinates of slavery in the South. Rather than showcasing the Southern regionalism typical of the antebellum slave narrative, the narrative tracks Aaron's travels through a relatively restricted geographic range in New England. We never learn where Aaron escaped from in the South, and the opening of the text suggests an ambiguity regarding Aaron's status as a former slave while grounding its rhetoric in Aaron's supposed testimony to the editor ("Aaron says").[72] The narrative is cobbled together from a number of different print sources, combining excerpts from slave narratives, newspapers, sermons, scripture, and anti-slavery lectures. Most notably, it uses the slave narrative form to offer a series of moral lessons on Christian hospitality as well as to stump for the Liberty Party. The narrative opens with a clear indication of the presumed market value of Aaron's story, and the author's desire to sell his book. Ventriloquizing Aaron, the author/editor writes, "Now reader, Aaron wants you to buy this book."[73]

It is certainly possible that the author/editor titled the narrative after *Light and Truth* because potential purchasers in the region would have been familiar with Lewis's text. While the narrative makes reference to other New England cities and towns, Maine dominates Aaron's story. Readers learn that Aaron "has been pretty much all through the State of Maine," and follow his travels through Portland, Kennebunk, and even Hallowell, Lewis's own hometown.[74] The publication history and textual locales of Aaron's story suggest that the author/editor of *The Light and Truth of Slavery* may have even lived in proximity to Lewis himself. Given such local connections, this act of citation may also be read as an act of slander against Lewis, in which the anonymous author/editor of *The Light and Truth of Slavery* turns the learned freeman and local "colored historian" Robert Benjamin Lewis into Aaron, an illiterate former slave.

While there is no direct textual influence of Lewis's *Light and Truth* on *The Light and Truth of Slavery*, the author of Aaron's story cribs more than Lewis's title: he also cribs Lewis's image (see Figures 2.2 and 2.4). The first page of *The Light and Truth of Slavery* includes an illustration of Aaron that was clearly modeled after Lewis's portrait. The image of Aaron reproduces the turban on Lewis's head in the lithograph, as well as his black coat and wide white collar. But, importantly, in *The Light and Truth of Slavery*, Lewis/Aaron has been stripped of his Masonic garb, symbols of learnedness, status, and community. The image's caption states, "Reader, here is the picture of the poor, way-faring, degraded Aaron."[75] Marcus Wood notes that the "poor, way-faring, degraded" status of Aaron is reflected in the crude and cheap image technology used to produce the image. While Lewis's portrait was a detailed lithograph,

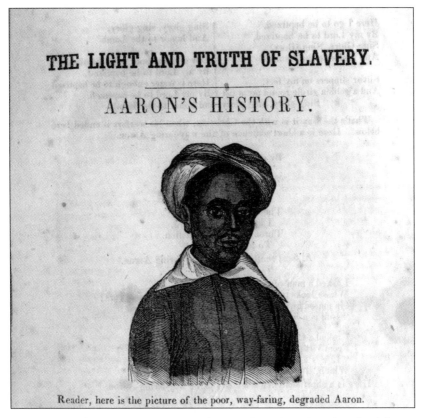

THE LIGHT AND TRUTH OF SLAVERY.

AARON'S HISTORY.

Reader, here is the picture of the poor, way-faring, degraded Aaron.

Figure 2.4. The "poor, way-faring, degraded Aaron," in *The Light and Truth of Slavery: Aaron's History* (Worcester, MA, 1845–1847). Courtesy of the American Antiquarian Society.

Aaron's image is a woodcut. Although Wood does not make the connection between Lewis's portrait and Aaron's image, he notes that Aaron's image is "so poor and degraded as to give no rendition of Aaron at all; the entire face is swallowed up in one mass of black printer's ink," leading to an "eradication of personal identity through poor technology."[76] This act of degraded image reproduction might be read as another personal attack on Lewis himself, in which the ethnologist's distinguished lithograph portrait is transformed into a crude, inferior woodcut, representing not a learned freeperson, but a degraded slave.

Ultimately, then, Aaron's image transforms a portrait of a freeman from one of nobility in *Light and Truth* back into an image of degeneracy and inferiority. In other words, Aaron's image attempts to claim Lewis's portrait, and his ethnology, for the visual archive of racist science and popular culture. But in reproducing Lewis's image, albeit in crude woodcut form, a trace of the counter-visual archive of racial science still persists, perhaps most notably in the reproduction of Lewis's direct, resistant gaze in and through Aaron's image. The image also powerfully registers the threat and danger of intellectual productions by free people of color, especially histories of African intelligence and nobility like *Light and Truth*, as perceived by white New Englanders during the period.

It is notable that Aaron's narrative and image also strip Lewis of his "Indian parentage," highlighted in the original lithograph and in the front matter of Lewis's book. There are many possible reasons for this, from the need to transform Lewis into a believable slave narrator to white interest in distancing Black and Native politics from one another. No matter the cause, the effect of this act is clear: in detaching Lewis from his Native ancestry, the woodcut image performs the kind of polygenetic "separation of the races" that appeared in popular print. While (white) ethnological texts were clearly most interested in establishing the superiority of the white race, these texts also routinely worked to separate non-white peoples from one another. Already in *Notes on the State of Virginia*, Jefferson sought to align Native Americans with whites, rather than with Africans in the early republic. In so doing, he attempted, to use Frank Wilderson's language, to oust Africans from the social itself.[77] The act of stripping Aaron/Lewis not only of his Masonic garb, but also of his Native ancestry points to the perceived threat of Black-Native solidarity in Jacksonian America and the danger that forms of speculative kinship among Black and Native peoples posed to white supremacy.

Finally, the removal of indigenous identity from Aaron/Lewis's image reveals something provocative about Lewis's own trafficking in "Indian character" as a form of cultural and racial appropriation. Lewis's portrait was produced amid the rise of a growing pictorial industry of the Native American in the 1830s United States, through exhibits like George Catlin's Indian Gallery, in natural history museums and exhibits, and in the staging of Native American sketches and melodramas like John Augustus Stone's *Metamora; or, The Last of the Wampanoags* (1829). An industry of visualizing and exhibiting Native peoples also took shape through the dissemination of portraiture in publications like Thomas McKenney and James Hall's *History of the Indian Tribes of North America* (1836–1844) and in various images in the print sphere, through traveling exhibits featuring Native culture and sometimes actual Native peoples, through the appearance of Native Americans on the lecture circuit, as well as the visual display of captured Native leaders on the streets of American cities.[78]

In addition to highlighting an actual ancestral connection, Lewis used Native ancestry as a savvy visual and rhetorical tool, since the popular discourse about the "noble savage" could actually work to dignify Black subjects. Piggybacking on a tradition of dignified Native portraiture and a related visual culture of the "noble savage" visible even in Morton's *Crania Americana*, visual cues of Native identity were sometimes used to lend a sense of nobility to the visual representation of African Americans. Such visual rhetoric may have even subtly signaled Lewis's indigeneity to another place: Africa.

While Robert Benjamin Lewis anticipated and fought against the degradation of the Black and Native image to which his own image was submitted in Aaron's narrative, other black ethnologists found degeneracy to be a rhetorically powerful language with which to rally the race and to make whites understand the effects of their actions down South and their inaction up North. In his 1837 *Treatise on the Intellectual Character, and Civil and Political Condition of the Colored People of the United States*, Hosea Easton offers a series of ekphrastic accounts of black bodies and visages literally de-forming under the weight of racism and anti-black violence; this rhetoric of deformation counterintuitively wallows in the degradation of blackness in the name of black kinship and collectivity.

Easton was a Massachusetts intellectual, activist, and Methodist preacher who was alternately passionate and pessimistic about the future of African Americans, enslaved and free, in the United States. Like David Walker's 1829 *Appeal*, Easton's 1837 *Treatise* is as much a scathing political commentary on race relations and racism in Jacksonian America as it is an ethnological account of the biblical and ancient history of the races. At the beginning of his *Treatise*, and at several points throughout, Easton notes that the colored population in the United States is a wronged and injured people and locates this injury in two sites: the first is the original injury of stealing Africans from their home and thus their "losing their country and their birthright," while the second is the ongoing racism and prejudice experienced by blacks within the United States at the hands of whites.[79] In the *Treatise*, Easton notes that he has had "sufficient opportunity to know something about prejudice, and its destructive effects" as a black person born and raised in Massachusetts.[80]

The *Treatise* contains many examples of anti-black racism and prejudice drawn from Easton's own experience, ranging from his time in Boston, where he participated in black community organizing and politics and co-founded the Massachusetts General Colored Association in 1826, to the burning down of his own church in Connecticut by a white mob in 1836. This was a period when African Americans in New England actually made important progress: the 1830s witnessed the birth of a number of black churches, the founding of several political and literary institutions, successful efforts to secure schooling for black children, and the establishment of black-owned businesses that contributed to financial security for some members of the community in places like New Haven, Middletown, Hartford, and earlier, in Boston. But at the same time, New England became a hotbed of racist activity as white Americans lashed out against the strengthening political organization of the region's free black population. The anti-black mob violence of the 1830s was also deeply influenced by white panic over worsening economic conditions across the country. The dark rhetoric of Easton's own *Treatise* registers the Panic of 1837, which was particularly devastating for nominally free African Americans already living in conditions of economic precariousness.

In the midst of these stressful and dangerous times, Easton became ill and passed away just two months after the *Treatise* was published. He was only thirty-eight years old. His experiences with anti-black mobs and his tragically short life are testaments to the devastating effects of racism delineated in his own *Treatise*. In the 1844 edition of *Light and Truth*, Robert Benjamin Lewis himself cites prejudice as the cause of Easton's early death, noting that he, and his three brothers, all "met a premature grave, on account of the cursed prejudices existing against them in their own town, by reason of their complexion."[81] This passing reference to Easton's death may indicate that Lewis was reading Easton's ethnology as he prepared the revised and expanded 1844 edition of *Light and Truth*. Lewis's biographical treatment of Easton suggests that although Easton passed away at a young age, like both David Walker and William Apess, his *Treatise* would continue to shape the development of black ethnology into the 1840s.

The Magnified Freeman

In addition to providing a monogenetic account of the origin and history of the races, Easton's *Treatise* is also an important textual intervention into the racist visual culture of antebellum print culture and racial science, a visual culture that Easton understood as helping to produce the vicious anti-black violence and life-threatening prejudice that wreaked havoc on black communities across the Northeast. Easton's ethnology is a deeply visual text. Throughout, he replaces the racist placards of black deformity that lined the bookstore windows and barrooms of Boston with an ekphrastic archive that places the blame for black degeneracy on white actors and violence.

While Lewis turned to the emerging technology of lithography to intervene in ethnology, print also served as a key medium through which black ethnologists challenged the rise of the American school of ethnology, as well as the racist images of black character in antebellum popular culture. The battle against the visual culture of black degeneracy, which was waged *through* print culture, also challenged the consumption of anti-black imagery among the white lower classes in the North. Easton's anecdote in the *Treatise* about the use of racist cartoons as a kind of wallpaper (or ceiling-paper) in Boston public houses further points to the existence of a white working-class print culture in which anxieties about black labor and fears of proximity to black people in Northern cities were played out. On the ceiling, the public house staff and patrons drew on the newspaper's own form of juxtaposition, reproduction, and arrangement to produce a visual print archive composed completely of prejudicial images. In this way, the papered ceiling served as a site that also condensed and intensified the anti-black imagery of the press and broader print sphere.

Although the *Treatise*, which was printed cheaply as a pamphlet, contains no actual images, Easton is engaged with questions about race and visuality throughout the text: he uses print to reflect on the binds of black visibility and to imagine other forms of visuality for black subjects. In one powerful section of his *Treatise*, Easton meditates on the double bind of black subjects, trapped between regimes of invisibility and spectacular hypervisibility. Writing on forms of racist pedagogy in the North, Easton argues that white men who have been instructed "from youth to look upon a black man in no other light than a slave" cannot "look upon him in any other light."[82] According to Easton, the white "looks" that "light" and frame the black subject also work to "magnify" the black (man's) body to monstrous proportions whenever he is seen in any other "sphere of action than that of a slave." The large, monstrous body of the freeman is seen as one that cannot fit into any public space anywhere: "mechanical shops, stores, and school rooms, are all too small for his entrance as a man." At the same time, the grotesque form of the huge, hulking freeman works to exclude him from the very category of the human. Through the penetrating, exacting gaze of white Americans, the freeman is magnified "so large that they [white Americans] cannot be made to believe that he is a man and a brother." While the visual framing of the Northern freeman as a monster makes it impossible to incorporate him into public space, in the South, the slave experiences an opposite fate: he is shrunk down so that he can be fit into the confined, private spaces of enslaved labor. Easton writes, "If he be a slave, his corporeality becomes so diminished as to admit him into ladies' parlors, and into small private carriages, and elsewhere, without being disgustful on account of his *deformity*, or without producing any other discomfiture."[83] This image of deformity and diminishment of corporeality signifies in several ways: in addition to explicitly referencing the confinement of black laboring bodies within "ladies parlors," "private carriages," and related spaces of domestic service, this scene also recalls the experience of slaves packed into the hold in the Middle Passage as well as the disfiguration of enslaved bodies under regimes of labor and punishment on the plantation.

Crucially, Easton's language of corporeal magnification and diminishment is enabled by a cultural imaginary produced by the visual technologies of the microscope and the telescope. The telescope's magnificent ability to bring distant bodies from across the galaxy into proximate view, and its ability to reveal possible life on other planets, played an important role in the American imagination in this period, producing new cultural visions not only of outer space, but of earthbound objects and bodies as well.[84] The 1830s also saw an explosion of popular interest in the microscope, and new technical developments that increased the ability to manipulate the microscope as well as improvements to resolution power situated the microscope at the center of a number of emerging scientific fields. Despite the fact that very few ordinary people owned a microscope, this new technology spawned a rich microscopic imaginary in the popular press and imaginative literature.

In addition to the inclusion of items on and advertisements for microscopes and telescopes in major newspapers and periodicals, African American and abolitionist periodicals routinely ran treatises on optical instruments and also reprinted philosophical meditations on the cultural—and existential—significance of instruments like the telescope and the microscope. Optical instruments, the *Liberator* suggested, offered a window onto new and previously unknown worlds both on Earth and across the galaxy, but they also forced society to meditate on and ask about the place of the human in (and beyond) our world.[85] In the *Liberator*, and across American periodical cultures, microscopic images were often described in the terms of small and normally invisible beings becoming huge, monstrous, and unsettling, of tiny fleas appearing as large as the "hugest elephants," and of teeming swarms of animalcules otherwise invisible in water, saliva, food, and other apparently inert substances.[86] Easton takes the terms of monstrosity and the grotesque as they were produced through the optical powers of the microscope and uses them to refract the optical bind of black Americans in the North and the South. The microscope's ability to make visible otherwise invisible beings resonated for African Americans in the antebellum period. Through the lenses of an imaginary optical instrument, Easton reflects on the impossibility of black existence in America, trapped between conditions of invisibility and a cruel "diminishment of corporeality" under slavery and forms of spectacular hyper-visibility and surveillance under liberal "freedom" in the North.

Easton's comments on the "diminishment of corporeality" under slavery were also part of his ongoing interest in the damaging corporeal effects of slavery. He notes, for example, that the "slave population labor[s] under an intellectual and physical disability or inferiority."[87] Throughout the text, disability is figured through the language of injury, which serves a double rhetorical function for Easton: a critical term in US law, "injury" indicates the right of black subjects to redress in legal contexts; at the same time, "injury" points to the bodily and psychological harms produced by regimes of Southern enslavement and Northern prejudice, which Easton calls "slavery in disguise." Here Easton intervenes into dominant discourses of ethnology: shifting the question of "negro inferiority" from biology to slavery itself, he reveals that slavery, not biology or God, is responsible for the physical and intellectual "deformation" of the colored people. Eighteenth-century theories of environmentalism continued to provide powerful resources for black intellectuals in the nineteenth century since they could be mobilized against polygenesis.

Like his imaginative vision of the magnification and diminishment of black corporeality, the issue of slave reproduction and kinship is framed through a powerful, visual example, creating another ekphrastic moment that recalibrates the visual archive of black inferiority. Easton offers an account of the traumas of the enslaved mother in distinctly visual terms, focusing on the effects of her witnessing of unimaginable violence and brutality. Inviting his readers to "think of" this poor, prospective mother and to "feel as a heart of flesh can feel," Easton directs them to bear witness to what she witnesses, to "see her weeping eyes fixed alternately upon the object of her affections and him who accounts her a brute—think how she feels on beholding the gore streaming from the back, the naked back, of the former, while the latter wields the accursed lash, until the back of a husband, indeed the whole frame, has become like a loathsome heap of mangled flesh."[88] He then laments the fact that enslaved women—and prospective mothers—are forced to repeatedly bear witness to such horrible scenes of violence inflicted upon their kin. Easton tells us that he believes in the general axioms that "mind acts on matter" and that "mind acts on mind." It is thus the psychological traumas induced by the *act of witnessing* the whipping of slaves that produces a "deformity" in the mother's unborn child: Since mind acts on matter, and mind on mind, "is it a matter of surprise that those mothers who are slaves, should, on witnessing the distended muscles on the face of whipped slaves, produce the same or similar distensions on the face of her offspring, by her own mind being affected by the sight; so with all other deformities."[89] This is a powerful chain of impressions, in which the observation of the "distended muscles on the face of whipped slaves" impresses itself on the mind of the prospective mother, which then produces the "same or similar distensions" on the face of her child. The child's deformed face, produced out of the traumatic witnessing of slavery's violence, emerges as a counterimage to the visual archive of deformed visages in racial science as well as the images that Easton references of the "negroe's deformity" in the popular press.

Easton's interests in the severe and sometimes fantastical morphological effects of slavery and prejudice on the colored population continue through to his very last statements in the *Treatise*. In closing, Easton eschews a definition of freedom that is tantamount to the mere abolition of slavery. Rather, he argues for what he calls the "true emancipation," which would involve not just the complete overthrow of slavery in a legal act of abolition, but also the active involvement of whites in reviving and bringing back to life the beaten down, half-dead population of the nominally free and the formerly enslaved. Only then, according to Easton, will the physical and mental capacities of the black population begin to improve.

In a truly incredible conclusion to the text, Easton again reveals his fidelity to an environmentalist understanding of heredity and contemporary languages of physiognomy. He suggests that under true emancipation the bodies and visages of degraded black subjects would literally begin to transform:

> The countenance which has been cast down, hitherto, would brighten up with joy. Their narrow foreheads, which have hitherto been contracted for the want of mental exercise, would begin to broaden. Their eye balls, hitherto strained out to prominence by a frenzy excited by the flourish of the whip, would fall back under a thick foliage of curly eyebrows, indicative of deep penetrating thought. Those muscles, which have hitherto been distended by grief and weeping, would become contracted to an acuteness, corresponding to that acuteness of perception with which business men are blessed.[90]

Like many other examples discussed throughout this book, this passage reads like science fiction. By highlighting emancipation's role in inciting literal morphological transformations, black ethnologists were not only interested in establishing the inherent humanity of black subjects, but also engaged in highly experimental meditations on the human itself. For Easton, reform includes both the reformation of the bodies that have long suffered under slavery in the South and prejudice in the North and the reformation of the souls (both black and white) that were crushed under the barbaric regimes of slavery. Here, Easton expands the definition of "reform" to include the literal re-formation of African American bodies and spirits. Easton's is thus a deeply visual, and embodied, understanding of the project of Emancipation and Reconstruction.

But despite this moment of utopian transformation, Easton's is not, ultimately, an account of the triumph of black agency and vitality. Indeed, it seems likely that Easton's *Treatise* has largely fallen through the gaps in the study of early African American writing because it does not fit within models of black resistance and agency that have long dominated scholarship.[91] Easton's discourse is puzzling and challenging precisely because it excludes an account of black resistance, suggesting, rather, that African Americans will be "stuck" without a complete structural transformation of American society. Indeed, instead of an argument insisting on the fitness of the race under slavery, readers are offered an account of the enslaved and the free as being together a degraded and degenerate population. The *Treatise* is thus moored in the bleak existential realities of black life in 1830s America. In one chilling moment in the text, Easton includes a speculative and philosophical statement about his own being: "I wonder that I am a man."[92] In this way, Easton emerges within an early genealogy of Afro-pessimist thought, a genealogy that recognized the black subject's complete exclusion from humanity and civil society, of being a "slave" even when nominally free, and of slavery as social death. In sum, Easton recognized, as Jared Sexton has discussed, that black social life is always lived within the context of black social death.[93]

But the *Treatise* not only registers the pessimism of black intellectuals in the 1830s: it is also an attempt to make that pessimism productive for black politics. In this way, it is perhaps most appropriate to frame Easton's pessimism as a calculated strategy; in politics and activism, Easton was deeply committed to fostering collectivity and fellowship among the black communities in which he worked, preached, and organized. In this way, the *Treatise*'s pessimism emerges as a carefully crafted rhetoric, aimed at establishing and sustaining forms of speculative kinship and sociality beyond the page.[94]

Black ethnology might itself be understood as a deeply social genre, in which speculative kinship also took shape through intimate connections among writers, in personal exchanges and through the circulation and reading of texts. While responses to the history of racial science are often viewed within the black-white dyad—as responses, for example, to individual white naturalists like Thomas Jefferson and Samuel George Morton—the history of black ethnology marks an important moment when black writers on science begin speaking to one another in a sustained way. During his life, Benjamin Banneker produced knowledge largely in isolation from a black community beyond his family, but the genealogy of antebellum black ethnology chronicled in Chapter 1 brought Banneker into the fold of a form of speculative kinship, produced through scientific writing and acts of memorialization. While some of the figures addressed in this chapter encountered one another in person—in the "colored" spaces of New England and through the itinerancies produced by race, labor, poverty, and preaching in the region—others met only virtually through texts. Even after writers like Walker, Apess, and Easton passed away, their ethnological texts continued to provide forms of virtual kinship, knowledge, and solidarity for other intellectuals and readers of color.

Throughout the 1830s and 1840s, black ethnologists constructed robust networks of kinship through personal exchange and through the practice of citation itself. For example, while it is certainly the case that David Walker used Thomas Jefferson to authorize his *Appeal*, subsequent black ethnologists used Walker's text to authorize their own texts, citing from, riffing on, and expanding his polemic and his evidence. Likewise, it is clear that James Pennington had read Hosea Easton's *Treatise* before penning his own ethnology in 1841 and that Robert Benjamin Lewis incorporated information about Easton and his *Treatise* into the 1844 edition of *Light and Truth*. The printer of that 1844 edition, Benjamin F. Roberts, was also Hosea Easton's nephew. The 1844 edition of *Light and Truth* included mini-biographies of David Walker and Maria Stewart. These biographies stood as evidence or "proofs" of black intelligence in Lewis's biography, but they also trace forms of kinship and solidarity among writers and intellectuals of color across New England.

Black ethnologies were also embedded in networks of actual and speculative kinship with Native Americans. Robert Benjamin Lewis wrote about William Apess in his 1844 *Light and Truth*, and it is possible that Apess's ethnological appendix in *A Son of the Forest* shaped Lewis's own ethnological investigations, especially his speculations that Native Americans were the descendants of ancient Jews.[95] It is also very likely that Apess met David Walker, and possibly Maria Stewart, during his time on the reform lecture circuit in Boston and in the course of interactions with the anti-slavery movement. These intellectual forms of kinship between African Americans and Native Americans were buttressed by shared histories of descent in New England. As mentioned earlier, Robert Benjamin Lewis was of Native and African descent; Hosea Easton had Narragansett and Wampanoag ancestry on his father's side, and African and white ancestry on his mother's side.[96] Ethnology proved to be a powerful discourse for writers of color, especially for writers of mixed descent who turned to ethnology's discourse on Africans and Natives to produce the beginnings of an Afro-Native writing tradition rooted in the biological, political, and intellectual kinship of people of color. Images like Robert Benjamin Lewis's portrait also challenged the separation of "Africans" from "savages" in polygenesis through the bold visualization of an Afro-Native subject, a distinctly visual experiment in speculative kinship.

The Science of Art

As this chapter has traced, antebellum black writers turned to ekphrastic writing techniques to challenge damaging visual representations of blackness in popular culture and science, to compensate for limited access to the means of image production, and to imagine diverse forms of kinship among peoples of African descent as well as indigenous peoples in North America. Cheaply printed texts also promised a level of circulation that individual works of art, photography, and lithography often could not: while Robert Benjamin Lewis's portrait is a stunning intervention into the visual archive of ethnology, replacing the absolute divisions between African Americans and Natives in that science with a visualization of an Afro-Native subject, it is likely that the cost of lithography prohibited wide circulation of the image itself.

While printed text often served as a surrogate for visual images in anti-racist science, black artists also produced important forms of visual evidence that could be used to combat biased science. Chapter 5 chronicles, among other things, how art education opened the door to scientific learning among black women in antebellum Philadelphia, while providing a pathway for intervening into physiological discourses about race and gender. James McCune Smith's writing in the 1850s also displays the place of visual art within fugitive science. McCune Smith treats works of art as pieces of evidence with just as much authority as scientific studies. In his essays, the observations of artists often appear right alongside citations from medical and scientific authorities. For example, in his 1859 ethnology, "Civilization," McCune Smith states that it was an artist who first suggested to him that the American climate was transforming all blacks and whites into the "physical type" of the nation's "Aboriginal inhabitants." This scientific "fact" was something that the artist himself learned through his art, while taking "casts of many distinguished American Statesmen."[97] Contrary to earlier articulations of Afro-Native solidarity in the mixed-race milieu of the early nineteenth century Northeast, such arguments about whites and blacks transforming into Native Americans run much closer to the appropriations of "Indianness" that became increasingly common as Native tribes were dispossessed and removed to federally designated reservations into the mid-century. Despite ongoing references to Native Americans in black writing in the 1850s, by this decade, much of the collaboration and solidarity that marked the earlier writings of Lewis, Easton, and others, had disappeared. By the 1850s, black writers, like whites, were busy mythologizing the "vanishing Indian."[98]

McCune Smith proceeds to invite readers of the *Anglo-African Magazine* to become similarly involved with scientific discovery *through* art, noting that the accuracy of his hypothesis that Americans are becoming Native Americans may be "tested" by "an examination of any Daguerrian National Gallery." Here, McCune Smith transforms the art museum itself into an important site of scientific exchange and knowledge production. While the history of the museum is also one of segregation and exclusion, McCune Smith suggests that it was a potentially democratic space that could serve diverse needs and ends for people of African descent. As ostensibly public spaces, art galleries and some academies, natural history museums, and traveling exhibits could also serve as important sites for education and learning, which could be furtively experienced by black patrons.

William J. Wilson was another contributor to the *Anglo-African Magazine* who saw an infinite number of possibilities within the space of the gallery, and looked toward the establishment of a museum of black art that could be used for both scientific and artistic purposes. In his "Afric-American Picture Gallery," a series that ran in conjunction with McCune Smith's essays in the *Anglo-African Magazine* in 1859, Wilson offers readers an imaginative textual tour of a virtual gallery of artwork on various subjects related to black life in the US and across the diaspora. In addition to the gallery being a fictional construction within the textual space of the *Anglo-African*, the series was printed without any actual images, though verbal descriptions abound. In the Picture Gallery, Wilson's pen name "Ethiop" becomes the name of a fictional character turned gallery proprietor, curator, and docent, who leads readers through a survey of paintings, statues, and sketches featuring black subjects.[99] These works of art include "heads" of important people of African descent, Southern landscapes, and paintings of a slave ship, a slave church, and Mount Vernon. Some of Wilson's sketches may have been taken from his viewing of original paintings and portraits in artist studios, small galleries, natural history museums, and possibly even private homes, but most were drawn from reproductions that appeared in print.[100]

For Wilson, the gallery was a space that was particularly well suited to visualizing the forms of speculative kinship at the heart of black ethnology. Embedded in the series is a fascinating parodic ethnology of the white race. Delineating the degeneration and downfall of this horrible, weak part of the human race, this mock-ethnology places Wilson in the tradition of David Walker's sarcasm and James W. C. Pennington's mocking critique. Throughout the series, portraiture and sculpture also become tools for engaging with the project of speculative kinship and intervening in ethnological discourses. For example, in one installment, Ethiop's viewing of a statue of Benjamin Banneker in the gallery provides an occasion to make an imaginative connection to the early national scientist, with Ethiop's "mind traversing back to the days of Banneker." Thus, like Walker, Pennington, and McCune Smith, Wilson contributed to the imagination of a "Banneker Age" in the antebellum period. Moreover, in addition to installing a statue of Banneker in the center of his gallery, Wilson is highly invested in memorializing noted eighteenth-century figures of African descent, including Phillis Wheatley, Crispus Attucks, and Toussaint L'Ouverture.

Throughout the Picture Gallery, portraiture and sculpture are given scientific status and treated as media that can produce accurate representations of physiognomic typologies of the race and thereby challenge the visual racial hierarchies evident in racial science and popular culture. In the gallery, Wilson creates an interesting ambiguity, in which engraved portraits drawn from the print sphere are transformed into sculptural busts. While the "head" of Phillis Wheatley could certainly signify a portrait in nineteenth-century parlance, in the virtual space of his gallery, Wilson invites readers to imagine these portraits as distinguished works of sculpture. By transforming engravings and lithographs into sculptural busts, Wilson sought to lend permanence to the visual representation of black subjects—albeit, ironically, through another ephemeral form: the magazine. Attempting to transcend the ephemerality of periodicals as well as the degradation of the black image in racial science and visual culture, Wilson's ekphrastic experiments transformed black bodies and faces into durable visual archives of humanity.

Finally, Wilson's imagined gallery gives a glimpse of a small, but growing group of black professional artists practicing both in the United States and in artistic communities abroad.[101] The gallery's ekphrastic experiments with sculpture resonate particularly with the work of Afro-Native sculptor Mary Edmonia Lewis. Born a freewoman of Chippewa (Ojibwe) and African descent, educated at Oberlin before a scandal forced her departure, and connected to William Lloyd Garrison and other Boston abolitionists, Lewis traveled to Europe in 1865 and eventually settled in Rome. There, she opened a studio and began producing her art among a community of expatriate artists (see Figure 2.5).[102] Like Robert Benjamin Lewis, Edmonia Lewis used the ground of the visual to engage in a project of speculative kinship that delineated the connections—and forms of autonomy—between African Americans and Native Americans.[103] For example, Lewis's *Forever Free (The Morning of Liberty)* (1867), depicts a former slave with his arm reaching up to the sky standing next to a kneeling woman, her hands clasped together in prayer (see Figure 2.6). Both figures appear

F.ᴸᴸⁱ D'ALESSANDRI CORSO Nº 12, ROMA.

Figure 2.5. Fratelli D'Alessandri, carte de visite of Edmonia Lewis, ca. 1874–1876, Rome, Italy, albumen silver print on paper. Courtesy of the Walters Art Museum, Baltimore.

Figure 2.6. Edmonia Lewis, *Forever Free (The Morning of Liberty)*, 1867, marble. Courtesy of the Howard University Gallery of Art, Washington, DC, and Kirsten Pai Buick.

to be looking up in gratitude to God on the occasion of Emancipation. The dress and straight hair of the woman suggest that she may be of African, Native, or of mixed descent. The whiteness of marble further complicates the already complex racialization of Lewis's subjects in *Forever Free*, while the racial indeterminacy and proximity of the figures point to, among other things, the many forms of kinship binding Native American and African American peoples to one another, including a shared history of subjection at the hands of the US government. In other works, like *The Wooing of Hiawatha* (1866) and *The Marriage of Hiawatha* (1866), Native history is given its own autonomy and specificity, while works like *Hagar in the Wilderness* (1875) are more closely connected to the specific experiences of black women under the conditions of enslavement, as well as efforts among African Americans to claim ancient Egypt for people of African descent. Ultimately, Lewis's art presents a complex vision of race in the United States, one that refuses the visual codes of polygenesis as well as related ethnological codes in visual art. Further, her sculpture hints at Afro-Native identities in the United States while still maintaining the distinct histories of Black and Native peoples in North America.

Black sculpture and its ekphrastic siblings also made interventions into the visual cultures of nineteenth-century racial science. The neoclassical style popular in the early nineteenth century lent a mythological aura to Lewis's subjects, but it also allowed her to classicize Black and Native bodies. In racial science across the Atlantic, from Virey's *Histoire naturelle* (1801) to Nott and Gliddon's *Types of Mankind* (1854), visual illustrations of classical statues were often placed next to crude depictions of non-white peoples, especially Africans. By contrast, in Edmonia Lewis's sculptures, as in William J. Wilson's imagined ones, the visual archive of degeneration in racial science and popular culture is replaced by neoclassical Black and Native figures that rival or even exceed the fitness and beauty of white people cast in stone. The surviving cartes de visite of Edmonia Lewis also indicate her interest in crafting and controlling her own image in the public sphere. Used as calling cards and to promote her professional stature as an international sculptor, they stand, in Kirsten Pai Buick's terms, at the intersection of black "celebrity" and "specimen" (see Figures 2.5 and 2.7).[104] Like the use of lithography by Robert Benjamin Lewis in

Figure 2.7. Henry Rocher, carte de visite of Edmonia Lewis, ca. 1870, albumen silver print, 9.2 x 5.2 cm. National Portrait Gallery, Smithsonian Institution / Art Resource, NY.

the 1830s, the use of photography, with its claims to "truth" and objective representation, would prove central to further re-visions of racial science and anti-black imagery throughout the mid- to late nineteenth century. In this context, Du Bois's turn-of-the-century photo album, *Types of American Negroes*, can be seen as the photographic culmination of a long nineteenth-century history of revising and re-visioning racial science.

3

Experiments in Freedom

Fugitive Science in Transatlantic Performance

Just as antebellum racial science depended on its circulation through visual culture, performance also contributed widely. Throughout the period, the popular stage doubled as a scientific laboratory, where theories of race were both produced and disseminated to a mass audience. Racial science was a popular and diverse field of inquiry whose cultural power derived not from its status as a hegemonic or institutional science, but from its popularization through printed texts, images, and performance. Despite the limited circulation of Samuel George Morton's *Crania Americana*, his theories—and skulls—were widely disseminated through more popular forums throughout the 1840s and after Morton's death in 1851.[1] The public could view Morton's skull collection at the Academy of Natural Sciences in Philadelphia and the craniologist's friends and allies presented his work in print and on stage, most notably in George Gliddon and Josiah Nott's 1854 publication of *Types of Mankind*, as well as through Gliddon's popular mummy lectures, in which the ethnologist-adventurer showcased skulls, offered theories on the polygenic origins of the races and the Caucasian roots of Egyptian civilization, and unwrapped mummies ransacked from Egyptian tombs before a public audience.

Race scientists often doubled as scientific showmen, traveling with ethnological charts, human skulls and other comparative specimens in tow. Other nineteenth-century entertainments, from the minstrel show to the freak show, contributed to the popular dissemination of racial science through the representation of black and other non-white peoples as biologically and intellectually inferior, just as the print sphere helped to popularize the visual "types" of racial science. Operating in the same cultural milieu and in many cases on the same performance circuits as race scientists, quack doctors, and scientific showmen with questionable credentials, black performers and lecturers regularly forged creative responses to the popular performance of race science. This chapter approaches racial science through the lens of performance, chronicling how African American performers and lecturers rejected racial science's attempts to categorize and fix their bodies through a counterarchive of black performance. It also begins the work of excavating the history of intersections between black performance and scientific lecturing in both the United States and Britain.

Because of the ephemeral nature of performance as well as the near invisibility of African American science before the Civil War, I take a necessarily creative approach to the archive. Inspired by the bold leaps and experimental engagements with history that characterize the field of performance studies, this chapter stitches together a dynamic—if sometimes elusive—genealogy of black performance. Following a paper trail of ticket stubs, pamphlets, newspaper columns and announcements, broadsides, and other printed texts and ephemera, I chronicle how Henry Box Brown, Frederick Douglass, William Wells Brown, and some lesser-known figures countered the widespread circulation of racist science in popular entertainment and print culture through dynamic performances of fugitive science. Though the focus throughout will be on lectures, traveling acts, popular theater, and other forms of performance that have left printed traces, I also offer some more speculative readings that gesture toward what Diana Taylor refers to as the "repertoires" of performance—that is, those aspects of performance that cannot be recorded.[2] Even as live performance eludes complete capture within the archive, a shadow archive of fugitive science in performance is sketched in glimpses in this chapter, revealing itself at certain points, while remaining opaque at others.

Performances of fugitive science in the United States often trafficked in an Atlantic imaginary produced, in part, by the globally oriented discourses of racial science, while black performances abroad made more material connections to the transatlantic networks of science and abolition. Starting with the history of Henry Box Brown's travels and performances in England, this chapter proceeds to chronicle a set of encounters in which solidarity between black America and the British proletariat was articulated through the transatlantic networks of popular science. The historical trajectory of what follows, from the 1830s through the 1850s, is not meant to be wholly comprehensive or even chronological; rather, the account focuses on some key flashpoints that bring into focus a dynamic genealogy of fugitive science in transatlantic performance.[3] Throughout, the "popular" refers to those forms of literature, science, and performance that reached a large and diverse audience through the increased democratization of the print sphere and the rise of mass entertainment venues.

The 1845 founding of P. T. Barnum's American Museum signals the entrenchment of science within an emerging popular culture. With Britain witnessing a similar explosion in the popular performance and dissemination of science during this period, the 1830s through the 1850s mark an especially fruitful time for transatlantic engagements with science. Subsequently, when the Civil War began in 1861, such transatlantic networks started to break down, as the nation looked within and sought to mobilize the tools and methods of natural science for an increasingly nation-based science. However, before the beginning of science's tethering to the project of nation-building, fugitive science traveled far and wide, across public and private, professional and nonprofessional, and national and international spaces.

Performing Racial Science

The late eighteenth-century shift from natural history to comparative anatomy had a dramatic impact on the study of human difference, helping to usher in increasingly biological theories of race in the antebellum period, theories rooted in the physiology and morphology of the body. Natural history was a science of surfaces and skin, driven by the belief that racial differences were produced by varying climatic conditions in different geographical regions. Comparative anatomy went deeper, seeking to locate human differences, and inequalities, in the internal structures of the body. In *The Order of Things*, Michel Foucault argues that the nineteenth century witnessed the creation of a dimension of depth in the natural sciences, which moved from taxonomic systems of natural history that sought to make animal and plant species wholly visible to the human eye to a comparative anatomy that increasingly understood living beings to be composed of "dark, hidden, and interior forces."[4]

Since comparative anatomy was interested in making the invisible visible, it found a convenient ally in the theater and other forms of popular spectacle. Mass entertainments regularly played upon the drama of appearance—including stage tricks and magic performances that made objects appear and disappear—while various shows, from the freak show to the minstrel show and other forms of popular theater, doubled as staging grounds for exhibiting human difference and making the supposedly deep and essential differences of black bodies hyper-visible on the antebellum stage. Jayna Brown notes that nineteenth-century racial theories were not only popular theories, but also "from their inception, decidedly spectacular."[5] Throughout the antebellum period, when spectacular performances of racial difference were popular and pervasive, the line between science and entertainment was constantly being blurred on stage: curious audiences may have gone to public dissections and other morbid displays of human difference in order to gain knowledge, but they were also drawn to these exhibitions for their entertainment and shock value.[6]

Moreover, in addition to being popular, theories of racial science were also thoroughly transatlantic. Spreading through intellectual currents, correspondence and travel across the Atlantic, racial science was also transatlantic because of its entrenchment in popular science and entertainment circuits that crisscrossed the ocean. Theories of racial descent and evolution regularly made their way onto the transatlantic stage both in scientific lectures and in various forms of popular entertainment, including the theater, the circus, zoological exhibitions, minstrel shows, and the then emerging freak show.

Rather than understanding the transatlantic stage as a venue where racial science was simply represented (or, re-presented) to a mass audience and recycled into various popular entertainments, we might approach it as a kind of public laboratory, a vital space of experimentation where alternative theories of race, and resistance to them, were not only disseminated, but also produced and negotiated through performance. Indeed, the antebellum stage served as an important site for the production of experimental knowledge in a number of different fields, including phrenology, magnetism, astronomy, physiology, and anatomy.

Lecture and entertainment circuits were especially central to the midcentury rise of popular anatomy, which made scientific and medi-

cal knowledge about the human body increasingly accessible to work-
ing- and middle-class people. Chronicling the rise of popular anatomy
in the early nineteenth century, Michael Sappol illuminates various
means for the production and exchange of anatomical knowledge:
thus, traveling surgeons and anatomists offered lectures to the public,
audiences paid to witness public dissections, autopsies were routinely
performed with members of the community in attendance, and published reports of postmortem dissections of accused criminals often
contributed to, and extended, the spectacle of criminal execution after
the death of the condemned.[7] The theater of dissection was also an
important part of medical education and professionalization, and, as
Sappol notes, as early as the 1760s, the anatomical theater was already
blurring professional science and public entertainment. He cites, for
example, "William Shippen, Jr., [who] caused the first North American
anatomical theater to be constructed in Philadelphia, for the instruction of his medical students, but his theater was also used to stage a
dissection of [conjoined] twins for a public, ticket-buying audience."[8]
Anatomical museums were also established in major American cities
throughout the late eighteenth and early nineteenth centuries. These
museums walked a thin line between providing useful information
about anatomy to working-class and middle-class visitors and serving
as sensational exhibitions of "freaks," oddities, and curiosities. Barnum's
American Museum on Broadway in New York, which featured human
and non-human oddities, wonders from the natural world, lectures and
performances, including minstrel shows, had been an anatomical museum before Barnum purchased it in the early 1840s.[9] By the 1850s, it
thus became increasingly difficult to disentangle professional anatomy
from both popular anatomy and the nineteenth-century sideshow that
Barnum made famous.

Freak shows and minstrel shows were also sorts of anatomical theaters. The theatrical display and spectacularization of black and black-
faced bodies was, in part, about locating blackness in the exceptional
morphology and peculiar movements of racialized bodies. Paralleling
the methods of comparative anatomists, both freak shows and minstrel
shows constructed a normative body ideal through the delineation of
"abnormal" types.[10] Showmen, anatomists, and white minstrel performers all worked hard to make the supposed internal essence of racial dif-

ference visible in the display and manipulation of animated bodies (both alive and deceased) on stage.

The methodological alliances among comparative anatomy, minstrelsy, and the freak show were solidified in 1836, when P. T. Barnum organized a public autopsy of George Washington's supposedly 161-year-old nurse, Joice Heth, shortly after her death. Hoping to appease skeptics who did not believe that Heth could be as old as Barnum claimed, he contracted New York surgeon David Rogers to perform the dissection in the amphitheater of the City Saloon, which sat next to Barnum's American Museum on Broadway. He then sold admission tickets at fifty cents a head.[11] Before her death, Heth had been exhibited as a curiosity under the possession of R. W. Lindsay and was sold to Barnum in 1835. Exhibiting Heth, "the most astonishing and interesting curiosity in the World," throughout the country, Barnum transformed Lindsay's failing exhibit into a national sensation, proved himself to be a masterful promoter, and used the success of the tour to kickstart his career and entrance into the annals of American celebrity.[12]

While Heth's public autopsy still has the power to shock, it was surely an unsurprising development for antebellum audiences.[13] Advertised as a "living skeleton" and compared to the mummies that were beginning to circulate in the United States as part of a growing cultural and scientific obsession with Egypt, Heth was already being figured as a post-mortem subject by Barnum in the year before her death.[14] When she was exhibited, spectators were encouraged to "play doctor" by meticulously surveying and studying her body to verify her old age. These scenes eerily echoed the slave auction block, where potential purchasers determined the "soundness" of black captives by conducting invasive pseudo-medical exams on the spot.[15] News reporters also visited Heth in order to verify her age and to provide readers with anatomical surveys of her body that were both extensively detailed and, at times, disturbingly grotesque. For example, the *New York Sun* reported, "From the length of her limbs and the size of the bones, it is probable that she was a large, stout woman, in her day; but now, she comes up exactly to one's idea of an animated mummy. . . . Her feet have shrunk to mere skin and bone, and her long attenuated fingers more resemble the claws of a bird of prey than human appendages."[16] In this way, Heth's body was regularly "dissected" by the penetrating clinical gaze of doctors, journalists, and a morbidly curious

American public. Her person was submitted to a nightmarishly long autopsy that was initiated before she had even passed away.

Despite attempts at ocular mastery through such forms of spectatorship, the act of visually locating race in the body was a slippery task.[17] We might wonder, At that final, gruesome exhibition of Heth's person, did spectators witnessing the brutal dismemberment of her body affirm the physiological difference, and inferiority, of black bodies, or did the horrifying scene remind audience members of their shared mortality and similarity to the body before them? From minstrel shows to abolitionist lectures, talks on racial science, public autopsies, and public executions of black subjects, performances of racial difference were likely to raise more questions than they answered.

Black performers regularly trafficked in—and worked to emphasize—the ambiguity of race, while resisting the public spectacularization and visual consumption of their bodies. When black musicians, dancers, lecturers, and other performers stepped on stage, they occupied a space that was routinely used to visually assess the physiological capabilities and limits of blackness through both "legitimate" performances of racial science and various nonscientific dissections of black character and anatomy in popular entertainments, particularly on the minstrel stage. The legacies of determining soundness on the slave auction block also haunted public spaces of black performance. In response, black performers developed a number of strategies. Daphne Brooks conceives of performative acts of veiling the body in the terms of "spectacular opacities," which "confound and disrupt conventional constructions of the racialized and gendered body" while shrouding the body from the "imposition of transparency" produced through spectacularization: "This cultural phenomenon [of spectacular opacity] emerges at varying times as a product of the performer's will, at other times as a visual obstacle erupting as a result of the hostile spectator's epistemological resistance to reading alternative racial and gender representations. From either standpoint, spectacular opacities contest the 'dominative imposition of transparency' systematically willed on to black figures."[18] The contestation of imposed transparency through spectacular, yet opaque performances of and with the body also challenged attempts to externalize and fix blackness within evolutionary hierarchies through the public exhibition of racialized bodies. Whereas racial science made bodies hyper-visible on stage, in visual images, and in print, black performers challenged this regime of forced visibility, refusing racial science's attempts to make race fully transparent—and knowable—through the display of their bodies. Spectacular opacity was a particularly important tool for black women, who were subjected to harsher regimes of forced visibility and exploitation on transatlantic stages. As the public exhibition of women like Joice Heth as well as the notorious exploitation of Sarah Baartman both signal, black women's bodies have often carried the burden of proving the supposed inferiority and pathologies of blackness itself.[19]

Despite attempts to fix racialized and gendered bodies on stage—and, more specifically, to fix race through the display of sexual difference— race remained a wildly floating signifier across multiple and adjacent performance spaces. Throughout the antebellum period, black performers took advantage of the indeterminacy and ambiguity of race to produce alternative theories of blackness. Unhinging blackness from the "truth" of the body, these performers uncoupled race from an impoverished concept of the biological body. Both explicitly and implicitly, early black performance responded to emergent regimes of racist science through what Brooks calls "spectacular performances" of freedom. Rejecting the idea that the body could serve as a scientific proof that revealed an invisible and essential truth about race, these performers used their bodies as "instrument[s] of ontological deception."[20] Unhinging blackness from the supposed truth of the body while challenging race science's restrictive conception of the body as a mere prison or container, they transformed the body into a powerful site of liberation and transformation. Early black performers thus loosed the body from the ossifying grasp of antebellum racial science, while suggesting other meanings and purposes for their persons. While comparative anatomy sought to racialize the inside and outside of bodies, situating racial difference not only on the skin, but in internal structures and organs, the restive, flitting movements of early black performers continually rejected the interiorization of race by putting blackness on the move. Indeed, with its focus on the gestural and fleeting, there may be something radically anti-essentialist about performance per se, even performance that seeks to naturalize race as biological.[21] Black performers, including dancers, lecturers, and actors, regularly opposed the popular science and performance of black morbidity by staging multiple fugitive sciences. Fugitive science, here, signifies both the robust counterarchives of science performed by African Americans on stage, as well as a wider repertoire of gestures, movements, and practices that challenged racial science's attempts to make their bodies signify and stand in for the essential truth of race.

While scientific lectures, minstrel shows, freak shows and a host of other popular performance genres attempted to fix the bodies of African Americans and other non-white people into static, racist taxonomies, the complex choreographies of antebellum black performance on adjacent stages continually evaded such efforts. Some black performers and lecturers took an even more direct approach to racist science by incorporating popular sciences into their lectures, shows, and acts. Paradoxically, these figures drew inspiration from the wide diffusion of popular science in mass entertainment venues, including problematic stagings of racial science. On the antebellum stage, fugitive science both drew from and exceeded the science of race.

Black Phrenology

Phrenology held a particularly prominent place in the performance of fugitive science. Often regarded today as a pseudoscience, phrenology was a deeply contested, yet legitimate scientific field in the early to mid-nineteenth century. Indeed, phrenology's correlation of intellectual faculties with particular cranial zones influenced ideas about the localization of psychological function in early brain science. Far from its parodic presentation as the "science of bumps" or "bumpology," phrenology was rather, as Nathaniel Mackey notes, the premier "science of the mind" in the nineteenth century.[22] Popular parodies of phrenology in the early nineteenth century reflect not so much the illegitimacy of phrenology, but rather the forms of popular contestation and anxiety that plague all emergent scientific fields.

Founded by the German physiologist Franz Joseph Gall in the late 1700s and rooted in his research on the anatomy of the brain (not just the bumps on the surface of the head), phrenology was first popularized by Gall's assistant, Johann Spurzheim, in the early 1800s. He lectured throughout Great Britain in 1814 and set out on a grand lecture tour of the United States in 1832. Although he died just three months after his arrival in America, Spurzheim's visit clearly left its mark.[23] Phrenology enjoyed a meteoric rise throughout the 1830s, especially after the prominent Scottish phrenologist George Combe gave a lecture tour in 1838. While Combe became something of a celebrity during his time in the United States, his popular phrenology lectures reached a wider audience in 1839 when the Phrenological Society of New York transcribed, collated, and printed them under the title *Lectures on Phrenology, By George Combe, Esq., Including Its Application to the Present and Prospective Condition of the United States.* Combe further satiated the public's interest in both phrenology and his own magnanimous "character" with the 1841 publication of a memoir of his American travels, *Notes on the United States of North America: During a Phrenological Visit in 1838-9-40.* Subsequently, a number of practical phrenologists began to practice in the United States, and several books offering novices instruction on examining heads and producing phrenology charts were published. Itinerant phrenologists crisscrossed the country giving readings in private homes, at public exhibitions, and before audiences on the antebellum stage. By midcentury, phrenology had been transformed into the quintessentially American science, an irony given the field's European origins. Just like the "American" school of ethnology, phrenology in the United States was produced through a transatlantic network of scientific exchange and knowledge production. However, phrenology continued to be understood as distinctively American due to its popularity across the country and its imbrication in American popular culture.

In the United States, phrenology was deeply dependent on antebellum performance cultures: popular among both the elite and working classes, phrenological readings of celebrities were widely reported in the press, and readings were often performed in public. The dramatic and "hands-on" element of phrenological examinations—in which a careful exploration of an individual's skull would reveal hidden aspects of their personality and character—made them particularly amenable to stage performances. Phrenology also figured in the American minstrel show, which expertly absorbed and adapted elements from all spheres of popular culture, including popular science. An 1859 minstrel songbook printed in New York included a song titled "Phrenology," in which the prominent American phrenologist Lorenzo Fowler appears as "Massa

Fowler," and the singer recounts a visit to his office "for to get my head examined":

> He put his thumb upon a bump, an den begin to Quivery
> He looked me deep in de eye, an it made this darkey shiver
> He said de bump ob *eativeness* was very large developed;
> Said de bumps war altogeder like a jawbarelup.[24]

Poking fun at both the patient and the phrenologist, the rest of the song details the patient-singer's attack on Fowler after the phrenologist dared to suggest that his head, or "knowledge-box," was completely hollow. It also makes phrenology itself an object of comic derision. And there may have been other, more personal reasons for attacking "Massa Fowler," given phrenology's popularity among American social reformers, including abolitionists. Putting phrenology in blackface was a clear attempt to delegitimize the field for its inclusivity and its anti-slavery leanings. At the same time, the posing of mock-phrenologists in blackface encoded a cultural anxiety that phrenology might be, or become, a black science.

On the minstrel stage, phrenology signified in myriad ways. The representation of African American interest in phrenology was part and parcel of critiques of black education and elevation that were standard in antebellum minstrel shows. The striving of African Americans for professional expertise and expressions of scholarly knowledge were persistent objects of mockery and parody on the minstrel stage. But the staging of phrenology-themed minstrel songs and sketches may have also registered and responded to the actual existence of black phrenologists traveling on adjacent performance circuits. Indeed, references in the *North Star* suggest that black phrenologists were traveling the country as early as the 1840s. The December 22, 1848, edition of the newspaper reported:

> During the month of October last, a series of scientific lectures was delivered in this city [Rochester] by DR. HENRY H. LEWIS, under the auspices of an association of colored citizens, who eagerly improved the opportunity of listening to one who, though not boasting of Anglo-Saxon blood, had by dint of application qualified himself to impart a knowledge

of phrenology, mesmerism, and other interesting branches of science; with the two former he evinced a familiarity both in the lecture room and the social circle at once gratifying and instructive.

In the July 7, 1848 issue of the *North Star*, Martin Delany reported that his own head had been examined by a fourteen-year-old African American boy named Simon Foreman Laundrey, whose "examinations compare well with experienced and competent professors of the science of phrenology." Not only did Laundrey "examine heads" and "read out the organs," but he also delivered lectures on phrenology and was preparing a scientific work for publication titled the "Geography of the Brain." According to Delany, Laundrey "offered his services to examine my cranium, and passed his little hands over the organs, reading them with as much facility as Fowler or Melrose." Referring to him as a "natural phrenologist," Delany emphasized Laundry's skill and expertise to readers of the *North Star*. He also recommended that the young man take to the road with his practice and use his performances to raise funds to attend a "literary institution" like Oberlin. Indeed, the public act of "reading organs" by a young freeman would have resonated for white and black audiences, who could see it in terms of the larger struggle of African Americans for elevation through education. More specifically, the performances of Laundry and other black phrenologists signified on mid-nineteenth-century narratives about literacy: "reading organs" allowed African American practitioners of phrenology to perform alternative modes of literacy. Moreover, such acts of autonomous, skillful "reading" in public spaces challenged regimes of literacy and education that sought to surveil and discipline black subjects.[25]

These brief references to traveling black phrenologists in the *North Star* appeared in the context of a larger pro-phrenology agenda in Douglass's paper, as well as in the later *Frederick Douglass' Paper*. Douglass's support for phrenology was made explicit in his 1854 commencement address, "The Claims of the Negro, Ethnologically Considered," at Western Reserve College in Ohio. In the speech, Douglass evoked Combe's landmark study, *Constitution of Man* (1828), as a pragmatic tool for African Americans to combat the dangerous scientific racism of Nott and Gliddon's *Types of Mankind*. Douglass's reclamation of phrenology through Combe's text is striking, especially given the proximity between phrenology and craniology. Indeed, the "soft science" of head bumps and the "hard science" of skulls often overlapped. Combe's 1838 lectures looked and sounded extremely similar to contemporaneous lectures on craniology. Like Gliddon and other lecturers on polygenesis, Combe showcased human skulls, using them to display the visual difference and inferiority of non-white groups to public audiences. During Combe's stay in the United States, he visited and became friends with Morton, even contributing an essay and phrenological chart to *Crania Americana*. Combe's contribution to the volume did much to tether phrenology to craniology, and by association, to the history of scientific racism.

While phrenology may be cemented to craniology and scientific racism in the contemporary historical imagination, in the antebellum period, some African Americans, as well as Anglo-American women, latched onto phrenology as a radically inclusive and "democratic" science.[26] First, phrenology held that anyone could become a practitioner of head-reading. Combe speculated that Native tribes who mechanically flattened their children's heads might be "instinctive phrenologists" (or what Delany referred to as practitioners of "natural phrenology"), cultivating mental faculties through the physical manipulation of the head and thus the brain.[27] Phrenology's focus on self-transformation also made a natural link to American social reform movements rooted in philosophies of personal improvement and moral responsibility, including mainstream abolitionism. And finally, phrenology's emphasis on physiological and psychological adaptability as well as the individual's power for self-transformation posed a serious challenge to racial science's attempts to make racial traits fixed and immutable.[28] Despite the powerful fraternity between craniology and phrenology, black abolitionists attempted to hold onto a phrenology that could not be subsumed by racial science. Indeed, in Douglass's newspapers we see the emergence of what the minstrel stage seemed to fear—namely, the transformation of phrenology into a black science, wrested from its association with craniology and oriented instead to the politics of anti-slavery and social transformation. Through phrenology, Douglass imagined ways that the individual's power for self-transformation might expand into larger political transformations. Across many of his publications—including *My Bondage and My Freedom*, the *North Star*, and *Frederick Douglass'*

Paper—Douglass mobilized phrenology as a fugitive science that destabilized the racist science of craniology from within its own methodology. By uncoupling phrenology from craniology, Douglass, Delany, and the traveling African American phrenologists they mention detached phrenology from racist science, mobilizing it instead for a set of experiments oriented toward black elevation and emancipation.

Atlantic Imaginaries of Racial Science

Performances of fugitive science in the Unites States also worked collectively to produce a rich transatlantic imaginary that linked African Americans to people of color across the world—sometimes, ironically, through racial science's own emphasis on the global distribution of racial groups across the continents. In his 1854 speech discussed above, Douglass turned race science's global imaginary against itself. Throughout "The Claims of the Negro, Ethnologically Considered" Douglass made an impassioned argument against the specious and destructive claims of the emerging fields of racial science, including craniology and ethnology, as well as comparative anatomy, more broadly. This was not the first time Douglass had spoken out against race science; he had also done so in some earlier speeches.[29] To prepare "Claims of the Negro," Douglass studied the texts of the American school of ethnology as well as earlier tracts like Samuel Stanhope Smith's 1787 essay on the climatic production of race.[30] He also consulted M. B. Anderson, a white ethnologist who taught at the University of Rochester.

Douglass's speech condemned the virulent racism of polygenesis, particularly its power to "read the negro out of the human family."[31] It was also penned as a direct response to Nott and Gliddon's *Types of Mankind*, which had been published earlier that year. Throughout the speech, Douglass speaks of Nott and Gliddon's book with marked disdain, noting that "perhaps, of all the attempts ever made to disprove the unity of the human family, and to brand the negro with natural inferiority, the most compendious and barefaced is the book, entitled 'Types of Mankind,' by Nott and Glidden [sic]. One would be well employed, in a series of Lectures, directed to an exposure of the unsoundness, if not the wickedness of this work." Throughout the speech, Douglass wages a vicious attack on Morton, Nott, and Gliddon, as well as on Louis

Agassiz—the leading members of the American school of ethnology—exposing these figures as charlatans, mere "Southern pretenders to science," whose blatant political biases make their writings unreliable and utterly unscientific. According to Douglass, racism ousts "the Notts, the Gliddens, the Agassiz[es], and Mortons" from the ranks of science.[32]

Despite the vitriol that Douglass unleashes on ethnology, he does not reject nineteenth-century science as a whole. In fact, he goes on to celebrate the new inventions and cultural possibilities that emerge from the popular diffusion of scientific knowledge and technological innovations. In a stunning argument for the unity of the races, Douglass laments that the true tragedy of polygenesis is that it seeks to rip people apart whereas the popular diffusion of science and technology had been so recently successful in encouraging what he calls the "magnificent reunion of mankind in one brotherhood":

> It is somewhat remarkable, that, at a time when knowledge is so generally diffused, when the geography of the world is so well understood—when time and space, in the intercourse of nations, are almost annihilated—when oceans have become bridges—the earth a magnificent hall—the hollow sky a dome—under which a common humanity can meet in friendly conclave—when nationalities are being swallowed up—and the ends of the earth brought together—I say it is remarkable—nay, it is strange that there should arise a phalanx of learned men—speaking in the name of *science*—to forbid the magnificent reunion of mankind in one brotherhood. A mortifying proof is here given, that the moral growth of a nation, or an age, does not always keep pace with the increase of knowledge, and suggests the necessity of means to increase human love with human learning.[33]

Here, Douglass offers his listeners a word of caution about the practitioners of the American school of ethnology, that "phalanx of learned men" who speak "in the name of science." For Douglass, this racist "phalanx" does not represent the ideological underpinnings and biases of science in toto, but instead represents a dangerous perversion of science itself. Far from rejecting the march of science, Douglass invests hope in the social and political possibilities enabled by the wider diffusion of scientific inquiry across an ever-shrinking world. Having radically diminished the distance between geographically isolated populations around the world, scientific and technological advancements are ushering in a post-national age in which provincial "nationalities are being swallowed up" by the technological compression of time and space. He offers listeners a fantastical vision in which the entire world is transformed into a scientific lecture hall, the "hollow sky" its domed ceiling, under which all peoples across the world, a "common humanity," can meet in "friendly conclave." Thus, in the middle of a speech attacking racist science, Douglass offered his audience a strikingly utopian view of popular science as a tool for social amelioration and global alliance. Douglass favors a science that would be animated by the power of human "love" instead of racial hate, a radically egalitarian science that would forge—instead of break—affective and political bonds not only among groups within the United States, but across the globe. Throughout, ethnology also offers Douglass a language through which to connect African Americans to diverse and scattered populations of African descent across the diaspora. But whereas polygenesis trafficked in a global discourse that fixed the races in evolutionary time and denied their connection to one another, Douglass uses this discourse to imagine forms of solidarity among Afro-diasporic people in the US and to connect them to people of color across the world.

Douglass's image of an enormous and grand scientific lecture hall, to which all peoples across the globe are given access, stands in stark opposition to actual practices of admittance to lectures in the United States during the period. Britain was by no means a racial utopia, but there admittance to such venues was more reliable for black patrons. Douglass's imaginary lecture hall also glimpses the transatlantic imaginary upon which more material experiments with fugitive science were built. The imaginary scaffolding of Douglass's "hollow sky a dome," for one, materializes in the actual domes under which black travelers spoke, performed, and engaged with science while traveling abroad, as well as with the Great Exhibition in the Crystal Palace, which African American travelers visited in 1851. Throughout the 1840s and 1850s, many former slaves and freemen and women visited and toured Great Britain, in addition to the fugitive slaves who traveled there to avoid recapture by former owners after the passage of the Fugitive Slave Act in 1850. Free African Americans traveled abroad to lecture on anti-slavery topics, fundraise for black churches, schools, and political organizations, and help build international opinion against the institution of slavery in the United States.[34] The reasons former slaves traveled abroad were often simultaneously political and personal, providing an important platform for activism, but also a route of escape from the United States.

In contrast to the United States, where racial science constrained black engagement with natural science, former slaves and activists found greater freedom to engage with natural science abroad. The vibrancy of popular staged science in Britain, for example—from mechanics' galleries to scientific lectures, exhibits, and various public displays of experimentation—shaped and energized black engagements with science. African Americans also benefited from national exhibits of science. For example, fugitive slaves William Wells Brown and William and Ellen Craft visited the Great Exhibition in the Crystal Palace in London in 1851. A forerunner to the world's fairs and expos that became hugely popular later in the century, the Great Exhibition displayed achievements in the arts, sciences, and industry drawn from England and across the world.

But African Americans did not just passively absorb science abroad; they also participated in it and made contributions. As will be detailed in Chapter 4, Martin Delany made a discrete—and recorded—contribution to the proceedings of an international statistics conference in London in 1860. In 1859, he and a group of black men from the United States toured present-day Nigeria, where, among other things, they collected data to help determine the possibilities of resettling African Americans there. Henry Box Brown's scientific contributions, which I discuss below, were considerably more eccentric than Delany's, but they may have been more influential given their popular reception among British working-class audiences. And William Wells Brown and the Crafts did not just tour the exhibits at the Crystal Palace: they also performed under its glass dome by strategically displaying their bodies alongside various exhibits, including displays of American "progress" as well as visual representations of classical slavery. For example, American sculptor Hiram Powers's *Greek Slave*, which was featured at the Great Exhibition, was a popular sculpture of a white female Greek slave that ignored the identities and experiences of enslaved black women in the nineteenth century.[35]

Noting that the Great Exhibition contained a "more various assemblage of the human race, than ever before was gathered under one roof," Brown further recognized that non-white visitors to the Crystal Palace could make interventions into the ethnological exhibits on display, as well as problematic displays of slavery like Power's sculptural representation of "white slavery."[36] In the Crystal Palace, the bodies of Brown and the Crafts may have served as spectacles like so many other "exhibits" there, but the presence and strategic touring of their persons also challenged the colonial ordering of the races across the exhibition itself, especially pseudo-ethnographic depictions of Western civilization that anticipated the anthropological displays of non-white peoples in world fairs and expos in the late-nineteenth- and early twentieth century. According to Lisa Merrill, the strategic public touring of fugitive slaves like Brown and the Crafts in the American section of the Great Exhibition staged a particularly powerful critique of American achievements in the arts, science, and industry. The presence of Brown and the Crafts as visitors to this exhibit exposed the fact that US civilization was actually mired in the barbarities of enslavement.[37]

Back in the United States, de facto forms of segregation barred African Americans from similar exhibition venues across the Northeast. Carla Peterson notes that access to public exhibits and public services in antebellum New York, including transportation, was often determined according to the whims of individual gatekeepers and operators: admission to an exhibit one day did not guarantee access on another.[38] For example, while a replica Crystal Palace was erected in New York in 1853, African Americans could not be sure of their admittance to its exhibits.[39]

In an environment of uneven and unpredictable access to public spaces and institutions, print sometimes served as a surrogate for public displays of science and related forms of exhibition in the United States. Throughout his career, Frederick Douglass was particularly interested in using the printed page as a kind of surrogate, a space that, among other things, compensated for denials of access to "public" science. *Frederick Douglass' Paper* provided accounts of the Great Exhibition in London for readers without means to travel abroad, included updates on the construction of New York's Crystal Palace, and encouraged local readers of the paper to visit Barnum's traveling panorama of the Crystal Palace before it closed in Rochester.

Douglass's reprinting of European science in his periodicals, together with his citation of transatlantic science in his lectures, also served an important authorizing function, contributing to his learned reputation while helping to further establish his status as a cosmopolitan traveler, just back from the United Kingdom, something that the great most of Americans could not claim in the 1850s. James McCune Smith's medical training in Scotland in the 1830s similarly afforded him an elevated status back in the United States. By the time of the publication of his post-Reconstruction memoir, *My Southern Home*, in 1880, William Wells Brown had also given himself the title of "MD," which legitimated the medical knowledge he obtained while working as an enslaved medical assistant to his first owner, while using his transatlantic encounters with science and medicine to reinforce his identity as a learned black man in the postbellum South.[40] In his travel narrative from 1852, Brown had happily reported that he observed three black men among the medical students at a lecture when he visited the Medical School at the University of Edinburgh.[41] His subsequent claiming of the title of "doctor" suggests that while Brown valued medical training gained from formal education, he also believed that such training could be gained from the "school of slavery," through knowledge stolen by the enslaved. And it is in this context, in which medical training is stolen by enslaved people, that we might better understand Brown's sometimes puzzling burlesquing of medicine across his writing, an act that trafficked in representations drawn from the "medical minstrel show" but also linked black knowledge (fugitive knowledge) to black criminality (fugitivity). Unlike professionally trained physicians like McCune Smith, Brown did not deny the connection between fugitive science and criminality; he embraced it.

Fugitive Science at the Fringe

As knowledge stolen and put to work in diverse contexts in the name of freedom, fugitive science also defines the career of Henry Box Brown, the former slave, author, and traveling showman who keenly understood the power and appeal of popular science and sought to use it for his own ends. And no one better represents the transatlantic dimensions of fugitive science than Brown. In her definitive analysis, Daphne Brooks argues that Brown used theater, performance, visual art, and visual technology to disassemble dominant narratives of the black body and confining spectacles of slavery. Focusing on the transatlantic staging of his moving panorama, the *Mirror of Slavery* (1850), Brooks shows how Brown manipulated "the corporeal to produce a renegade form of escape artistry," an ongoing performance of freedom that "transcended the discursive restrictions of the slave narrative and redirected the uses of the transatlantic body toward politically insurgent ends."[42] Brooks brilliantly figures Brown as an antebellum performance artist who boldly worked in and across multiple kinds of media, "leaping" from "one art form into the next in his quest for emancipation."[43] Here, I would like to extend Brooks's presentation of Brown as a renegade multimedia performance and escape artist by focusing on his particularly artful appropriations of popular science. In Brown's hands, popular science was transformed into yet another medium for emancipation. Rather than dismissing science as an always ideological, racist formation, Brown understood popular science to be an assemblage of different fields and practices that could be dismantled, reassembled, and redirected toward the performance (art) of emancipation.

Brown became a celebrity, first in the United States and later in Britain, for his sensational, nearly unbelievable escape from slavery: in March 1849, he mailed himself to freedom by traveling from Richmond, Virginia, to Philadelphia, Pennsylvania, in a wooden box sent through a private mail service. Brown's fantastical tale of escape quickly captured the popular imaginary, and he soon began his career onstage by speaking about and then replicating his dramatic escape on the abolitionist lecture circuit. In addition to delivering his personal testimony, Brown would jump out from inside the box used in his escape and then delight audiences with a rousing song. Brown's story reached a wider audience with the 1849 publication of his *Narrative of the Life of Henry Box Brown*, in which his story was heavily mediated—and "boxed" in—by his white amanuensis-editor, Charles Stearns. Stearns was a fiery evangelist, an archetypal figure of the Second Great Awakening, who used Brown's narrative as an opportunity to link the struggle against slavery to the politics of millenarianism, while advocating the overthrow of the Union and its replacement by a Christian government. Feeling confined by the heavy editorial control of his life's narrative by both Stearns and the American Anti-Slavery Society, Brown split from mainstream abolition and began to organize various lectures and performances in collaboration with James C.A. Smith, a free black Southerner who helped organize Brown's initial escape in Richmond. While science was not a key aspect of these early performances, Brown quickly found himself in direct competition with advocates of polygenesis on the antebellum lecture circuit. For example, Brown's panorama circulated in Boston at the same time as George Gliddon's own panorama on the hierarchy of the races, *Egyptian Collection and Grand Moving Transparent Panorama of the Nile.* Gliddon, of course, went on to co-author *Types of Mankind* with Josiah Nott, and that popular text on polygenesis would be widely cited by pro-slavery advocates in the years leading up to the Civil War.

Looking to escape an increasingly hostile and dangerous environment in the United States following the passage of the Fugitive Slave Act in 1850, Brown took his act to England, where he turned to British popular science in order to transform his lectures into highly experimental and hybrid performances, which combined a performative "Africanist" mysticism with the mysticism of mesmerism and other popular sciences and did so in a way that dramatized his distance from the various abolitionist scripts that had confined him in the United States. In addition to increasing his autonomy and distancing himself from the liberal wing of mainstream abolitionism, which sought reform not revolution, Brown used popular science—which bore closer connections to labor and the working class in Britain than in the United States—to forge alliances with the British proletariat, especially workers in the cotton mills. After less than a year touring in the United States, Brown would go on to spend the next thirty-five touring in England. Unleashed from the abolitionist framing of his body and editing of his narrative, or what John Sekora refers to as the "white envelope" of the antebellum slave narrative, Brown obtained increasing creative control over his performances across the ocean.[44] He also regained narrative control over his own story in print, when he republished his narrative in Manchester in 1851. While the 1849 Boston edition downplayed Brown's authorial role—the title page maintained that the narrative consisted simply of a "statement of facts" dictated to an editor who fashioned them into artful prose—the 1851 title insisted that the narrative was fully "Written by Himself." Such statements of autonomy were absolutely central for formerly enslaved writers, who wrote against widespread suspicions about their capabilities to both read and write. These authors were also writing against the former negation of their personhood under slavery, the ultimate act of criminality upon which the institution was created and sustained—what Fred Moten refers to as stolen life.[45] In Brown's words, "They robbed me of myself."[46] During his time in Britain, Brown became increasingly performative in declaring his autonomy and increasingly experimental in incorporating different media and content into his act. While his narrative may have emphasized the power of self-possession, Brown's performances pointed at the same time to its limits. Likewise, even as slave narratives helped to establish the autonomy and personhood (owning of the self) of formerly enslaved authors, early black performance routinely hailed a larger collectivity through dynamic, ecstatic performances that challenged liberal concepts of possessive individualism.[47]

Opening the Black Box

The European travels of Frederick Douglass, William and Ellen Craft, and William Wells Brown all occurred under the sponsorship of the American Anti-Slavery Society (AASS), and their visits were intended to help strengthen ties between the AASS and the liberal, mainstream wing of British abolition. Douglass found a favorable reception for his lectures among the working people of England, Scotland, and Ireland, but his visit was, at times, circumscribed by the demands and expectations placed on him by the abolitionists. Abroad, Douglass was often forced into the role of a distinguished ambassador from the United States and "displayed" at various social events, including balls, fairs, and other gatherings of polite society. In these spaces of polite decorum—as well as at reform rallies where slavery was not on the agenda—subversion became a necessity. According to Richard Blackett, black visitors often used public platforms at reform gatherings that were not focused on the abolitionist question to attack slavery, condemn British sympathizers of US slaveholding practices, and display their independence from the institutional frameworks of the AASS.[48]

A few African Americans used their travels in the United Kingdom to forge transatlantic connections through the British labor movement.

These figures worked to build solidarity with factory workers, who, like enslaved people in the United States, were engaged in highly exploitative forms of industrial labor.[49] Henry Box Brown's travels were distinctive because of his lack of affiliation with any abolitionist or reform organization and for the frequency with which he toured the rural regions of England, especially in the northwest, where he routinely performed for factory workers. Due to the sheer number of lecturers, performers, and other entertainers competing for audiences in the entertainment capital of the country, London proved a difficult place for African American lecturers and performers to gain a foothold. For Brown, the north of England provided an open market where he was able to establish his reputation as a performer and carve out a successful career for himself on the road. In addition to touring with a number of different panoramas, including the *Mirror of Slavery*, a panorama of the Indian Mutiny of 1857, and one on the Civil War, Brown lectured, sang plantation melodies, and even performed a dramatic restaging of his 1849 escape, shipping himself in a box from Bradford to Leeds. He was hugely popular in the northern factory districts, and workers' guilds and mechanic institutes often invited him to return for repeat performances. Low-paid, exploited factory workers clearly saw their own condition reflected and amplified in the figure of a former slave from the American South. Moreover, many of these workers were materially linked to American slaves through the thread of cotton itself, from cotton fields in the US South to cotton mills in the United Kingdom. In the 1851 English edition of his narrative, which was printed in Manchester and sold during his performances, Brown added an introduction designed to hail his English audience: "It is not at all unlikely that the great unsettledness which of late has attached to the prices of cotton . . . will lead to arrangements being entered into, through the operation of which the bondman will be made free."[50] Referring to recent crises in the global cotton economy, Brown argued that the dispossessed of America and England were entangled in the same world system and went on to suggest that it was this very connectedness on the world stage—enabled through the transnational cotton economy—that was likely to lead to "arrangements of which the bondman will be made free."[51] In this powerful rallying cry to the English workers, Brown suggests that a global capitalist economy rooted in speculation and enslaved and exploited industrial labor may bring about its own collapse.

Workers were also surely drawn to the many sections of Brown's narrative—appearing in the 1849 narrative and again in the 1851 narrative—in which he describes not the brutalities of agricultural labor on the plantation, but the toils and hardships of life for slaves working in mills and other manufacturing sites in the US South.[52] Scenes like this one, in a Virginia grain mill, would have clearly resonated with the experiences of English factory workers, who toiled under cruel owners and managers, suffered under horrible conditions, and often had little to eat and wear:

> We followed these abject beings to their quarters, and such a sight we had never witnessed before, as we had always lived on our master's plantation, and this was the first of our journeys to the mill. These Slaves were dressed in shirts made of coarse bagging such as coffee sacks are made from, and some kind of light substance for pantaloons, and this was all their clothing! They had no shoes, hats, vests, or coats, and when my brother spoke of their poor clothing they said they had never before seen colored persons dressed as we were; they looked very hungry, and we divided our bread and meat among them.[53]

Brown's act of witnessing here anticipates the ethnography of urban, industrial poverty that would develop decades later in the United States, most notably in Jacob Riis's 1890 exposé, *How the Other Half Lives*. Brown himself had been sent away from his parents "to work in a tobacco manufactory" in Richmond—a fact that helped to strengthen the bond between Brown and his proletarian audiences.[54]

Brown's tour in the factory districts made a clear impact on his audiences. In the 1887 autobiography of Samuel Fielden, the socialist-turned-anarchist, who was convicted for his involvement in the 1886 Haymarket Riot in Chicago, recalled seeing Brown's performances when he was a child laborer working in a cotton mill in Todmorden in West Yorkshire:

> For some years before this time of which I now write there had appeared in my native town at different times, several colored lecturers who spoke on the slavery question in America. I went frequently to hear them describe the inhumanity of that horrible system, sometimes with my father, and at other times with my sister. One of these gentlemen called him-

self Henry Box Brown; the gentleman brought with him a panorama, by means of which he described places and incidents in his slave life, and also the means of his escape. . . . He claimed that he had been boxed up in a large box in which were stowed an amount of provisions, the box having holes bored in the top for air, and marked, "this side up with care." Thus he was shipped to Philadelphia via the underground railroad, to friends there, and this was why he called himself Henry Box Brown. He was a very good speaker and his entertainment was very interesting.[55]

Fielden notes that the lectures by Brown and others "had a very great effect on my mind, and I could hardly divest myself of their impressions, and I used to frequently find myself among my playmates dilating much upon the horrors of slavery."[56] This powerful childhood scene, in which Fielden recalls being unable to "divest" himself of the impressions made by Brown and other black lecturers, gives a sense of the impact Brown had on proletarian audiences in the factory districts. Fielden also singles out Henry Box Brown's performance as a formative moment in his own journey to becoming a transatlantic revolutionary.

It appears that Brown's flashy Orientalist-Africanist costume and flare for the dramatic made his visit to Todmorden a particularly memorable one. Fielden recalls, "He used to march through the streets in front of a brass band, clad in a highly-colored and fantastic garb, with an immense drawn sword in his hand."[57] After Brown ended his professional partnership with James C. A. Smith in the early 1850s, his act became increasingly spectacular and eccentric: it began to look less like a typical anti-slavery performance and more like other mass entertainments populating the British circuit. Dressed in a turban, brightly colored clothing, dripping with jewelry, and brandishing a sword, Brown transformed himself into Henry Box Brown, the "African Prince."[58]

In yet another transformation, Brown began to incorporate experiments in mesmerism, animal magnetism, and biology into his Africanist-inflected stage performances. The "African Prince" was soon being billed as the "African Biologist."[59] As Fielden's account suggests, Brown's unique self-stylization as an "African Biologist" made him extremely popular among his working-class audiences. Rather than allying himself with the bourgeois movement of mainstream abolitionism, as other African American visitors did during their travels, Brown cast his lot with the industrial workers of England, performing and working among them for three decades before returning to the United States. Given the extreme popularity of staged science in Great Britain during the period, in both urban cities and rural towns, Brown's turn to science made his act both recognizable and appealing to British audiences. Popular science also suggested a new politics and new political affiliations.

In the 1850s in the United States, popular science was closely linked to mass spectacle and commodification, and it helped to reinforce the growing divisions between the working class and the bourgeoisie under industrialization. Popular spectacle, commodity culture, and popular science were also wedded in Britain, but there, movements also existed that sought to forge a genuine working-class science. Iwan Rhys Morus has chronicled the establishment of galleries of practical science in London, where "those barred from entry into elite social institutions could witness, and even participate in, the productions of experiment."[60] Working people were encouraged to visit exhibitions and listen to lectures for education and elevation. Mechanics' institutes fostered the production of both artisanal and scientific knowledge and sought to link these knowledges to worker's struggles and efforts to organize.[61]

Brown was repeatedly invited to perform by workers' institutes and organizations. His eccentric and creative experiments with popular science on stage helped to link the plight of African Americans to that of the British proletariat. In addition to emphasizing the solidarity between factory laborers, especially at cotton mills, and slaves of the American South, Brown's performances meditated on the politics of labor in other ways. Having traveled across the country for years in order to eke out an existence for himself and his family—Brown married a white woman in England and had children with her—his performances were clearly work, and hard work at that. At the same time, Brown's self-stylization as an eccentric, flamboyantly dressed "African biologist" was also a defiant gesture of refusing the mundane, soul-crushing labor of both the factory and the plantation.[62] In so doing, Brown provided a model of worker's resistance that reconfigured the relationship between science and labor, suggesting that popular science might be used to imagine a form of resistance and emancipation that rejected labor altogether.

While London remained the epicenter of popular science in performance, scientific lecturers also frequently toured in England's smaller cities and towns. Given the popular craze for all things scientific, it should not come as a surprise that Brown, that master showman and multimedia artist, would find a way to incorporate science into his act, transforming scientific experimentation into a praxis of solidarity and resistance. As Jeffrey Ruggles notes, Brown's first "stage experiment" was conducted on March 2, 1859, in Brentford, a suburb of London. Assisted on stage by the American mesmerist Sheldon Chadwick, who billed himself as "Professor Chadwick," Brown's staging of experiments in "mesmerism and biology" was both "excellent" and "successful," according to the *West London Observer*. [63]

Brown continued to offer lectures on "electro-biology" (mesmerism on stage) throughout the 1860s. While we cannot be exactly sure of the content of Brown's stage experiments, we can make some educated guesses. First, Brown's famous box would have taken on new meanings in the context of his performances of electro-biology. In his study of electrical experiments and exhibitions in the nineteenth century, Morus gives us a vision of a Victorian England where little electrical machines and apparatuses appeared virtually everywhere, in lecture theaters, galleries, museums, and other public spaces.[64] In this context, Brown's box finds a place alongside the various electrical apparatuses and other mysterious "black boxes"—to use Bruno Latour's phrase—that accompanied scientific showmen throughout the period.[65] Since hypnosis stood at the center of the mesmerist's repertoire, it is likely that hypnotic trances also figured prominently in Brown's performances. In such acts, the mysterious, charismatic mesmerist would induce trances in audience members and then display control over their actions. We should think seriously about the subversive implications of a former slave controlling the movement of white bodies on the Victorian stage. The spectacle of Brown taking "possession" of his audience members raised the specter of Brown's former condition as a slave in the United States, and enacted that chilling line, turned refrain in his 1849 and then 1851 narrative: "They robbed me of myself." On stage, Brown's mesmeric trances conjured the spirit of the enslaved in the United States and the memory of stolen life from the transatlantic slave trade. Exploiting the associations between mesmerism and mysticism, as well as between blackness and conjuring, Brown's act provided a visceral study of the politics of captivity while emphasizing his own agency and freedom from slavery and adjacent regimes of unfreedom.

Brown's performances of mesmerism also revised the religious metaphors that had framed and determined his story of escape in the United States just a few years previously, when printed songs and visual culture drew a sympathetic connection between Brown's trials and the persecutions and resurrection of Christ. The metaphorical—and affective—link between Brown and the suffering of Christ was further formalized, and visualized, in an 1850 lithograph of Brown's "un-boxing," published in Boston and titled, "The Resurrection of Henry Box Brown at Philadelphia" (see Figure 3.1). Brown likely sold this lithograph at his performances, alongside song sheets of his famous "Hymn of Thanksgiving" and "Escape from Slavery of Henry Box Brown." The lithograph was also reproduced for the 1851 edition of Brown's book, where it appeared as the frontispiece, guiding the expectations of readers of the narrative, especially the account of Brown's escape, which he revised so that it complemented the frontispiece image. Thus, the English edition radically transforms the straightforward recounting of his "un-boxing" in the 1849 narrative through the grand Resurrection metaphor presented in the lithograph. However, rather than further dramatizing Brown's Christ-like suffering or heightening the theme of salvation in the narrative, Brown uses the Resurrection metaphor to promote his marvelous "resurrections" on the British stage. In other words, the 1851 narrative uses the discourse of resurrection—of being raised from the dead—to advertise Brown's miraculous stage shows while suggesting his own Christ-like celebrity status.

In England, Brown's "resurrection" was transformed from a Christian allegory to a stage trick. Brown regularly drew from both stage magic and popular science to distance himself from the Protestant, moralistic imperatives of mainstream American abolition that had kept him "boxed in" after his 1849 escape. However, we should not presume that Brown's investment in popular science was wholly secular. Rather, his experimental remixing of mystical sciences with stage magic and conjuring displayed a different kind of "spiritual" investment, one that, among other things, challenged the increasing secularism of midcentury

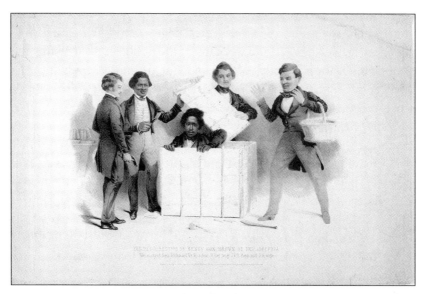

Figure 3.1. "The Resurrection of Henry Box Brown at Philadelphia," Boston, 1850. Courtesy of the American Antiquarian Society.

natural science. Through his staging of a mystical, apparently "Africanist" science on stage, Brown distanced himself from the moral suasion of abolitionism, while posing challenges to the evacuation of the spiritual and the supernatural from science itself. As in Martin Delany's novel, *Blake; or, The Huts of America,* which I discuss in the next chapter, Brown enacted a mystically inflected science, a fugitive science oriented toward the praxis of freedom that was also a critique of the dry rationality that was increasingly defining natural science by the middle of the nineteenth century.

Unfettered from the demands and constraints placed on him by the religious and moral models of abolitionism in the United States, Brown was able to use the popular lecture circuit in England—composed of a wide and wild assortment of mass entertainments—to continually experiment with his routine, incorporating and melding together mesmerism and electro-biology with black knowledge and mysticism. His billing as the "African Biologist," as well as "Professor Henry Box Brown," were not derogatory or derisive commentaries on his pretensions to authority and expertise. Rather, lecturers in both the United States and Britain regularly took on the title "doctor" or "professor," even when they did not hold any professional or medical degree, and these figures were not necessarily dismissed as charlatans by the public. Indeed, before the professionalization of science and medicine in the second half of the nineteenth century, scientific expertise was extended to a surprisingly broad range of practitioners. When Brown's son was born in Bristol in 1864, his birth certificate even listed his father's profession as a "lecturer in mesmerism."[66] It is apparent that Brown gained both respectability and eventually financial security from his performances: a census record indicates that in 1871, Brown was living in Manchester with his Cornish wife and their three children and was doing well enough as a lecturer and performer to have a servant working and living at his residence.[67] In 1875, Brown and his family moved back to the United States; in the 1880s they resettled in Canada where Brown continued to incorporate science and medicine into his performances.[68]

Faced with the surprise of Brown's embrace of popular science, Jeffrey Ruggles strains to find an adequately political explanation for his doing so. Since Brown's turn to mesmerism and electro-biology had no immediately apparent connection to slavery or to the science of race, Ruggles concludes that Brown was personally distant from slavery: "By the time of the Emancipation Proclamation, Brown had emancipated himself, in a sense, from his personal history of enslavement. When he presented electro-biology, it did not matter that he had been a slave, for mesmerism was an act with no particular connection to slavery."[69] However, rather than viewing science as a nonpolitical domain, or as an escape from politics, we might consider how science as experiment and practice helped to link mesmerism and electro-biology both to Brown's ongoing project of self-transformation and emancipation, as well as to the political and scientific movements of the British working class. Here I understand "practice" to be a form of "politics without a proper locus," as Saidiya Hartman conceives it. Since enslaved and nominally free people were regularly barred from the political as it was traditionally conceived, their acts and resistances often registered in seemingly apolitical domains and were "measured *against* notions of the political and its central features: the unencumbered self, the citizen, the self-possessed individual, and the volitional and autonomous subject." Thus, Hartman shows how the concept of practice "enables us to recognize the agency of the dominated and the limited and transient nature of that agency."[70] This, in turn, allows us to challenge the seemingly apolitical nature of Brown's turn to science by recalibrating the political itself. Brown's eccentric performances of science, his experimentation with a number of different of scientific fields—in short, his enactment of a dynamic, fugitive science—illuminated that science was itself a performative domain. In so doing, he cleared a space for African Americans both to intervene in ongoing debates about the science of race and to link popular science to ongoing emancipation and labor struggles in transatlantic contexts. Transforming the popular stage into a site of experimentation, his performances suggested material ways that natural science might be linked to resistance, rather than to domination.

Performing Plantation Science

John Ernest has argued that the British edition of Brown's narrative is the performative one, in which Brown's "public performances are built into the narrative."[71] In addition to reprinting advertisements for his shows, endorsements for his panoramas, and letters about his escape from firsthand witnesses, the edition reproduces songs that Brown sang during his performances, including his famous "Hymn of Thanksgiving," first performed after his first, dramatic "unboxing" in the Philadelphia Anti-Slavery Office in 1849.[72] The 1851 narrative seeks to legitimate Brown's status as both a respected performer and "emerging antislavery celebrity."[73] It is also itself an archive of performance, offering a robust record of the songs, stories, and panoramas that structured his spectacular shows.

The archive of performance contained in the 1851 narrative illuminates yet more evidence of Brown's engagement with natural science, including an explicit intervention into the discourse of racial science. The narrative concludes with his adaptation of Stephen Foster's "Uncle Ned" titled "The Escape from Slavery of Henry Box Brown," a song that Brown performed publicly and also sold as a broadside. In this "commemoration of my fete in the box," Brown revises both the minstrel tradition and the sorrow song tradition (where the coffin-like box delivers one to renewed life instead of the grave) to offer a rousing account of his liberation. The chorus celebrates Brown's spectacular escape as well as his refusal of plantation labor:

Brown laid down the shovel and the hoe,
Down in the box he did go;
No more Slave work for Henry Box Brown,
In the box *by Express* he did go.[74]

After the reproduction of the song lyrics, a curious appendix is included at the narrative's end, prefaced with this editorial note: "The allusion in my song to the shovel and the hoe, is founded on the following story, which forms the slave-holders' version of the creation of the human race."[75] Brown's slaveholder creation story is a polygenetic one, in which the races were created separately in multiple acts by God. Indeed, Brown's story in the appendix might be read as a mock-ethnology that signifies on the narratives of biblical creation that were fabulated by pro-slavery ideologues:

The slave-holders say that originally, there were four persons created (instead of only two) and, perhaps, it is owing to the christian account of the origin of man, in which account two persons only are mentioned, that it is one of the doctrines of slave-holders that slaves have no souls: however these four persons were two whites and two blacks; and the blacks were made to wait upon the whites. But in man's original state when he [was] neither required to manufacture clothes to cover his nakedness, or to shelter him from storm; when he did not require to till the earth or to sow or to reap its fruits, for his support! but when everything sprung up spontaneously; when the shady bowers invited him to rest, and the loaded trees dropped their luscious burdens into his hands; in this state of things the white pair were plagued with the incessant attendance of the two colored persons, and they prayed that God would find them something else to do; and immediately while they stood, a black cloud seemed to gather over their heads and to descend to the earth before them! While they gazed on these clouds, they saw them open and two bags of different size drop from them. They immediately ran to lay hold of the bags, and unfortunately for the black man—he being the strongest and swiftest—he arrived first at them, and laid hold of the bags, and the white man, coming up afterwards, got the smaller one. They then proceeded to untie their bags, when lo! in the large one, there was a shovel and a hoe; and in the small one, a pen, ink, and paper; to write the declaration of the intention of the Almighty; they each proceeded to employ the instruments which God had sent them, and ever since the colored race have had to labor with the shovel and the hoe, while the rich man works with the pen and ink![76]

In this tongue-in-cheek account, the division of manual and intellectual labor between the white and black race is explained away by a peculiar and completely contingent act by God. The "curse" of enslavement and hard labor cannot be ascribed to biological difference, to Ham's Curse, or to God's design, but is rather the result of a purely chance event: the first black man on earth opening up the "wrong bag." Through both his song and mock-theory, Brown satirizes polygenesis, a technique that stretches back to the satirical treatments of ethnology by David Walker and James W. C. Pennington and looks forward to William J. Wilson's mock-ethnology in his 1859 "Afric-American Picture Gallery." Through satire, Brown reveals the absurdity of polygenetic theories, which fly in the face of basic lessons of the creation story in scripture, in which, Brown notes, only two persons are mentioned, not four. It should not come as a surprise that rather than offering a direct critique of race science, Brown offers a highly performative and creative *satire* of polygenesis, a satire that both reveals the laughable absurdity of such theories—or ideologically motivated, fictional stories—and suggests that polygenesis was the production of pro-slavery ideology more than science.

In addition to intervening in polygenetic discourses that justified regimes of enslavement in the plantation South, the narrative also records Brown's former imbrication in and subsequent liberation from adjacent regimes of plantation science and agriculture. The narrative offers a window onto some of the many technical aspects of growing and processing tobacco, while foregrounding the centrality and expertise of enslaved laborers in the production of this major plantation commodity.[77] Brown was born and raised on a tobacco plantation outside Richmond, Virginia where he worked as a house servant. Although he was likely spared from working in the tobacco fields on the plantation, Brown's master died when he was fifteen years old and he was subsequently sent to work in a Richmond tobacco factory. While recounting his experiences at the Richmond plant, Brown outlines the tough working conditions at the factory for its workers, much like the reports of the English factory inspectors that led to the passing of the British Factory Acts in the 1830s–1850s and that Karl Marx cites throughout *Capital* (1867). After offering a brief report on the factory's conditions, Brown moves on to outline the detailed production process required to bring tobacco to market. He emphasizes that his work and that of his fellow workers was skilled labor, rooted in both artisanal skill (made, in Brown's terms, "with the hands") and technical competency (in the "machine house"). Later in the narrative, tobacco work is elevated to the status of a full-fledged profession. After determining to escape from the master who sold his first wife, Brown shares his current frustrations and future plans with Samuel Smith, the Richmond shopkeeper who would go on to assist Brown with his escape: "I said to him if I were free I would be able to do business such as he was doing; he then told me that my occupation (a tobacconist) was a money-making one, and if I were free I had no need to change for another."[78] Through Smith's identification of Brown as a "tobacconist," the narrative transforms tobacco labor into a highly skilled occupation while at the same time revealing Brown's rejection of the regimes of plantation agriculture and industry to which he had been subjected as a slave.

Through its insertion of black expertise into networks of plantation agriculture as well as its incorporation of Brown's performative interventions into the "plantation science" of polygenesis, the 1851 narrative records Brown's transformation of both antebellum race science and plantation science into transatlantic sciences of emancipation. Once in England, Brown liberated himself from the racial sciences and plantation sciences that had confined and rooted him in the United States, taking flight in highly speculative and experimental forms of popular science in the United Kingdom. Freed from the constant surveillance of race science and its subjugating categories in the United States, Brown used both the transatlantic stage and the page to consider how other forms of science—from mesmerism to electricity experiments and beyond—might be used to imagine other futures of blackness.

Science in/as Performance

The transatlantic performance of fugitive science included both actual performances and the construction of a robust transatlantic imaginary in early African American cultural production, an imaginary enabled by the globally oriented discourses of race in ethnology as well as the travels of African Americans within and outside the United States. During this golden era of popular science, from the 1830s through the 1850s, the connections between black performance and science were many and diverse. In both the United States and Britain, scientists of all kinds competed for audiences with abolitionist lectures and various forms of black performance. At times, such competition produced fascinating forms of intersection, and in the case of racial science, even occasional moments of confrontation. In her study of nineteenth-century craniology, Ann Fabian recounts one such scene in 1830s Philadelphia. One evening, during his 1838 tour of the United States, George Combe arrived to present his lecture at the Philadelphia Museum only to discover that the floor above the lecture hall had been rented to the wildly popular Frank Johnson and his band, recently returned home from a European tour. Johnson was a prominent black composer, bandleader, and musician from Philadelphia, who gained national and international fame for his compositions, especially his dances and military marches. While Combe counted five hundred Philadelphians at his lecture, he reported that Johnson's concerts easily drew in some two to three thousand people. To add insult to injury, Combe complained, "The music is so loud that it often drowns my voice, and when the audience above applaud with their feet, I have no alternative but to stop till they have done." Fabian uses this scene to demonstrate the competition among entertainers that "characterized commercial entertainment in the United States in the 1830s and 1840s."[79] But it is also a beautiful example of black art quite literally interrupting the dominant discourse of antebellum race science. This scene of sonic disruption also troubles our assumptions about the rigid divide between scientific and cultural production in the period.

This scene becomes even more interesting when we consider that Frank Johnson's band had just returned home from a European tour that had been a grand success. Johnson and Combe encountered each other in Philadelphia, an important scientific metropole in the United States with substantive connections to other cities where scientific Enlightenment ruled, especially London and Edinburgh. Since scenes like this one were happening on both sides of the ocean, Johnson and Combe could have just as easily encountered one another in Scotland. Throughout the antebellum period, transatlantic black performance regularly confronted and challenged racial science. Frank Johnson was not a scientist, per se, but that night, his music made a significant contribution to the discourse of phrenology, a field with its own complex and vexed relationship to the science of race.

4

Delany's Comet

Blake; or, The Huts of America *and the Science Fictions of Slavery*

While some black travelers hoped to escape hostile conditions in the United States after the passage of the Fugitive Slave Act in 1850, others traveled abroad to raise money to support themselves and various reform organizations, while spreading the word of abolition among an international audience. Into the 1850s, African American travelers also continued to comment on and participate in European science. Martin Delany, who arrived in England in 1859, just after having led a group of African Americans on an exploratory expedition to West Africa, was especially interested in drawing connections between natural science and the struggle for emancipation.

The presence of an American-born black explorer of Africa in Britain created quite a stir in the press and in intellectual circles. Fashioning himself as an imperial explorer in the British style, Delany was also able to establish an international reputation for himself as a scientist. In July 1860, Delany received a royal commission from the British government to attend the International Statistical Congress in London as an honored guest. This annual meeting was presided over by the Prince Consort of England and it gathered together leading scientists and dignitaries from around the world, including representatives from Great Britain, Continental Europe, the United States, and Brazil. While only men were invited to participate in the meeting, a paper by Florence Nightingale, encouraging the transnational systematization of hospital statistics, was read in absentia.[1] Delany spoke on record at least three times during the week-long proceedings: he publicly thanked the congress for their hospitality and sympathy toward his race, discussed his recent travels in West Africa and the sanitary conditions in that part of the continent, and presented a paper on the spread of cholera based on his experiences with the Philadelphia cholera epidemic of 1854. However, it appears that members of the congress were more interested in the novelty of Delany's presence at the event than in his actual contributions to the proceedings.

In the July 28, 1860, issue of Britain's chief medical journal, the *Lancet*, Delany's paper on cholera epidemics received only one curt line in the summary of the proceedings from the "Sanitary Section" of the congress: "Dr. Delany, a coloured gentleman from Canada, made some important observations on the spread of cholera."[2] However, an article entitled "A Physician of Colour" appeared in this same issue of the *Lancet*, and in it, the author used the remarkable inclusion of a black representative at the Statistical Congress as evidence for the exemplary progressiveness of the field of medicine: "Medicine, which has always shown a noble preference for the universal interests of humanity over the minor divisions and classifications which limit charity and impede active benevolence, was with peculiar felicity represented at the late Congress by physicians, not only of every nation, but of every race."[3] "Dr. Delany, a physician of African blood," reportedly received the heartiest welcome of any of the representatives.[4] According to the *Lancet*, Delany so impressed the congress attendees because his "intellectual cultivation" was beautifully combined with all of "the most strongly marked physical characters of his race."[5] Delany was treated that week as an object of intense scientific curiosity: a real, living "physician of African blood" and a spectacular specimen of black manhood.

Indeed, it was the physical presence of Delany's "strongly marked" body at the congress that caused a six-month media scandal in English, Scottish, and American newspapers.[6] In his opening comments to the scientists and other representatives assembled at the meeting, Lord Henry Peter Brougham turned to the American diplomat George Mifflin Dallas and abruptly called his attention to the fact that a black man from America was an acting member of the congress. Reportedly, the audience cheered loudly in response to Brougham's pointed comment, which was intended as a sly critique of the continued legality of slavery in the United States.[7] In an article on the "Dallas and Delany affair" in *Douglass' Monthly*, Frederick Douglass teased out the significance of Brougham's cryptic comments: "It was saying: 'Mr. Dallas, we make members of the International Statistical Society out of the sort of men

you make merchandize of in America."[8] Brougham's public acknowl-
edgment of Delany outraged Dallas as well as the two other American
representatives at the congress, Dr. Edward Jarvis of Massachusetts and
Judge Augustus Longstreet of Georgia. A proud Southerner, Longstreet
promptly withdrew from the meeting and sent off irate letters to US officials and British newspapers. After learning of the offense taken by the
American delegates, Brougham returned the second day of the congress
with an apology, insisting that he had "merely meant to call to notice
an interesting or a statistical fact, viz.: that there was a negro in the as-
sembly."[9] Brougham's response is telling. While his original comments
obliquely suggested his own anti-slavery sympathies, this rejoinder be-
lied the true value of Delany's presence at the Statistical Congress. He
was an object of curiosity, an interesting "statistical fact."

Brougham's treatment of Delany as a "fact" collected among other interesting data sets at the Statistical Congress echoes Frantz Fanon's discussion of the experience of being sealed into a "crushing objecthood"
by the white gaze in *Black Skin, White Masks*. Fanon writes, "I came
into the world imbued with the will to find a meaning in things, my
spirit filled with the desire to attain to the source of the world, and then
I found that I was an object in the midst of other objects."[10] For Fanon,
these routine moments of objectification, of being frozen, or "fixed" "in
the sense in which a chemical solution is fixed by a dye," constituted
the "facticity" or "fact of blackness." The "fact of blackness" aptly describes Brougham's aggressive fingering of Delany ("Look, a Negro!") at
the Statistical Congress.[11] Delany publicly resisted his transformation
into a mute object for the exacting, penetrating gazes of the white scientists and statisticians in attendance. According to Delany's comments
to his biographer, he took Brougham's comments not as an objective
statement, but as a "disparaging allusion" to his personhood.[12] In response to being pointed out as a "negro" to Dallas, Delany stood up
and asserted that he was not a "negro," not a "fact," but a "man": "I rise,
your Royal Highness, to thank his lordship, the unflinching friend of the
negro, for the remarks he has made in reference to myself, and to assure
your [R]oyal [H]ighness and his lordship that *I am a man*."[13] Frederick
Douglass's comments on the Brougham incident further illuminate the
boldness with which Delany addressed this international audience. According to Douglass, Delany "rose, with all his blackness, right up, as

quick and as graceful as an African lion, and received the curious gaze of the scientific world."[14] In a manner that recalls the portrait of Robert Benjamin Lewis discussed in Chapter 2, Delany resisted the "curious gaze of the scientific world" even as he received it, turning it back on those who looked at him. In so doing, Delany asserted that he was a man, but also a force with which to be reckoned.

While Delany's actions at the International Statistical Congress were certainly remarkable, as the international press coverage of the event attests, they were in no way anomalous.[15] Indeed, Delany regularly rejected black "facticity" while forwarding substantive critiques of both the destructive prejudices of antebellum racial science and the Eurocentric biases of Western science. In an impressive array of lectures, literary texts, scientific treatises, and political essays, Delany presented himself as both a political agent and scientific practitioner, actively resisting his transformation—by law, science, and capital—into an object. But far from evading or rejecting antebellum science, Delany's radical politics depended on a dynamic engagement with a wide range of scientific fields, including comparative anatomy, ethnology, natural history, and astronomy.

In this chapter, I chronicle how Delany actively linked scientific revolution to race revolution throughout a lifetime of activism and writing. Delany's substantive engagements with natural science offer new ways to think about his literary experiment, *Blake; or, The Huts of America*. The past several years have witnessed an exciting renaissance in Delany scholarship focused on a range of topics, including *Blake* and transnationalism, property, the politics of seriality, early Black Nationalism, hemispherism, and Afrocentricism.[16] Considering the novel in the context of its publication in the *Anglo-African Magazine*, which published many scientific tracts, we can see that it was also deeply engaged with the politics of nineteenth-century science and sought to harness the revolutionary potential of natural science for political experiments in black transnationalism and universal emancipation.

Through its registering of the vicious racism of racial science in the 1850s, *Blake* is very much a product of a post–*Types of Mankind* America. At several points in the novel, Delany attacks racist sciences as conducted in support of slavery, revealing the capriciousness and amateur nature of these investigations. In his account, racial science is revealed to be rooted in an incoherent and cruel set of violent acts flagrantly conducted on black bodies. But Delany's fiction also imagines the formation of a utopian speculative science to be used in the struggle against slavery. Drawing from a wide variety of scientific fields, methods, and experiments, *Blake* envisions the construction of a fugitive science, a highly experimental, itinerant set of practices and tools mobilized and deployed in the freedom struggle of both enslaved and nominally free peoples. Moreover, Delany uses fugitivity to wage an attack on Western epistemology, revealing blackness to be an errant, disruptive force that stands at the heart of Western science itself.

While fugitive science might be understood in terms of the representational and thematic landscape of *Blake*, fugitive science also names Delany's method—his highly creative engagements with science and his mobilization of an eclectic, diasporic science both in *Blake* and in his life, as well as the significant formal experimentalism of the text itself. Read in this scientific context, *Blake* is recast as a deeply experimental, highly ambitious speculative fiction, a proto-science fiction that challenged impoverished conceptions of race and the human. While scholars have rightly delineated the novel's complex mapping of transnational spaces, the novel also puts forward an existential and cosmic vision of fugitivity that spans not only the US South and Cuba, but stretches throughout the globe and across the galaxy. Delany used fugitive science to imagine both a new science and a new world.

Martin R. Delany, MD

Delany is often cited as an important progenitor of Black Nationalism and as the author of *Blake; or, The Huts of America* (1859–1862), a radical novel of transnational slave revolt and one of the earliest novels published by an African American. *Blake* was published serially in the *Anglo-African Magazine* and the *Weekly Anglo-African*; it was never published as a stand-alone novel in the nineteenth century. Unduly committed to the enfranchisement of African Americans, Delany spent his life engaging in different types of political and writing projects when and as they seemed most amenable to forwarding the struggle for black liberation. To nineteenth-century Americans, Delany was best known for his militant political commitments to black emigration, for co-editing the *North Star* with Frederick Douglass, and for his senior position in the Civil War, where he served as the highest ranking African American officer in the Union Army. He was also known for taking a huge amount of pride in his African heritage. Douglass famously said, "I thank God for making me a man simply; but Delany always thanks him for making him a *black* man."[17]

Although his robust engagements with science and medicine have been largely ignored by scholars, nineteenth-century writings and speeches about Delany regularly highlighted his medical expertise and status as a respected scientist both within and beyond black communities in the Northeast. In her 1868 biography of Delany, Frances Rollin (writing under the pen name Frank A. Rollin) includes an incredibly detailed account of Delany's medical training, scientific writings and lectures, and practice of medicine. Rollin met Delany in South Carolina while he was serving as the head of the Freedman's Bureau in Hilton Head. After Delany approached her about writing his biography, offering her access to his speeches and papers as well as payment, Rollin agreed in the hope that it would help launch her literary career.[18] For his part, Delany was clearly seeking to extend his Civil War celebrity with a flattering biography in which he could fashion his image as a courageous Civil War hero for a Reconstruction audience and for posterity—and the spine of the first edition of Rollin's biography did indeed deliver this message: "Major Delany" appears in a crest with stars and stripes and an eagle perched on top.

While Robert Levine rightly cautions scholars against using Rollin's biography as an objective and reliable account, the volume does much to flesh out Delany's scientific commitments.[19] In fact, the biography's bias—filtered through Delany's own postwar perspective—reveals that he viewed his scientific and medical background to be an absolutely central aspect of his own life and his politics. After being raised and educated by his mother in Charlestown, Virginia (now West Virginia), and later in Chambersburg, Pennsylvania, a young Delany moved to Pittsburgh in 1831 to continue his studies and to improve his career prospects. He soon began to study medicine under Dr. Andrew N. Mc-Dowell. Although he did not, according to Rollin, "complete this course of study," he began to practice dentistry and used the surgical skills he gained "whenever immediately necessary."[20] Levine notes that by 1837, Delany was listed in the *Pittsburgh Business Directory* as "DELANY, MARTIN R. Cupping, Leeching and bleeding."[21]

After a tour of the South, he returned to Pittsburgh and ventured into publishing. In 1843, he founded the *Mystery*, a weekly newspaper that covered black struggles in Pittsburgh and beyond. Delany's first ethnological essay, his account of the origin and descent of the races, appeared in the paper. Anticipating W. E. B. Du Bois's 1920 argument in *Darkwater: Voices from Within the Veil*, Delany figured the world as belonging to its "darker peoples," since two-thirds of its population were "colored." Rollin claims that Delany's first ethnology generated much discussion and controversy, particularly his "novel declaration of the preponderance of numbers of the colored races of the world."[22]

In 1847, Delany transferred ownership of the *Mystery* to the AME Church in Pittsburgh, which began publishing the weekly paper under a new name, the *Christian Herald*, later renamed the *Christian Recorder*.[23] Delany himself moved on to the *North Star*, which he co-edited with Frederick Douglass for a year and a half. Most of Delany's time at the *North Star* was spent on the road. In early 1848 he embarked on a trip to the Midwest, during which he worked to secure subscriptions for the paper, spoke at anti-slavery meetings, visited black communities, organizations, and institutions, and contributed regular reports about his "Western Tour" to the *North Star*. Delany severed his connection with the *North Star* just a few months later, after his famous break with Douglass over the issue of emigration (Delany was sympathetic to the cause; Douglass was not).

With another experiment drawn to a close, Delany jumped to the next one and was admitted to Harvard Medical School in 1850. Coincidentally, the Swiss immigrant, zoologist, and recent convert to polygenesis, Louis Agassiz, had also just recently arrived at Harvard. While Agassiz spent the next two decades building his career at Harvard, Delany was not allowed one more year. Acting under pressure of the faculty and student body, Dean Oliver Wendell Holmes ejected Delany from the program, along with two other African American men and one white woman.[24] Toyin Falola notes that even though he did not complete his course of study, Delany took the title of "doctor" anyway.[25]

This was a common practice at the time since medical licensing was not standardized. Given Delany's pride and political commitments, it is also likely that he relished the opportunity to usurp a professional title normally reserved for white men.

Rollin notes that after leaving Harvard, Delany "traveled westward" and embarked on a scientific lecture tour, speaking on physiology, comparative anatomy, and ethnology:

> [He] lectured on physiological subjects—the comparative anatomical and physical conformation of the cranium of the Caucasian and negro races,—besides giving class lectures. These he rendered successful. While his arguments on these subjects were in strict conformity to acknowledged scientific principles, *they are also marked by his peculiar and original theories.* For instance, he argues on this subject that the pigment which makes the complexion of the African black is essentially the same in properties as that which makes the ruddy complexion of the European, the African's being concentrated rouge, which is black. This he urges by illustrations considered scientifically true. He maintains that these truths will yet be acknowledged by writers on physiology.[26]

Delany likely drew on his medical courses at Harvard in composing his lectures. He soon landed back in Pittsburgh, where he continued to practice medicine and gained acclaim for his treatment of cholera. This period also marked the beginning of Delany's interest in several programs for the founding of independent black states outside the borders of the United States. Although Delany had been exposed to the emigrationist politics of William Whipper and Lewis Woodson in Pittsburgh in the 1830s, his own commitments to the cause of black separatism did not solidify until the 1850s. Delany's experience of institutional racism at Harvard—of being accepted within the ranks of an elite white institution and then disposed of in a moment's notice—must have contributed to his political radicalization. Harvard taught Delany at least one important lesson: if African Americans sought education and elevation, they would have to build their own institutions to do so.

The Fugitive Slave Act of 1850 provided additional reasons to support the emigration cause and helped to spur the organization of a National

Emigration Convention as well as a number of black emigration interest groups.[27] Delany observed that the Fugitive Slave Act had made free African Americans utter aliens in their own land. Under such inhospitable conditions, he argued that African Americans could either suffer in the United States or leave the country and put pressure on the slaveholding states from abroad. At first, Delany rejected Africa as a site for removal and instead favored resettlement in South America. His hemispheric vision of the early 1850s was premised on the idea that African Americans could enter into a union with the oppressed peoples of South America to counter the empire of the United States. His first major public statement in favor of emigration appeared in his 1852 tract, *Condition, Elevation, Emigration, and Destiny of the Colored People of the United States*. *Condition* demonstrates how Delany and other prominent African American political figures of the time picked up on and appropriated the notion of Manifest Destiny to legitimate and imagine a black empire in the Americas. In *Condition*, Delany goes beyond a pragmatic suggestion that African Americans might better pressure the Southern plantocracy from outside the racist structures of the United States, arguing that one day diasporic peoples might "form a glorious union of *Southern American States* 'inseparably connected one and forever.'"[28] Here, Delany's creative geographical imaginary anticipates the kind of revolutionary mapping that appears in *Blake*. In *Condition*, the South is wrested from its associations with enslavement, racism, and disenfranchisement to become a black tropical empire in the Southern hemisphere, a safe haven for the "colored races" and, at the same time, a threat to slaveholding interests in the North (which is from this perspective, the US South). Also as in *Blake*, *Condition* challenges contemporary slave narratives that privileged linear forms of flight from South to North. Instead, Delany suggests that fugitives should flee *deeper* into the South, knowing "he has safety" there.[29] In these ways, *Condition* is animated by a spectacular vision of a tropical empire filled with fugitive slaves, a permeable and penetrating Global South that threatens to creep into the Northern hemisphere.

In 1853 and 1854, Delany continued to argue for the virtues of South American and Caribbean emigration, most notably in his 1854 address, "Political Destiny of the Colored Races." However, by the mid-1850s,

Delany abandoned his scheme to construct a fugitive empire in Latin America in order to focus his energy on resettlement efforts in Africa. Ironically, Reverend Thomas Bowen's *Central Africa* (1857) and David Livingstone's *Missionary Travels and Researches in South Africa* (1857), two texts that anticipated the British "scramble" for Africa later in the century, also helped to rekindle an interest in African colonization among black intellectuals and activists in the United States and Canada during the late 1850s. Delany's African interests were concretized in 1858 when he left the United States as the leader of a black expedition party to West Africa. He was commissioned by a board of expatriation advocates that had emerged out of the 1854 National Emigration Convention in Cleveland to study and report back on the possibilities of establishing a cotton economy in West Africa run by African Americans. Delany and the board hoped that an alternative, black plantation system—in which African cotton would be sold to British manufacturing firms— could compete with and ultimately topple the agricultural economy of the US South. Although all kinds of proposals and counter-proposals were made for emigration to sites around the globe in the 1850s, this scheme is particularly unique in its investment in a plantation economy for the express purpose of causing total destruction to the plantation complex of the US South.[30]

Delany and his party visited present-day Nigeria and parts of Liberia during their several month stay. In the expository section of his *Niger Valley Report*, which was written in 1860 and published in 1861, Delany writes that he was asked by the Emigration Board of Commissioners to make a "scientific inquiry" into the "topographical, geological, and geographic" qualities of the region in order to determine whether it would provide hospitable ground for a settlement of expatriated African Americans.[31] In the report, Africa is held up as a promising site where African Americans might forge a model nation that would prove the race's superior capacity for self-government. Delany embraces cotton as the key to African American political and economic success in the future. He goes on to make a plea: "We only want additional labor; give us that and we shall very soon cultivate our own cotton."[32] It becomes clear in these pages that Delany imagined a society in which transplanted African Americans would serve as managers in the fields, overseeing the labor of native Africans. Delany's vision of a black empire in Africa was thus ironically saddled with the exploitations and enclosures of the New World plantation system. Before leaving Lagos, Delany and his party even signed a treaty with the King of Abeokuta, granting the exploring party land rights among the Igbo people so they could begin to establish their plantation experiment in the region.[33]

In 1860, Delany left Africa for England, where he sought an alliance with British manufacturers who were increasingly anxious about the threat that sectional conflicts in the United States posed to the American cotton supply.[34] In response to supply problems, the textile industry formed the Cotton Supply Association (CSA) to search for alternative cotton sources around the globe. Delany received enthusiastic support for his African cotton scheme from the popular press and from major firms in England. Although he signed contracts with some cotton dealers, the African plantation experiment never came to fruition. The outbreak of the Civil War put an end to this and many other emigration schemes in the US. The Civil War also gave Delany a powerful reason to reinvest in the struggle for black enfranchisement within the borders of the United States.

During his trip to Britain in 1860, Delany lectured widely on his expedition. Not only did his African travels and exceptional status as a black physician from America bring him recognition among British officials, abolitionists, and manufacturers; he also became something of a local celebrity in the medical and scientific community. Rollin reports that Delany visited the "learned astronomer" John Lee and attended his "annual festival of Reform," where an elected committee chose "Dr. M. R. Delany, the African explorer," to serve as the event's honorary president.[35] Delany's popularity also prompted his invitation to the International Statistical Congress as well as a subsequent invitation to the Social Science Congress in Glasgow, which he attended during his two-month stay in Scotland.[36] The scandal that his presence produced at the congress in London only worked to increase his popularity, as the event was widely reported on by the British press. By the time of his return to the United States in late 1860, Delany had established himself as a respected physician, capable businessman, able lecturer on topics scientific and social, and courageous African explorer. He was a transatlantic celebrity.

Delany's Comet

On the other side of the Atlantic, Delany was also widely touted for his scientific and medical abilities, particularly in the pages of early African American newspapers and magazines. In his editorial note to *Blake,* which appeared in the inaugural issue of the *Anglo-African Magazine* in January 1859, the magazine's editor, Thomas Hamilton, introduced readers to this exciting new serial novel and its author by referring to the many scientific enterprises of "Dr. M. R. Delany," including his leadership of a "scientific corps of colored gentlemen, 'The Niger Valley Exploring Party'" (see Figure 4.1).[37] In addition to highlighting the scientific purposes of the African expedition, Hamilton calls attention to Delany's "new theory of the Attraction of Planets," which appeared in that very same issue of the *Anglo-African*. The first chapter of *Blake* to follow Hamilton's introduction further demonstrates Delany's commitment to the tools and methods of modern science: it includes a diatribe against conjuring and the dangers of superstitious knowledge. Given Hamilton's presentation of Delany as a "man of science" and emphasis on his novel astronomical theories, readers were likely to approach *Blake* as a novelistic treatment of science, a kind of science fiction.

The *Anglo-African Magazine* was published in New York City from 1859 to 1860 under the direction of Thomas Hamilton. In 1859, Hamilton also began publishing the *Weekly Anglo-African* as a supplement to the monthly magazine. Under Hamilton's leadership, the *Anglo-African* became the premier journal of black intellectual culture in the period. Self-described as a monthly devoted to "the literature, science, statistics, and the advancement of the Cause of Human Freedom," the magazine included African American poetry, short stories, and serial novels, along with a variety of scientific treatises, statistical analyses, and ethnological tracts written by leading black intellectuals.[38] Thus, the *Anglo-African* was deeply engaged in contemporary scientific debates and promoted itself as a premier venue for black science. The scientific tracts it published were substantial texts that were clearly intended to do more than simply demonstrate that its authors were literate and thus qualified for the rights of citizenship. Rather, they presented substantial and weighty empirical evidence in opposition to the tenuous claims of antebellum face, to some other planet—most probably the moon. At the instant when that planet is at perigee, a 'rock,' or some other detached solid body (may they not be real *magnetic stones?*) having attained a positive intensity of sensible electricity, equal to that of the body of the earth, is impelled to the moon as a meteoric stone to us.

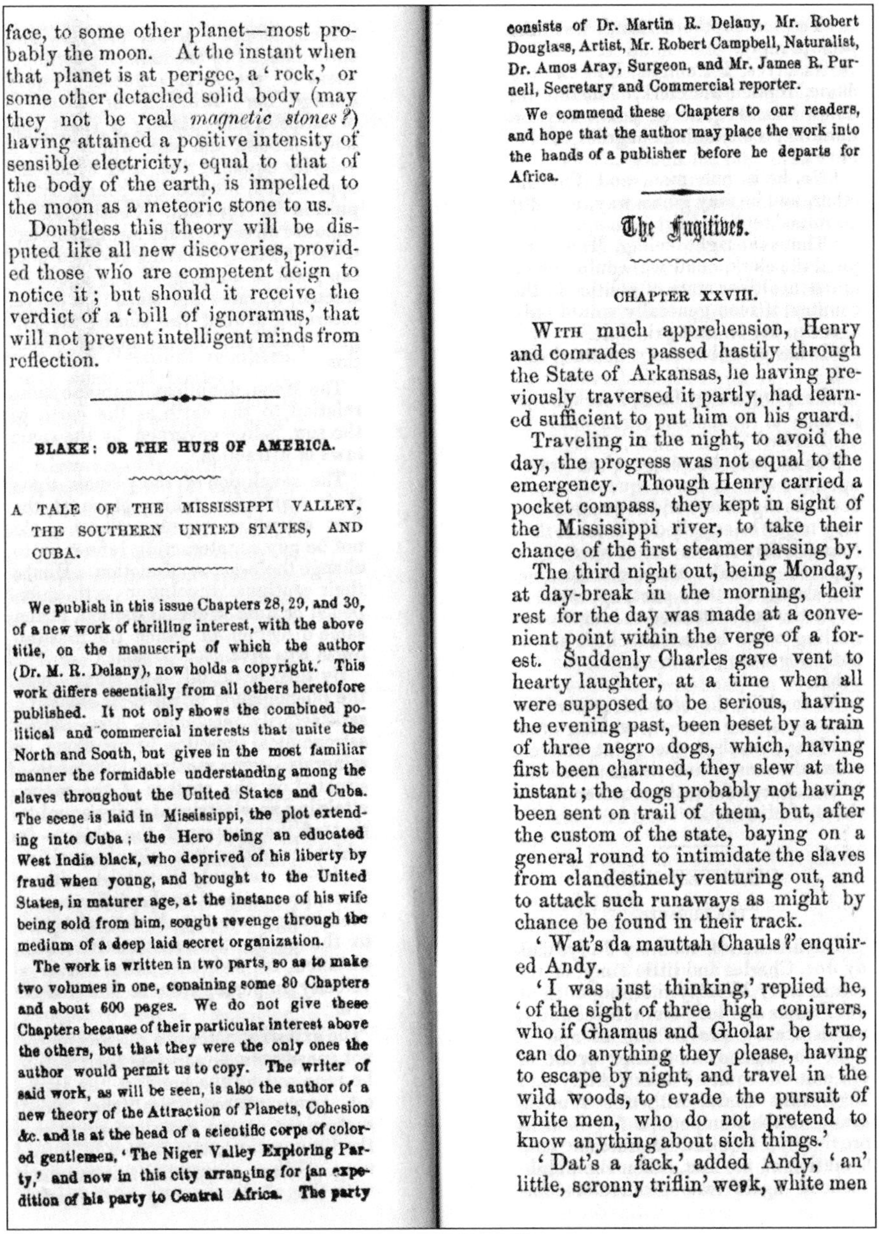

Doubtless this theory will be disputed like all new discoveries, provided those who are competent deign to notice it; but should it receive the verdict of a 'bill of ignoramus,' that will not prevent intelligent minds from reflection.

BLAKE: OR THE HUTS OF AMERICA.

A TALE OF THE MISSISSIPPI VALLEY, THE SOUTHERN UNITED STATES, AND CUBA.

We publish in this issue Chapters 28, 29, and 30, of a new work of thrilling interest, with the above title, on the manuscript of which the author (Dr. M. R. Delany), now holds a copyright. This work differs essentially from all others heretofore published. It not only shows the combined political and commercial interests that unite the North and South, but gives in the most familiar manner the formidable understanding among the slaves throughout the United States and Cuba. The scene is laid in Mississippi, the plot extending into Cuba; the Hero being an educated West India black, who deprived of his liberty by fraud when young, and brought to the United States, in maturer age, at the instance of his wife being sold from him, sought revenge through the medium of a deep laid secret organization.

The work is written in two parts, so as to make two volumes in one, containing some 80 Chapters and about 600 pages. We do not give these Chapters because of their particular interest above the others, but that they were the only ones the author would permit us to copy. The writer of said work, as will be seen, is also the author of a new theory of the Attraction of Planets, Cohesion &c. and is at the head of a scientific corps of colored gentlemen, 'The Niger Valley Exploring Party,' and now in this city arranging for an expedition of his party to Central Africa. The party consists of Dr. Martin R. Delany, Mr. Robert Douglass, Artist, Mr. Robert Campbell, Naturalist, Dr. Amos Aray, Surgeon, and Mr. James R. Purnell, Secretary and Commercial reporter.

We commend these Chapters to our readers, and hope that the author may place the work into the hands of a publisher before he departs for Africa.

The Fugitives.

CHAPTER XXVIII.

WITH much apprehension, Henry and comrades passed hastily through the State of Arkansas, he having previously traversed it partly, had learned sufficient to put him on his guard.

Traveling in the night, to avoid the day, the progress was not equal to the emergency. Though Henry carried a pocket compass, they kept in sight of the Mississippi river, to take their chance of the first steamer passing by.

The third night out, being Monday, at day-break in the morning, their rest for the day was made at a convenient point within the verge of a forest. Suddenly Charles gave vent to hearty laughter, at a time when all were supposed to be serious, having the evening past, been beset by a train of three negro dogs, which, having first been charmed, they slew at the instant; the dogs probably not having been sent on trail of them, but, after the custom of the state, baying on a general round to intimidate the slaves from clandestinely venturing out, and to attack such runaways as might by chance be found in their track.

' Wat's da mauttah Chauls?' enquired Andy.

' I was just thinking,' replied he, ' of the sight of three high conjurers, who if Ghamus and Gholar be true, can do anything they please, having to escape by night, and travel in the wild woods, to evade the pursuit of white men, who do not pretend to know anything about sich things.'

' Dat's a fack,' added Andy, ' an' little, scronny triflin' week, white men

Figure 4.1. Thomas Hamilton's introduction to Martin Delany's serial novel, *Blake; or, The Huts of America*, in the *Anglo-African Magazine* (January 1859), emphasizing the scientific writings and travels of "Dr. M. R. Delany."

racial science, as well as making contributions to scientific debates with no explicit connection to the science of race.

Installments of *Blake* first appeared in the *Anglo-African* in 1859, and then in the *Weekly Anglo-African* in 1861–1862, after the *Anglo-African* ceased publication in 1860.[39] Early readers of *Blake* would have encountered a number of scientific and statistical tracts published alongside installments of the novel in the magazine, including James McCune Smith's responses to Thomas Jefferson's *Notes*, George Vashon's essay on astronomy, and James W. C. Pennington's ethnological theories. The *Weekly Anglo-African* also ran articles on science, medicine, and statistics, and included a regular column from "BANNEKER" which reported on recent scientific and anti-slavery lectures in Philadelphia.[40] Banneker's column, written by the secretary of the Banneker Institute in Philadelphia (an organization I discuss in the following chapter), detailed lectures on topics as diverse as geology, astronomy, mathematics, "animal instinct," and the "circulation of the blood." The *Weekly* was especially keen on keeping readers updated on the activities of African American lecturers on science. The prominent teacher and lecturer at the Institute for Colored Youth in Philadelphia, Sarah Mapps Douglass, made repeated appearances in the *Weekly*. The July 23, 1859, edition included an article on Mapps's "course of lectures on Anatomy, Physiology and Hygiene" for a "class of ladies in Philadelphia" and the November 24, 1860, edition of the paper reported on the successes of Douglass's recent lectures on physiology in New York City.

In addition to articles on astronomy, ethnology, and statistics, *Blake*'s first readers also encountered Delany's own writings on astronomy for the *Anglo-African*. In his January 1859 article on "The Attraction of Planets," Delany laid out an elaborate and somewhat peculiar theory of the important role of electrical attraction and repulsion in the galaxy in order to disprove scientific theories about the possible "clashing of worlds," meaning the collision of the earth with another planetary body (see Figure 4.2).[41] While Delany's theory of the role of electricity in maintaining "the revolution of the great Planetary system" is concerned primarily with describing an astronomical phenomenon, his articulation of the role of circuits of energy in planetary revolution and of the transfer of energy between excited moving bodies bears an uncanny resemblance to *Blake*'s focus on fugitivity and revolutionary movements

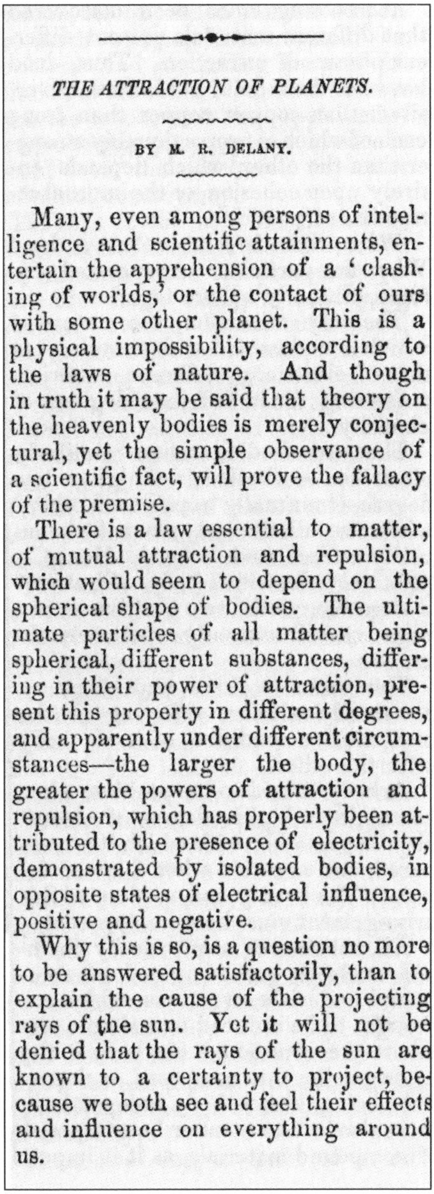

THE ATTRACTION OF PLANETS.

BY M. R. DELANY.

Many, even among persons of intelligence and scientific attainments, entertain the apprehension of a 'clashing of worlds,' or the contact of ours with some other planet. This is a physical impossibility, according to the laws of nature. And though in truth it may be said that theory on the heavenly bodies is merely conjectural, yet the simple observance of a scientific fact, will prove the fallacy of the premise.

There is a law essential to matter, of mutual attraction and repulsion, which would seem to depend on the spherical shape of bodies. The ultimate particles of all matter being spherical, different substances, differing in their power of attraction, present this property in different degrees, and apparently under different circumstances—the larger the body, the greater the powers of attraction and repulsion, which has properly been attributed to the presence of electricity, demonstrated by isolated bodies, in opposite states of electrical influence, positive and negative.

Why this is so, is a question no more to be answered satisfactorily, than to explain the cause of the projecting rays of the sun. Yet it will not be denied that the rays of the sun are known to a certainty to project, because we both see and feel their effects and influence on everything around us.

Figure 4.2. Martin Delany's "The Attraction of Planets," published in the January 1859 issue of the *Anglo-African Magazine* alongside *Blake*.

throughout the United States and across transnational spaces.[42] In fact, Delany's treatise, which focuses on the agitated movement and circulation of intergalactic bodies throughout space, immediately preceded "The Fugitives," the first chapter of *Blake* to appear in the magazine.[43] As in most of the novel, this chapter tracks the artful and nearly supernatural movements of the fugitive protagonist, Blake (who also goes under the pseudonym Henry Holland), who, directed by his pocket compass, skips across space and time, spreading word among diverse slave populations about an impending race revolution.

In "Comets," which appeared in the February 1859 issue of the *Anglo-African*, Delany continues to show interest in extra-planetary bodies in constant states of activity: "A comet must be a great sphere of electric fire in a constant state of action, which like the nucleus termed a 'thunder bolt,' flies darting, blazing and sparkling through space, leaving far behind streams of electricity, similar to lurid flashes of lighting amidst the darkness of clouds."[44] In both his fictional and scientific writings in the *Anglo-African*, Delany explores how fugitive bodies, which exceed the restrictive boundaries of the human, become vectors of force and affect change in a world that stretches beyond the South and the nation-state and reaches across the cosmos.[45] Moreover, throughout *Blake*, Delany explicitly links planetary revolution with slave revolution. Considered in the context of their original publication in the *Anglo-African*, Delany's serial novel and writings on astronomy work together to show readers how the mobilization of extra-terrestrial metaphysics and speculative science might help forge a practical science of emancipation here on earth. While *Blake* has long been considered a formally unorthodox work of early African American literature, Delany's substantial scientific interests and writings on popular astronomy in the *Anglo-African* illuminate further valences of the novel's experimentalism: Delany draws from science to craft a fantastical narrative that challenges the circumspect boundaries placed around the human in both antebellum science and literature. In *Blake*, speculative science transforms the archetypal fugitive slave narrative into speculative fiction.

Messenger of Light and Destruction

Delany composed *Blake* in the tense years following the passage of the Compromise of 1850, which sought to ameliorate tensions between the North and South over the status of slavery in territories newly acquired in the Mexican-American War. The Compromise also included the notorious Fugitive Slave Act, which legally required all citizens to aid in the return of runaway slaves even in states where slavery was outlawed. *Blake* registers, and exploits, international preoccupations with the threat of Southern expansion into the new territories of the United States as well as the annexation controversy of the 1850s, in which Southern slaveholders rallied for the conquest and annexation of Cuba as a US slave state.[46] Delany's novel follows the stealth travels and secretive meetings (or "secretions") of Henry Holland (Blake), who escapes from his master's plantation in Natchez, Mississippi, after learning that his wife has been sold to a Northern woman on her way to Cuba. Henry turns widespread confusion about the legal status of slavery following the Compromise of 1850 to his advantage, moving between the categories of "slave" and "freeman" in his revolutionary survey of the plantation South, as well as visiting states that correspond today to parts of the South, Midwest, and Southwest. As Jeffory Clymer notes, "Blake's travels are so varied that the narrative practically offers a tutorial in antebellum Southern geography," while Eric Sundquist speaks of *Blake's* "panoramic" view of slavery.[47] Much of the serial reads like a grand travel narrative, following Henry's movements across what feels like the entire Atlantic World.

Part 2 of the novel moves to the tumultuous political climate of Cuba, where a number of competing factions, including the Spanish colonial government, creole colonists, troublesome American "patriots," the free mulatto class, the servant class, and enslaved plantation laborers, struggle over the control and fate of the island. The constant threat of insurrection looms over the country as rumors of numerous plots and conspiracies circulate. While Henry is presented to readers in Part 1 as an exceptional slave who elevated himself from lowly origins in the US South, he is revealed in Part 2 to be an elite, freeborn person, the son of a black Cuban tobacco manufacturer who was sold into slavery in his youth while working on a slave ship. Dramatically unveiling himself as "Carolus Henrico Blacus," Blake is named by his new Cuban comrades as the "General-in-Chief of the army of emancipation of the oppressed men and women of Cuba."[48] He joins forces with his long lost cousin, the Cuban poet Placido, in organizing a plot to overthrow the slave-holding regime of the island.[49] Contemporary readers remain in the dark as to whether Blake's "deep laid secret organization"[50] for race war ever comes to fruition since the final chapters of the novel have not been located.

While the literary, political, and socioeconomic contexts of *Blake* have been thoroughly explicated by scholars, the novel's dynamic engagements with nineteenth-century science have been largely neglected.[51] In addition to didactic discussions of astronomy, natural history, and the speculative practices of New World conjuring, the narrative offers a trenchant critique of the cruel exploitations and dehumanizing spectacles enabled by the popular diffusion of the new physiological sciences linked to the midcentury emergence of biology. An early chapter offers a terrifying scene in which a Natchez planter exhibits one of his young slaves as a "curiosity" to neighbors and friends. Calling him "a queer animal," the planter forces the boy to trot "around like an animal" while being whipped: each lash signals to the boy that he should change his performance from song, to prayer, to whistle.[52] Figuring the planter as a "showman," the scene exposes the plantation as a cruel theater of experimentation on the bodies of enslaved people, while revealing the links between plantation science, racist public spectacles, and the freak show. But the narrative is equally attuned to the recuperation of science and the mobilization of a fugitive science, cobbled together from a range of scientific methods and fields and put to pragmatic use for liberation struggles. A repeated reference to Blake as a "messenger of light and destruction" is both striking and apt since the protagonist's project to "enlighten" his enslaved comrades is inextricably linked to his plans to topple the institution of slavery through a widescale uprising and race war.[53] Blake is routinely presented in his travels as a scientific investigator on a serious mission of research. Early in his expedition, readers are informed that Henry/Blake is both an "intelligent slave" and a "scholar" who "carefully kept a record of the plantations he had passed."[54] Henry's meticulous empirical observations aid him in concealing his identity, allowing him to pose as a local slave from a neighboring plantation "when accosted by a white," but they are also part of Henry's larger project of collecting data on the status and conditions of enslavement across the United States and in Cuba.[55] At each plantation visit, Henry poses a series of probing questions to enslaved informants about practices and life on the estate. But instead of summing up these interviews into properly scientific conclusions, Delany presents the information to readers as raw data. In other words, Henry rarely works through his data to offer a scientific conclusion from his experimental survey. Instead, plantation life and slavery appear to readers in all of their radical heterogeneity and does so in a way that reveals the impossibility of properly "accounting" for the diverse forms of life and modes of resistance practiced by enslaved peoples.

Henry's methods in revolutionary statistics were mirrored in the *Anglo-African* and *Weekly Anglo-African*, both of which complained about the racial biases and gross distortions of statistical studies and censuses during the period. For example, a condemning article titled "Lie Statistical" in the February 2, 1861, edition of the *Weekly* addresses the continued circulation of false data on the mortality of "mulattoes" in Boston, which had been fabricated by Josiah Nott: "Dr. Nott, of Mobile, next invented a series of statistical tables for Boston, showing that mulattoes were more short-lived than either the whites or blacks; and these tables, or rather, these results, appear periodically, many years after they were proven false by the conclusive statement that the bills of mortality in Boston at the time named in the table made no distinct entries of blacks and mulattos." As a corrective to such gross manipulations of empirical data for the cause of white supremacy, the *Anglo-African* produced its own statistical reports on black populations in the United States. In fact, in the February 1859 issue of the *Anglo-African Magazine*, installments of *Blake* were prefaced by a "Statistical View of the Colored Population of the United States—from 1790 to 1850." The "Statistical View" was run as a serial and appeared in subsequent issues with installments of *Blake*. The coexistence of serial science and serial fiction helps to illuminate the fluidity between "literature" and "science" in the *Anglo-African*. It also suggests that readers may have brought shared expectations and reading methods to both fictional and scientific articles appearing in serial form.[56] From a wider perspective, "serial science" challenges the privileging of the serial as a distinctively literary form in the nineteenth century and points to wider cross-animations of literary and scientific forms in nineteenth-century periodicals. Through the combination of Blake's figuration as a revolutionary statistician and the actual statistical data produced for the *Anglo-African*, black statistics emerged in the magazine as a central part of its political rhetoric.

In addition to transforming statistics into an emancipatory tool, *Blake* draws widely on astronomy to link the subterranean science of fugitivity to speculative sciences that were themselves resistant to the accounting methods of racist science and statistics. In some ways, Delany's "The Attraction of Planets" and "Comets" are speculative texts of exobiology that seem far from politics and, indeed, far from earth.[57] However, in *Blake*, astronomy is continually linked to escapes from and struggles against slavery, making for an "on-the-ground" inquiry that explicitly connects the movement of extraterrestrial bodies to the movement of human affairs and subjects. In addition to collecting vast amounts of information for his revolutionary research, Blake also disseminates popular scientific knowledge among enslaved populations, which includes practical tools for calculating escapes and mapping routes to freedom. In chapter after chapter, stars, constellations, and other celestial bodies appear as objects of investigation for free, fugitive, and enslaved people. Thus, for example, in a description of a serene evening in New Orleans, the moon is presented as an "object of impressive interest" to "the slave as well as those of enlightened and scientific intelligence."[58] Delany's interest in astronomy was clearly shaped by his affiliation with freemasonry, which sought out the secrets of universal knowledge in esoteric signs, numbers, symbols, and ancient artifacts.[59] Martin Bernal has argued that arguments made by African Americans about the invention of astronomy in ancient Africa made astronomical and astrological figures of prime importance to black freemasons during the antebellum period.[60]

In addition to the importance placed on astronomy by black freemasons in the North, practical knowledge of the stars was critical for enslaved people seeking to follow the North Star to freedom. Delany draws from the scientific knowledge base of black freemasonry to embed a pedagogical lesson about astronomy and navigation within his novel, a lesson directed at fugitive characters and possibly at fugitive readers as well. For example, a chapter titled "Studying Head Work" reads like an

elementary astronomy lesson, as Henry offers a group of fugitives detailed instruction on mapping constellations in order to locate the North
Star, "the slave's great Guide to Freedom."[61] The chapter also includes an
introduction to a "little round metallic box" called a compass as well as
step-by-step instructions on how the tool can aid in fugitive escapes.[62]
Henry promotes the compass as an absolutely essential tool for conducting fugitive science as it only costs "one-half dollar, or four bits, as
we call it, so that every slave who will, may get one."[63] We should not
discount the possibility that Delany wished for this and other similarly
didactic chapters to provide actual "lessons" to readers of the *Anglo-
African* who either sought to escape from slavery or planned to help
others do so. While Northern African American periodicals circulated
primarily among a free Northern audience, both white and black, editors clearly hoped that readers and agents would find ways to circulate
and distribute these papers and their ideas farther south. The novel thus
not only *represents* the science of fugitivity in its narrative plot, but also
attempts to will fugitive science into existence, figuring itself as a tool to
be used in actual escapes from and resistances to slavery. The narrative's
dizzying mobilization of fields, tools, technologies, stars, comets, virtually anything at hand, is an attempt to construct—or cobble together—a
dynamic and active fugitive science that pushes through the plane of
representation into the realm of reality.

While *Blake* provided readers of the *Anglo-African* with a veritable
instruction manual in the science of fugitivity, Henry's didactic lessons
are often condescending to his fellow travelers in the narrative, who
struggle to understand him both because of their lack of education and
their belief in superstitious practices that distort their ability to recognize reality and comprehend "truth." In a series of exchanges, Henry's
students repeatedly interrupt him with questions and distract him from
being able to directly communicate his important lessons. Mammy Judy,
whose investments in conjuring and Christianity are both viewed as un-
helpful, backward-looking practices throughout the novel, even accuses
Henry of performing witchcraft because she is unable to understand
him. Many scholars have been troubled by these scenes, in which the
"exceptional" fugitive attempts to school a group of backward slaves,
who are represented as laughably ignorant, minstrel-like characters.
These scenes are indeed vexed. At the same time, the representation of

the enslaved as both woefully ignorant and as the latent source of an intelligent revolution ultimately reveals the central crisis of epistemology
in the novel, which is caught between the "light" of rational, Western
science and the undeniable "dark" power of belief and religion. Which
method, the novel asks of its readers, will lead to revolt and ultimately,
universal emancipation? Which is the key to emancipation, belief in the
immanence of science or the supernatural?

This question plays out in the text through a series of heated dialogs
over the proper role of religion in the struggle for emancipation. Early
on the narrative, Henry condemns *both* Western Christianity and Africanist practices in the New World as superstitious belief structures that
block enslaved peoples from taking action against the slave power. "The
Fugitives" chapter includes a diatribe against the "silly nonsense of con-
juration" among slaves and ex-slaves:

> "Now you see, boys," said Henry, "how much conjuration and such fool-
> ishness and stupidity is worth to the slaves in the South. All that it does, is
> to put money into the pockets of the pretended conjurer, give him power
> over others by making them afraid of him; and even old Gamby Gholar
> and Maudy Ghamus and the rest of the Seven Heads, with all of the High
> Conjurers in the Dismal Swamp, are depending more upon me to deliver
> them from their confinement as prisoners in the Swamp and runaway
> slaves, than all their combined efforts together. I made it a special part of
> my mission wherever I went, to enlighten them on this subject."[64]

Delany's critique of conjuring and the detrimental effects of superstition among slaves is amplified by the fact that the chapter was
immediately prefaced in the *Anglo-African* by his astronomical theory
on the electrical attraction of the planets, in which a secular form of
scientific inquiry was modeled for readers. Delany was clearly attracted
to the idea of the revolutionary potential of a thoroughly modern
scientific revolution for emancipation, untethered from the supposedly outmoded and subjugated knowledges of the enslaved. While
the embrace of a distinctly secular science also resisted the conver-
sion imperative and Christian moralism of white abolitionist reform,
of which Delany was severely critical, at the same time, the realm of
the supernatural continues to motivate Blake's own movements and

activities on his revolutionary journey. Held in dialectical tension throughout the novel, "science" and "superstition" are transformed through their encounter. Ultimately, the narrative embraces a syncretic form of science that is further shaped by the mysticism of science and knowledge production in freemasonry.

In the end, then, the realm of the metaphysical cannot be shed from the novel since belief, even if focused on an afterlife or a realm beyond the earth, is an indispensable component of liberation in this one. After much debate, Henry finally assents that conjuring and Christianity are good insofar as their metaphysical pretensions can be used for the ultimate aims of freedom. He may disregard religious and other forms of spiritual belief, but continues to mobilize and deploy religious material practices that may forward the struggle for freedom. Thus, Henry/Blake exploits a shared knowledge base in the Bible when he deploys scriptural characters and verses in order to organize disparate plantation populations across diverse geographical spaces. Levine notes that although Henry is critical of Christianity, it is his "visionary insight into (not a rejection of) a scriptural phrase ['Stand still and see the salvation'] that provides him with the germ of his insurrectionary plot."[65] In one scene, Henry travels to the "mystical, antiquated, and almost fabulous Dismal Swamp," where a "number of the old confederates of the noted Nat Turner were met with" along with fugitive slaves, conjurers, and even some claiming to have been "patriots in the American Revolution."[66] The image of the conjurers as wizened, "frosty-headed, bowed old men" presents conjuring traditions as antiquated and out of step with modern methods of social change and revolution. The ceremonies of the conjurers appear as silly and almost pathetic rituals: a "fragment of green bottle glass" is claimed to be a "mysterious and precious 'blue stone'" while magic scales "declared to be from very dangerous serpents," appear under closer observation "to be those of innocent and harmless fish."[67] Despite the perceived bogusness of their practice, Henry allows the swamp conjurers to anoint him a priest of the order of High Conjurers. While indulging a "time-honored superstition" as well as, apparently, his own amusement, Henry later tells his comrades that he became a conjuror because "I'll do anything not morally wrong to gain our freedom."[68] While Henry may claim to prefer Western science to the superstitious knowledges of the enslaved, he repeatedly abandons the dry plane of rational knowledge production for a mystically inflected praxis of freedom. Metaphysics is shed from religion only to reappear at the heart of science.

The mystical secrets of *Blake* are also clearly linked to the sacred secrecy of freemasonry. While astronomy figures prominently throughout the text, Henry deliberately obscures, or in the terms of the novel, "secrets" its mystical content and its connection to Africanist conjure, radical astrology, and black metaphysics, more generally. On an evening when the stars are "shining unusually bright," Henry gazes intently at the "golden orbs of Heaven" from the deck of a steamship on the Mississippi River.[69] He is soon witness to a spectacular scene: "Now shoots a meteor, then seemingly shot a comet, again glistened a brilliant planet which almost startled the gazer; and while he yet stood motionless in wonder looking at the heavens, a blazing star whose scintillations dazzled the sight, and for the moment bewildered the mind, was seen apparently to vibrate in a manner never before observed by him." The magically vibrating stars and meteors fill Henry with "amazement" and lead him, initially, to "attach more than ordinary importance to them" since they have an "especial bearing in his case"—that is, since these natural, seemingly supernatural phenomena, have a particular importance for a fugitive slave calculating routes of escape and freedom with the help of stellar constellations. Henry suppresses this impulse and dismisses the supernatural explanation in favor of a didactic lesson in rationalism: the "mystery [of the scintillating stars] finds interpretation in the fact that the emotions were located in his own brain, and not exhibited by the orbs of Heaven."[70] However, Henry's rationalist explanations quickly reach their limits as the speculative roots of black metaphysics again reveal themselves to be at the core of Western science: the Africanist roots of astrology and astronomy linger close to Henry's rationalism. Throughout *Blake*, revolutionary movement and organization are animated by the "secreted" supernatural valences of science and epistemology.

Henry's movements further resemble the blazing stars dancing across the sky. He skips invisibly across entire states in the matter of a day, carefully "secrets" himself into the natural environment to camouflage himself from enemies or to hold discreet meetings, and then pops up into spectacular visibility when friends and acquaintances inquire into his location and fugitive activities. With his rapid metamorphoses and furtive movements, Blake appears to readers more as a vector of force than as a character who participates in and develops within a narrative plot. A chapter titled "A Flying Cloud" even compares Blake to a meteorological phenomenon.[71] Delany's engagements with speculative science repeatedly unsettles the primacy of "man," opening up the category of human agency to include nonhuman bodies and inhuman forces. Throughout the novel, fugitive bodies on earth and in the sky both vibrate and are traversed by what the political scientist Jane Bennett calls a "vibrant materiality" that emanates from all matter. She argues for the vital "force of things," or "the capacity of things—edibles, commodities, storms, metals—not only to impede or block the will and designs of humans but also to act as quasi agents or forces with trajectories, propensities, or tendencies of their own."[72] Vital materialism moves beyond the negative power of things to resist or hinder activity to show how objects additionally possess the power to act as positive agents; in Latour's terms, they are "actants" that affect other bodies in the world.[73] At the same time, the concept of vibrant materiality points to the forces that continually interact with, decompose, and recompose human subjects. Offering a different critical genealogy of a related concept, Fred Moten reminds us of the unsettling, "dispossessive force" of objects: "While subjectivity is defined by the subject's possession of itself and its objects, it is troubled by a dispossessive force objects exert such that the subject seems to be possessed—infused, deformed—by the object it possesses."[74] The "resistance of objects" includes that of enslaved peoples, as commodities whose speech and performance embodies a critique of self-possession, private property, and the theory of value.

Blake bears more resemblance to the vibrating comets, stars, and planets he observes from the Mississippi steamboat than to a properly developed character (see, e.g, Figures 4.3 and 4.4). His is what we might call, following Gilles Deleuze, an impersonal life.[75] Delany exchanges a novelistic world of well-developed characters for a dynamic field of impersonal forces that kickstart chains of activity and re-activity in the world. These subterranean and fugitive forces also go under the name of blackness, which, in Moten's terms, bears a privileged though not exclusive relation to an empirically defined population of people who are called black.[76] Blackness itself, however, is not empirical: it cannot be calculated or measured and is irreducible to the category of "Man,"

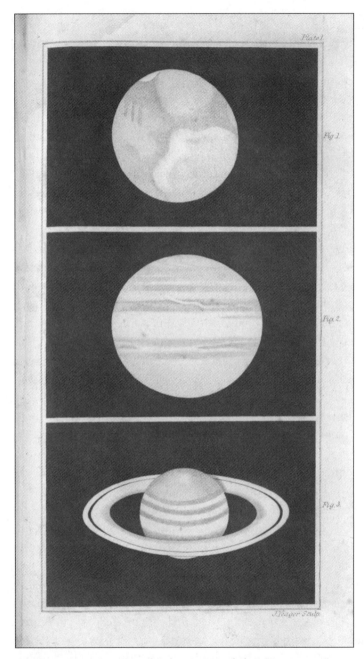

Figure 4.3. Mars, Jupiter, and Saturn in Herschel, *A Treatise on Astronomy* (Philadelphia, 1834), plate 1. Courtesy of The Library Company of Philadelphia.

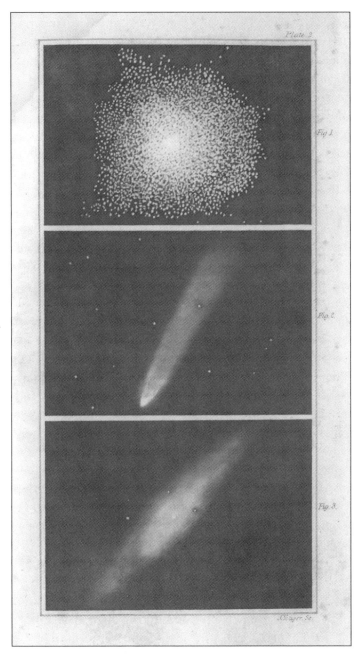

Figure 4.4. Comet and nebulae in John Herschel, *A Treatise on Astronomy* (Philadelphia, 1834), plate 2. Courtesy of The Library Company of Philadelphia.

which, as Sylvia Wynter writes, over-represents itself in Western culture as if it were the human itself.[77] In the introduction to the inaugural issue of the *Anglo-African*, in which *Blake* first appeared, editor Thomas Hamilton expands on the immeasurability of blackness: "The negro is something more than mere endurance; he is a force. And when the energies which now imbrute him exhaust themselves—as they inevitably must—the force which he now expends in resistance will cause him to rise; his force can hardly be measured today."[78] In *Blake*, the immeasurable, vital force of blackness challenges the scientific imperative to separate and classify the "races of mankind." In addition to the standard narrative of a slave becoming "man" (becoming-human), *Blake* is composed of a series of other becomings (becoming-panther, becoming-woman, becoming-black, becoming-comet), all of which strain against the purposefully inadequate and narrow conception of the human offered by polygenesis, which sought to reserve this status for a small, select group of people.[79]

Indeed, Delany's fugitive science posed a serious challenge to the anthropomorphism of both antebellum racial science and liberal abolitionism. The anti-humanism of *Blake*, which refuses to settle on an impoverished notion of the human as the final horizon for black politics, offered important challenges in its own moment as it does in ours, given the novel's rejection of traditional categories of personhood, and of the human itself, as the horizon of political, and no doubt, artistic activity.

Delany further presents a forceful critique of the formal constraints placed on African American authorship, while rejecting paradoxical demands placed on such works, especially fugitive narratives, to be both *truthful* (the documentary demand) and *fantastic* (the fictional demand).[80] William L. Andrews notes that fugitive slave narratives were required to conduct two proofs: (1) demonstrate the humanity of the narrator; and (2) demonstrate the reliability of the narrator as a "truth-teller."[81] *Blake* lays bare the impossible demand for fugitive narratives to be both believable and fantastic (beyond-belief), blurring and complicating the line between fact and fiction while favoring nonlinear accounts of multiple actors and a multitude of experiences over a progressive, developmental narrative about the novel's central protagonist. The narrative is additionally fragmented by a series of seemingly factual footnotes from the author, empirical observations about enslavement that fragment the plot and illuminate the bind of black authorship, trapped between the factual and fantastical (an "unbelievable, true tale of escape").[82] In order to escape that authorial bind, *Blake* enacts a radical empiricism at both the formal and thematic level, producing a speculative fiction that rejects the sociological bind of African American writing.

The Science Fictions of Slavery and Freedom

Delany's novel might, finally, be placed within and against the increasingly surreal nature of race science in the 1850s. By the 1850s, science and fiction often merged through the fantastical and bizarre claims of racial science. Indeed, the blatant anti-blackness of Nott and Gliddon's *Types of Mankind* (1854) and the works of a number of Southern scientists and physicians make Samuel George Morton's stalwart commitments to the tireless collection of data in the name of empiricism look almost admirable, by comparison. By the early 1850s, members of the American school of ethnology no longer cared to disguise the political biases of their work. A few years before Delany published *Blake*, Louisiana physician Samuel Cartwright went so far as to chastise Southern statesmen for *not* mobilizing race science within pro-slavery politics. More than simply providing scientific evidence for the necessity of maintaining slavery, science should take the place of politics in arbitrating the slavery question, according to Cartwright:

> As the premises cannot be settled by the parties themselves it would be better to refer them to the umpirage [sic] of comparative anatomy, physiology, chemistry, and history. Comparative anatomy, if interrogated whether the organization of the white and black man be the same or not, could put the question beyond controversy, *and leave the North and the South nothing to dispute about.* Physiology could say whether the laws governing the white and black Man's organism be the same or different. Chemistry could declare whether the composition of the same elementary substances, in the same proportions and combinations, [be] in the two races, or in different proportions and combinations. . . . What comparative anatomy discloses, history tells, chemistry proves, and the Bible reveals, that by a higher law than the Union, the Constitution, or any other human enactments, the negro is a slave.[83]

Cartwright insists that the sectional divides between the North and the South would quickly disappear if both parties would simply turn to the evidence provided by comparative anatomy and echoed in other fields: "The negro is a slave" by nature. Hence, the institution of slavery best fits the natural condition of black people.

During a time when racial science traversed many fields and methods, articulating human difference in multiple and often eccentric ways, Cartwright's was a thoroughly biological theory of race, which sought to extend racial difference from the skin into the internal structures and organs of the body. Cartwright's pernicious disease taxonomies effectively inscribed enslavement and inferiority onto black bodies. His was also a politically interested theory unabashedly designed for use in pro-slavery rhetoric. The Louisiana physician is best known today for his invention of a set of outrageous diseases that were supposedly endemic to African-descended peoples, an act that secured the doctor's status as an infamous figure within the annals of scientific racism. In his "Report on the Diseases and Physical Peculiarities of the Negro Race," first delivered at the Annual Meeting of the Medical Association of Louisiana in 1851, Cartwright coined the term *drapetomania*, or the "disease causing slaves to run away."[84] Composed from the Greek for "runaway slave" and "mania," the neologism was meant to signify the mental disease that caused slaves to "abscond from service." Transforming the perfectly natural desire of slaves to escape slavery into a "disease of the mind," drapetomania not only reinforced the physiological and mental inferiority of black peoples, but insisted that fugitivity was itself pathological. Cartwright goes even further in the "Report" in his description of another fictive disease, "Dyaethesta Aethiopis," which affects both the mind and body. Its symptoms included physical lesions on the body and a general lethargy of the mind. And it appeared to be contagious, Haiti serving as the primary example of its infectious spread across nation-states. Cartwright writes, "To narrate its symptoms and effects among them [Haitians] would be to write a history of the ruins and dilapidation of Hayti [sic] and every spot of earth that they have ever had uncontrolled possession over for any length of time."[85] Most prevalent "among free negroes living in clusters by themselves," this obscure, mysterious disease turns out to be the disease of black freedom.[86] While Cartwright's freedom illnesses clearly encode anxieties about black rebellion and self-government, the physician's 1851 report primarily serves as a panacea for anxious, fearful slave masters and plantation owners. Drapetomania and dysaesthesia are serious blights on the plantation economy, but both are completely curable. For sulky, detached slaves showing signs of the freedom illnesses, Cartwright recommends healthy doses of strict plantation management, work, sunshine, and if necessary, corporeal punishment to help patients adhere to their natural, and most salubrious, condition of servitude. In short, the doctor prescribes enslavement for the disease of black freedom.

From his descriptions of grotesque, nearly alien bodies to his outrageous taxonomy of invented diseases, Cartwright's writings illuminate the site where antebellum racial science veered into the realm of fiction. Indeed, there's something fantastical and nearly unbelievable about the report. In the 1850s, scientific essays and speeches by Douglass, McCune Smith and others attacked racist sciences on these grounds, exposing such scientific accounts as highly subjective and destructive fictions.[87] But the science fictions of antebellum race science were simultaneously challenged by early black speculative fictions, which deployed science itself to imagine alternative histories of enslavement and freedom. Delany's *Blake* is a willfully unrealistic account of nineteenth-century slave society, in which characters spectacularly skip across geographical spaces, time and space are magically compressed and expanded in the narrative plot, and Cuban poets are resurrected from the dead like zombies to take part in the organization of a transnational slave revolt. *Blake* offers an exhilaratingly alternative, fantastical history of slavery in order to imagine new worlds of freedom. At the same time, *Blake* transforms fugitivity from a black pathology (Cartwright's drapetomania) into a science of emancipation.

In "Racism and Science Fiction," the science fiction writer Samuel Delany briefly cites *Blake* as an important work of black proto-science fiction, writing that *Blake* "is about as close to an SF-style alternative history novel as you can get."[88] Just as *Blake* emerges at the intersection of science and fiction, Delany's science writing also walked that line. In 1879, near the end of his life and clearly tired once again of the limits of the liberal politics of race, Delany forged yet another bold scientific thought experiment. In his 1879 account of the origin and descent of the races, *Principia of Ethnology,* Delany argues that God created three original races ("white," "yellow," and "black") and that these races were destined by God to be separate and "indestructible" for all time. According to Delany, even miscegenation would not "dilute" the races, since the "stronger race" would absorb the other.[89] In the face of raging post-Emancipation arguments about the pending "extinction" of the black race from its gradual absorption into the white race through miscegenation, Delany insisted that blackness was here to stay. In what was clearly an intentionally provocative move—as most of his actions were—Delany walked a fine line between monogenetic and polygenetic arguments for the cause of black separatism. And in contrast to antebellum black ethnology's fidelity to a Christian worldview, Delany's *Principia of Ethnology* mobilizes a biblical argument for a thoroughly secular cause. Scholars have often dismissed this eccentric text, viewing it as a reflection of Delany's conservatism in the Reconstruction and post-Reconstruction era. But rather than an anomaly, this tract might be viewed more productively as a postbellum extension of Delany's lifelong experiments with science/fiction, in which he appropriates ancient African history, archaeology, and the discourse of ethnology to imagine another possible black future.

5

Sarah's Cabinet

Fugitive Science in and beyond the Parlor

While early African American print culture serves as an important record of black engagements with natural science before the Civil War, print's embeddedness in the public sphere skews the history of fugitive science toward scientific practices and writings by men. And from Hosea Easton to James McCune Smith, black men's contributions often reinforced, rather than complicated or critiqued, the androcentrism of racial science. Nonetheless, traces of black women's engagements with science have been glimpsed in previous chapters. The lay preacher, orator, and friend to David Walker, Maria Stewart, included ethnological arguments in her speeches and was particularly interested in illuminating the glorious roots of art, science, and civilization in Africa. Edmonia Lewis must have studied anatomy in some capacity in order to sculpt the human form.[1] In 1902, Lewis showed up among Pauline Hopkins's ethnological contributions to the *Colored American Magazine*, an indication that the project of speculative kinship continued to proliferate in black ethnology into the new century.[2] Hopkins's serial novel *Of One Blood: Or, the Hidden Self*, published in the *Colored American Magazine* beginning in 1902, also harnessed ethnology to imagine forms of speculative kinship between African Americans and Africans, forms of kinship forged through actual ancestry as well as the connective powers of mesmerism and parapsychology.

Despite these contributions, it is much easier to tell a story in which black women serve as the mute experimental subjects of nineteenth-century science. As discussed in Chapter 3, Joice Heth, the supposed nurse of George Washington, was exhibited by Barnum as an anatomical curiosity before she passed away in 1836; after her death, she was dissected publicly before a paying audience, becoming a postmortem "exhibit" on black centenarianism. Earlier in the century, Sarah Baartman, the South African Khoisan woman who was exhibited as a curiosity in England and France, was dissected after her death by the famous comparative anatomist, Georges Cuvier. Parts of her body were then put on display at the Musée de l'Homme in Paris. These stories continue to have the power to shock and appall, in large part because of their illustration of how the violent exploitations of racial science followed women like Baartman and Heth beyond the grave. In death, as in life, they served as experimental subjects. Baartman's story also resonates with the pathologizing of black women's bodies and sexuality that continues today in popular culture.

The "gender problem" in the history of antebellum racial science is, however, not just a problem of invisibility in the archive. The classic histories of US racial science, while central and still important studies, all reflect a glaring absence of attention to gender.[3] For example, in *The Mismeasure of Man*, Stephen Jay Gould shows that Samuel George Morton overrepresented women's skulls in non-white groups, but this observation does not extend to a more systematic analysis of the role of women and sexual difference in the history of racial science.[4] Beginning in the 1980s, feminist scholars began to question received wisdom about the long history of race and science in US contexts. Nancy Leys Stepan showed how in nineteenth-century craniology and phrenology, sexual difference was used to articulate racial difference and vice versa.[5] In Stepan's account, nineteenth-century investigations into human difference used an elaborate system of analogy, whereby black men became feminized and white women were aligned with the lower races. However, even Stepan's account absents black women from the history of racial science and its cultural work. Robyn Wiegman's 1995 book, *American Anatomies: Theorizing Race and Gender* further extended Stepan's arguments by chronicling how the mobilization of sexual difference in comparative anatomy's construction of race demonstrated "a broader transformation in the nineteenth century in which the discourse of sexual difference was increasingly used to articulate the social complexities of race and racial hierarchies."[6] Wiegman's study also points to the problematic occlusion of black women in accounts, including Stepan's essay, that rely on an analytical paradigm focused on "blacks and women."

While Wiegman's and Stepan's arguments have been central for scholars working in feminism, critical race and ethnic studies, and feminist science studies, their call for further investigation into the gendered dynamics of racial theory has had little effect on the scholarship of racial science: we still know too little about the role of gender and sexual difference in scientific investigations of race.[7] The absence of gender and sex in the historiography is especially odd since scientific theories of race are, fundamentally, about the reproduction of race.[8] As I have discussed in this book, scientific accounts of race and racialization in the nineteenth century were often undergirded by a theory of auto-reproduction, in which the races were imagined to reproduce in the absence of women. Largely due to anxieties about miscegenation as well a more general prudishness about human sexuality, early ethnological theories on the descent of the races occluded the actual sexual reproduction of race.[9] Modern scholarship has often reproduced this unfortunate matrix of occlusion. Through the lens of androcentric history, the twentieth-century criticism of racial science reproduced the vision of men reproducing themselves across time. Finally, when scholars have approached the gender question in racial science, they have incorporated gender only in terms of identity, rather than analyzing the larger role played by sexual difference in scientific theories of race.

Thus, the history of sex and sexuality in the history of racial science exists under a triple erasure: archival, historiographical, and conceptual. We might ask: Does the redress of this erasure require a more accurate history of racial science? In other words, is further recovery of Baartman, Heth and other women's stories of scientific subjection sufficient or even desirable? Baartman's personal history—and more problematically, her body—has become an obligatory passage point in scholarship on black women's sexuality, especially investigations into sexuality, race, and the visual field.[10] While scholarship has sometimes, albeit unintentionally, reified Baartman's body as an object (of science, of spectacle, and of the white gaze), the concept and the enactment of black performativity—including the counterarchives of racial science in performance chronicled in this study—open up a space for thinking about Baartman and her historical legacies in ways that untether her from both the history of racist science and its attending optics of racialization and sexualization, as well as from, perhaps, the tyranny of history itself. Moreover, while recent biographies have sought to restore Baartman's humanity by recovering her history, re-stagings of her story by dramatists, poets, and artists, as well as critical reflections on representations of Baartman in contemporary visual culture, have been perhaps more effective in loosening her person from the tenacious grasp of racist science and modes of display, while pointing out the various gaps in the archive that make the complete restoration of her history impossible.[11] Through her re-staging within the poetry, prose, visual art, and drama of African America, from Elizabeth Alexander to Suzan-Lori Parks, Baartman's body becomes, to use Soyica Diggs Colbert's phrase, a black theatrical body—a flexible body that through its repetition and reproduction not only illuminates the various gaps in the archives of black history produced out of the traumas of the Middle Passage and Atlantic slavery, but also reproduces those gaps in order to remake and repair Baartman's history.[12]

Baartman has haunted my own investigations of racial science. Despite attempts to supplement her story with other stories of black women's relationships to natural science and stage science, the problem of Baartman—which enfolds questions about justice, repatriation, and the representation of black femininity and sexuality—has continued to unsettle the story I have sought to tell here. The compulsory repetition of Baartman's history reveals less about her life, and more about the gaping silences and gaps surrounding black women's subjectivities and sexualities in the archive. In the face of such gaps, we need willfully speculative and creative accounts of black women's engagements with and challenges to racial science.

While historical recovery work constructs its own narratives and obfuscations, this chapter recovers a little-known black woman scientist in order to begin a conversation about the intersections of race, gender, and science in black women's intellectual cultures in the antebellum period. In what follows, I chronicle the life and work of another Sarah: the educator, abolitionist, science teacher, poet, and lecturer, Sarah Mapps Douglass. Douglass taught natural science and literature in the girl's preparatory department of Philadelphia's Institute for Colored Youth, published essays and poetry in abolitionist periodicals, founded and participated in a number of abolitionist, benevolent, and literary associations, and contributed artistic-scientific discourses and natural history paintings to the friendship albums of her friends and students. She spent decades teaching and lecturing on anatomy and physiology to audiences of black girls and women as well as to the parents of her students and other community members in Philadelphia. She was a pioneer of science education for African American women in Philadelphia. Taken together, Douglass's teaching, art, writing, and lecturing complicates our understanding of the contours and content of both women's science and domestic science in the nineteenth century, while further illuminating the rich cross-fertilizations among African American science, literature, and the arts more generally in the period. Moreover, Douglass's lectures on anatomy and physiology posed important challenges to the routine public staging of black women's biological inferiority in various forms of scientific, pseudo-scientific, and popular spectacle, including the forms of exhibition and experimentation to which Heth and Baartman were subjected.

Facing the many gaps in the records of Sarah Mapps Douglass's life and work, I have purposefully engaged in an expansive and creative reading practice of the existing documents related to her teaching, writing, activism, and lecturing. Since forms of knowledge production and experimentation in semi-private spaces like the black parlor, the church, and the classroom often resist excavation, speculation becomes an important methodological tool. Carla Peterson has argued that in order to reconstruct the lives and activities of black women, scholars must use an "approach that encourages speculation and resists closure" and that, "given [the] lack of documentation, speculation . . . becomes the only alternative to silence, secrecy, and invisibility."[13] Speculation also helps to situate Douglass beyond the immediate contexts of her work in the parlors and classrooms of Philadelphia, where she lived nearly her whole life. Thus, this chapter also seeks to connect her to broader discourses of race and physiology, framing her work as a response to the forms of experimental science that exploited Heth, Baartman, and countless other women of African descent in the nineteenth-century Atlantic World.

Black Science in Antebellum Philadelphia

The question of black women practicing science is of course part of a broader question about "women in science," a question that shapes investigations in the history of science and feminist science studies, as well as in contemporary discourses around access to the STEM fields. The perceived invisibility of scientific women in the nineteenth century has, in part, persisted due to long-held assumptions that nineteenth-century science was a masculine endeavor rooted in the public sphere. While science was perhaps most visible in the public sphere, it was in no way limited to that context. In the past decade, scholars have begun the important work of recovering British and Anglo-American women's engagements with botany, natural history, and other fields in the eighteenth- and nineteenth centuries, uncovering the vibrancy of a middle- and upper-class women's science in the period.[14] Other scholars have shown that in the early nineteenth century, female seminaries and academies began to incorporate a strong curriculum in geography, botany, natural philosophy, anatomy, physiology, and other natural sciences for girls and young women.[15] The rhetoric around domestic science— the attempt to bring scientific principles and rigor to the management of the domestic sphere, or to make homemaking a science—certainly sought to restrict women's engagements with sciences that were deemed public and masculine. Nevertheless, the rhetoric and textual production of domestic science also offered new possibilities for women's scientific and technical practice within the home and adjacent spaces.

Despite key excavations of Anglo-American women's scientific production and learning, black women's scientific practice in the period remains obscure. In a place like Philadelphia, black women's science was practiced in a number of domestic, organizational, and municipal arenas, including the classroom, the church, the garden, the parlor, and various learned and literary organizations. However, the semi-private nature of these spaces, which were self-consciously constructed to protect African Americans from the racism and violence of the public sphere, means that the range of activities practiced within them are often difficult to pin down.[16] In such a context, scientific practice must be inferred from educational records, organizational minutes, letters, and various manuscripts. Below, I also explore how three black women's friendship albums register some of the scientific activity in which nominally free black women engaged in the parlor, the classroom, and beyond.

The print sphere does offer some important hints about this obscure history. For example, the November 24, 1860, edition of the *Weekly Anglo-African* included a brief report on "Mrs. Douglass's Lectures" on anatomy and physiology, which had recently taken place in New York. "Mrs. Douglass" was Sarah Mapps Douglass, the educator, activist, and member of what has been called the "black elite" of antebellum Philadelphia.[17] Having taken courses at the Female Medical College of Pennsylvania in the early 1850s, after which she built a reputation as a lecturer on physiology in Philadelphia, Douglass was invited by a committee of distinguished intellectuals, including Patrick Reason, James McCune Smith, and Henry Highland Garnet, to offer a "course of lectures on Physiology" in New York. Although Douglass focused on disseminating information about anatomy, health, and hygiene to black women and young girls, she also lectured to mixed audiences. Given the composition of the lecture committee, this particular course of lectures appears to have been offered to an audience composed of both men and women.

Although fugitive science traversed cities, regions, and nations in the antebellum period, Philadelphia's reputation as the country's scientific capital and home to a large population of African Americans made it a particularly rich location for black experiments with natural science. The sheer number of scientific fields with which Douglass engaged throughout her career speaks to the natural confluence of scientific fields and their proximity to cultures of literature and art among black Philadelphians. In these contexts, which were very much those of black educational institutions and intellectual and literary societies, as well as the trades in which African Americans worked, the study of natural history naturally flowed into the polite tradition of flower painting, the occupation of sign painting and whitewashing opened the door to the fine arts, and hair-cutting led to bleeding, cupping, and dentistry. African American tradesmen, from barbers and hairdressers to carpenters and shoemakers, were all routinely combining the arts and sciences in their trades. Moreover, middle-class black women's practice of the "ornamental sciences," like needlework, painting, poetry, and music, were complemented and supplemented by exposure to scientific fields and study in formal and informal educational contexts, from schools to literary circles. And all of these artistic, scientific, and artistic-scientific endeavors, from needlework to anatomy, were variously mobilized within the fight for enfranchisement and elevation among freemen and women in Philadelphia.

As they did in other northeastern cities, African Americans in antebellum Philadelphia built rich community organizations and institutions, both on account of the pleasures of collectivity and as necessary responses to pervasive conditions of racial prejudice and exclusion from public institutions, organizations, and services. African Americans also networked with one another to share work opportunities and founded mutual aid and benevolent organizations to counteract forms of employment discrimination that were prevalent across the city. The majority of black workers in Philadelphia lived in conditions of poverty and precariousness. They worked, when they could find it, in low-paid occupations—as chimney sweeps, porters, garbage workers, ditch diggers, and in other forms of difficult, manual labor. When work was not available in the city, many black men took advantage of Philadelphia's location on the water and went to work at sea. Unlike white middle-class and upper-class women, African American women of all social classes worked outside of the home; a great many worked in domestic service in the homes of white families. Those who were spared the drudgeries of domestic labor often worked as washerwomen or dressmakers and seamstresses in their homes. A small number of women, including Sarah Mapps Douglass, became teachers. And of course, in addition to these forms of labor, black women were also responsible for the domestic work in their own homes, including caring for children.[18]

While black workers faced intense forms of employment discrimination as well as competition from established white ethnic groups and recent immigrants to the city, those with sufficient capital and connections were able to gain footholds in select trades. In this way, black Philadelphians carved out a number of entrepreneurial and trade niches in the city. Black men were particularly dominant in the barbering and hairdressing trade, as well as in shoemaking, tailoring, and carpentry; in these trades, African Americans often owned their own businesses and served both black and white clientele.[19] Such occupational niches were especially important since even educated African Americans were rarely able to secure apprenticeships with white tradesmen in the city. Some black business owners, shopkeepers, and tradesmen were able to attain a level of economic security that was not typical of the rest of the African American population in Philadelphia or in other northern cities. Indeed, scholars have written about the vitality of a small, but significant population of African American elite in Philadelphia, those who constituted the upper-echelons of the community.[20] However, "elite" in this context should be qualified by a recognition of the precariousness of life for even the most wealthy black Philadelphians, as well as a recognition of the pervasiveness of racial prejudice and anti-black and anti-abolitionist violence in Philadelphia during the period, most strikingly emblematized in the burning down of Pennsylvania Hall during the second annual Anti-Slavery Convention of American Women in May 1838, where both Sarah Mapps Douglass and her mother, Grace Bustill Douglass, were delegates. In short, as they are today, class and social status were highly complicated by race. In his 1841 tract, *Sketches of the Higher Classes of Colored Society in Philadelphia*, Joseph Willson defines the "higher classes" in terms of their level of involvement in and commitment to the black community, as well as their education, moral rectitude, family history, and social capital, rather than in terms of a strictly economic definition of class and station.

Philadelphia's "black elite" thus referred to respected black families—those with education and social connections—just as much as it included those families with significant amounts of wealth. For example, membership in benevolent societies, literary societies, and other voluntary associations both contributed to and solidified membership in the black elite. Those families in the "higher classes" usually attended St. Thomas African Episcopal Church, while the poor and working class attended Mother Bethel AME Church.[21] There were also huge differences in wealth among the black elite. The prominent sail maker James Forten and his family were significantly more wealthy than most of the families in their social circle. The identification of Philadelphia's "black elite" is also complicated by the proximity of the black working poor to upwardly mobile members of black Philadelphia. There was nothing like a middle- or upper-class black neighborhood in the city, and poor black folks often lived in alleys and tenements on the same streets as the "black elite."

Black Philadelphians practiced science in educational, social, and occupational settings. They also engaged with science in literary institutions and as hobbies, as well as becoming amateur scientists, if they had the means to do so. From blacksmiths to carpenters, black tradesmen and artisans practiced a number of sciences and technical skills in everyday contexts. Medicine was also regularly practiced in trade settings. While barbers and hairdressers doubled as cuppers, bleeders, and dentists, in their roles as servants and caretakers for white families, African American women routinely served as medical practitioners in the homes of their employers, as they did in their own. Throughout the 1840s and 1850s, advocates for women's medical education often discussed the important roles that women already played as nurses caring for the infirm and the dying at home. Black women also worked informally as healers in the community.

Among Philadelphia's black elite, a number of sciences—from astronomy to botany—were practiced in educational settings, in literary societies, and as amateur activities. Literary societies were particularly rich venues for the exchange of scientific ideas and theories. Philadelphia's Banneker Institute offered lectures on a wide variety scientific fields, including astronomy, ethnology, mineralogy, botany, and zoology.[22] The driving force behind the institute, Jacob C. White, Jr., was also an enthusiastic advocate of phrenology, and he prepared an essay on the subject in the late 1850s, which was read before members of the institute.[23] White was not the only black Philadelphian interested in phrenology. In his 1852 tract, *Condition, Elevation, Emigration, and Destiny of the Colored People of the United States*, Martin Delany notes that Dr. James Joshua Gould Bias was a practical phrenologist who published a pamphlet on the subject titled *Synopsis of Phrenology*.[24] A graduate of the Eclectic Medical College of Philadelphia, Bias worked as a physician and is also listed as a "bleeder" in the 1838 Register of Trades. Julie Winch notes that Bias's wife, Eliza, worked alongside him.[25]

The Forten family further shows how scientific interests were exchanged in family contexts and were passed down through the generations. Robert Bridges Forten, James Forten's son, was a self-trained astronomer who taught astronomy at the school of AME minister Daniel Alexander Payne, himself an amateur naturalist. Robert, like the most celebrated astronomers in the United States and in Europe, was also highly skilled in the technical aspects of the field: he built his own nine-foot telescope, grinding and setting the lenses himself. Forten used his telescope to teach astronomy to black youth, and it was also displayed for a time at the Franklin Institute in Philadelphia. Forten's interests in astronomy were not solely academic or abstract. Through astronomy, Forten also connected to the family trade: although Robert's father, James Forten, was not an astronomer, astronomy was intimately connected to the business of sail making, given its importance to navigation and exploration. In this way, Robert Forten continued in the family business. So did Robert's daughter, Charlotte Forten (Grimké), who joined Amy Matilda Cassey's household in Salem, Massachusetts, so that she could benefit from the city's strong school system. In Salem, she recorded in her diary that she was immersed not only in the classics of English literature, but also in the study of astronomy, geology, geography, and natural philosophy.[26]

Sarah's Cabinet

The rich artisanal-trade culture of black Philadelphia comes into clear view within the microcosm of Sarah Mapps Douglass's family, one of the small number of African American families in the city who could count themselves among the "black elite." Sarah's father, Robert Douglass, Sr., was a West Indian immigrant from St. Christopher (now St. Kitts) who owned a successful hair salon. One of Sarah's brothers, Robert Jr., studied painting at the Pennsylvania Academy of Fine Arts and studied abroad in Europe. Robert had some wealthy white patrons, and "several of his oil portraits were reportedly 'prized' by 'prominent families' in the city."[27] In the history of photography, Robert is also distinguished as one of the earliest African American daguerreotypists in the country, and he was among the very first to practice it in Philadelphia. Douglass's mother, Grace, was a milliner who sold hats out of her home and through the family business. Grace was a member of the well-known Bustill family, with long artisanal roots reaching back to the colonial period. Grace's father, Cyrus Bustill, was a former slave who had learned the baking trade from one of his owners. During the Revolutionary War, he reportedly baked bread for the Patriots, and after he was freed, he set up a bakery in Philadelphia at 56 Arch Street. Cyrus had attended

Quaker meeting with his owner, and after obtaining his freedom, he continued to attend, as would his daughter Grace and granddaughter Sarah.

Sarah's education and interests were clearly shaped by the vibrant artisanal trade culture of black Philadelphia, as well as her family's engagements with fine art. While Robert Jr. was the well-known artist in the family, Sarah was also interested in the arts, and she was known for her painting skills among her students and in the broader community. A March 14, 1844, notice in the *Pennsylvania Freeman* advertising Robert Douglass's studio also notes that pieces "on Linen, Silk, & c." by "S. M. D." (Sarah Mapps Douglass) were available for purchase at his studio. Using a term that traversed both art and science in the nineteenth century as it does today, the notice informs potential customers that "specimens" of Douglass's art could be viewed in the "Daguerrian Gallery." Sarah also contributed a number of floral watercolor paintings to the friendship album of her friend Amy Matilda Cassey as well as to the albums of her students, which I discuss below.

Like her friends and family members, Sarah was highly active in Philadelphia's anti-slavery and allied organizations, as well as in a number of intellectual groups.[28] She was one of the founding members of the interracial Philadelphia Female Anti-Slavery Society (PFASS) and also participated in the national abolitionist convention movement in the 1830s. In addition to her work in interracial organizations, she also co-founded and served in leadership positions in a number of African American women's associations, including the Female Literary Association (FLA), the first literary society founded by black women in Philadelphia. After years of friction and disenchantment with the complex dynamics of the interracial PFASS, Douglass threw her energy in new directions, including organizing the Philadelphia Woman's Association.

Douglass's life of teaching began when she was just in her late teens. After beginning to teach in a coeducational school founded by her mother and James Forten, Douglass left her home in 1833 to take a position teaching at a New York City school for girls that was sponsored by the New York Manumission Society.[29] Remaining there for only a year, she returned to Philadelphia and took over Grace Douglass and James Forten's school,[30] which she transformed from a coeducational to an all-girls school. Over the years, it grew in size and reputation, and by 1837, it was being recognized in the black press.[31]

Despite the community's recognition of Douglass's teaching, she was forced to rely on a number of financial supporters and benefactors to keep her school afloat, a situation that clearly frustrated her in her quest for autonomy in the classroom. Unable to sustain her school on her own, Douglass began teaching at the Institute for Colored Youth (ICY) in Philadelphia in 1853, joining her cousin, Grace A. Mapps, and Patrick Reason, both of whom had been recently employed by the school. At the ICY, Douglass was appointed head of the Girls' Preparatory Department, the class for young women who were not yet ready to enter the high school.[32] Despite the fact that the ICY was run by an all-white board of managers, the all-black teaching staff seemed to have much control over the daily operation of the school.

Given that Douglass remained at the school until she retired in 1877, it seems likely that the ICY afforded Douglass a relative amount of freedom in the classroom. The science-centered curriculum of the Girl's Preparatory Department also suggests that Douglass was in charge of setting the curriculum for her class. In 1852–1853, Douglass received medical training at the Quaker-sponsored Female Medical College of Pennsylvania, and later in the decade, she took courses at the Pennsylvania Medical University.[33] In addition to contributing to her own intellectual development and medical expertise, this training enabled her to teach her own students physiology, anatomy, and hygiene. The 1860 annual report of the ICY, which includes Douglass's book list for her class, reflects her commitment to providing her female students with a sound education in the natural sciences. In addition to the standard reading, grammar, and arithmetic textbooks, Douglass's class also used textbooks on anatomy, physiology, geography, and botany.[34] This was clearly a curriculum designed by Douglass. As a point of comparison, no science textbooks appear on the reading list for the Boy's Preparatory Department at the school. The library of the ICY, which was open to students, parents, and community members, included many other scientific titles, ranging from a large collection of scientific and natural history–themed books for schoolchildren to a number of full-length works by major American and European scientists.[35]

Douglass's interest in science and medicine did not suddenly emerge in the 1850s. After Samuel Cornish visited Douglass's primary school in 1837, he reported to the readers of the *Colored American* that there was a natural history cabinet in her classroom.[36] In his words, it was a "well-selected and valuable cabinet of shells and minerals." Acknowledging the knowledge and skill of the class's teacher, Cornish noted that the cabinet was "well-arranged and labelled." The presence of such a cabinet in the classroom, as well as Cornish's desire to single it out in his short write-up in the *Colored American*, indicates that Douglass's students were studying science. Making an even more explicit reference to the importance of Douglass's scientific knowledge in both the construction of the cabinet and its uses in classroom instruction, Cornish observed that "Miss Douglass" has "a mind richly furnished with a knowledge of these sciences, and she does not fail, through them, to lead up the minds of her pupils, through Nature, to Nature's God." Metaphorically linking the cabinet of curiosity—filled with meticulously arranged objects—to Douglass's own "richly furnished mind," Cornish constructs "Miss Douglass" as an expert in natural history, as well as its modes of collection and display.

Marie Lindhorst notes that an 1836 depiction of a Philadelphia black girl's school in the *National Enquirer* may also refer to Douglass's school. In addition to praising the teacher's methods, the writer mentions the presence of a "large case completely filled with minerals, shells, plants, and various other specimens."[37] While natural history cabinets were common in schools during the period, they took on added significance in African American schools and adjacent institutions. Although Philadelphia was home to a number of preeminent scientific institutions, including the Academy of Natural Sciences, the Franklin Institute, and the American Philosophical Society, African Americans were largely excluded from them through both formal and informal mechanisms. In other cases, they did not feel welcome in these supposedly "public" spaces. African Americans were also routinely barred from attending public lectures.

Despite these exclusions, the proximity of black Philadelphians to such important scientific institutions and networks did help to generate interest in science in the community and propelled them to create their own institutions and spaces for scientific activity and engagement.

For example, the Banneker Institute, which routinely held lectures on scientific topics, also expressed interest in putting together a natural history collection. Two weeks after hosting a lecture on the "branches of the kingdoms of nature, namely, Mineralogy, Zoology, and Botany," which drew heavily on Linnaeus, the group discussed a plan to begin "collect[ing] specimens in natural history."[38] In his *Sketches of the Higher Classes of Philadelphia*, Willson notes that the recently organized Gilbert Lyceum, a black literary and scientific society composed of both men and women, proposed the "collection of a cabinet of minerals, curiosities, &c., as soon as its permanent organization will admit of so doing."[39] Willson also mentions a new literary society that was being formed by James Needham to encourage the intellectual development of young black men in the city. Needham's plans included building a library, purchasing a "philosophical apparatus," encouraging "men of color to become professors in particular branches of science," and collecting a "cabinet of minerals."[40] Although Willson largely ignores them, women like Sarah Douglass were also involved with the networks of black amateur science and institution building in Philadelphia. Douglass was a member of the Gilbert Lyceum and also participated in the activities of the Banneker Institute. Although the Banneker Institute included only men among its official membership, several women were listed as contributing members in the Institute records, and female lecturers, including Douglass, also spoke before the group.[41] Throughout the antebellum period, African Americans in Philadelphia built exhibits, cabinets, and lyceums to compensate for their formal and informal exclusion from the city's public institutions, including libraries and museums. Some black schools also gave students access to scientific instruments and specimens. In Douglass's classroom, which offered what Erica Armstrong Dunbar refers to as a "protected space" for black women, students could not only study a "well-arranged" cabinet, but also discuss and experiment with science.[42] Douglass's enthusiasm for science education seemed to grow with the decades, as reflected in her curriculum, which shifted from the more traditional polite subjects of women's education to more rigorous academic fields, including anatomy, physiology, and natural history, as well as all of the subjects taught to the boys at the ICY, including Latin, Greek, geography, and mathematics. Kim Tolley has observed that science was actively represented in the curricula of female academies and seminaries. In fact, natural science was actually better represented in female classrooms than male ones. Since young women were not usually trained for college entrance as men were, their teachers, Tolley argues, were more likely to deviate from a standard classics curriculum and experiment with other subjects of study, including geology, astronomy, and natural history.[43] Thus, lack of access to higher education and the professions may have actually opened up a space for girls to experiment with different fields and avenues of scientific inquiry. While the scientific and medical professions were largely closed to women, Tolley notes that science teaching was an acceptable and well-trodden career path for women in antebellum America. Douglass almost single-handedly opened this pathway for black women in Philadelphia, not only by training her students to become proficient in science, but also by cultivating a new generation of black women who might gain access to scientific professions in the future. For example, Sarah Mapps Douglass's student Rebecca Cole trained at the Female Medical College of Pennsylvania, where Douglass also took courses. Cole became the first African American woman to graduate from that institution and the second black woman in the United States to hold a medical degree and practice as a physician. For her graduation in 1867, she submitted a thesis titled "The Eye and its Appendages" (see Figure 5.1).

As early as 1860, the ICY's board of managers was expressing an institutional commitment to the sciences, which may have been driven by Douglass herself. The 1860 Annual Report of the ICY expressed a desire to put together "a well-arranged cabinet of natural objects" for the institute. The Board of Managers also discussed the importance of hosting a series of public lectures on the "useful arts and sciences" in a room furnished with "suitable apparatus for experiments."[44] Among these furnishings was a cabinet that the board purchased from Sarah after her retirement.[45] This could have been the very same cabinet that Douglass had begun building at her school in the 1830s. If so, Sarah's cabinet represented over forty years of her own work in collecting and curating specimens of natural history.

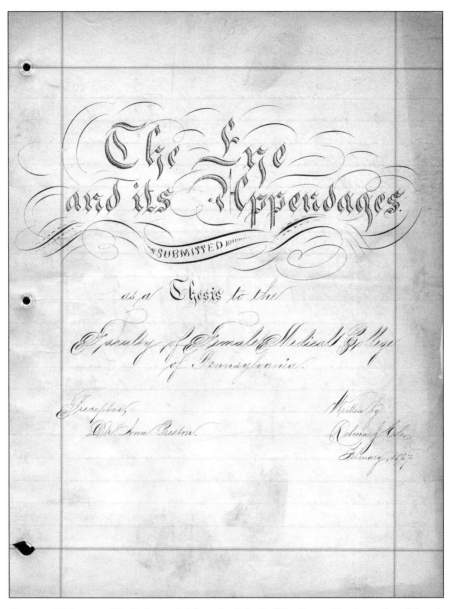

Figure 5.1. Title page of Dr. Rebecca Cole's medical thesis, "The Eye and its Appendages" (1867), Female Medical College of Pennsylvania. Courtesy of Legacy Center Archives, Drexel University College of Medicine, Philadelphia.

The Physiology of Resistance

Although explicit responses to racial science do not appear in the records related to Douglass's life and work, her lifelong commitment to supporting black women's health and morale through physiology and hygiene served as a practical challenge to the damaging stereotypes of black femininity circulating in scientific and popular discourses. Here, self-care stood in opposition to the damaging effects of an always gendered racism. Likewise, Douglass's lectures on physiology doubled as powerfully embodied performances of black women's humanity and intelligence. Just as Frederick Douglass did with craniology in "Claims of the Negro, Ethnologically Considered," Sarah Mapps Douglass turned nineteenth-century racial science against itself by orienting the fields of anatomy and physiology toward racial uplift rather than racial degradation.

As a pioneering health activist who understood the lack of access to formal education among the majority of Philadelphia's black population, Douglass participated in a number of adult education initiatives. After receiving instruction at the Female Medical College of Pennsylvania in the 1850s and at the Pennsylvania Medical University, an "eclectic" medical school focused on alternative medical practices, Douglass used her medical training not only in the classroom, but also to serve her community through lectures on anatomy and physiology. In addition to those she gave to parents and community members at the ICY, she also lectured before the Banneker Institute, and in 1860, traveled to New York to deliver a course of lectures. Given the fragmented record of Sarah's life and work, it is likely that many other lectures and public courses have gone unrecorded.

While newspaper reports and ICY annual reports consistently remarked on Douglass's superior skills in the classroom, her expertise in physiology and anatomy was also recognized by Philadelphia's black community, who benefited from her public courses on both topics. For example, Douglass routinely offered a course during the ICY's annual series of courses for parents of students at the school and other members of the community. These courses were part of the school's mission to provide broader community education and engagement and served as an adult night school for African Americans in Philadelphia. Douglass's teaching also extended beyond the classroom to visits to intellectual and other civic organizations. For example, on October 23, 1855, she lectured on anatomy at the Banneker Institute. The institute's connection to the ICY was strong, given that most of its members were graduates of the ICY. It also functioned as a continuing education venue, where young men and sometimes women could extend their studies beyond the walls of formal educational institutions. In other words, this member-driven organization allowed its members to engage in forms of autodidacticism and collective study that would not have been possible within the pedagogical and disciplinary structures of the ICY. The Banneker Institute records suggest a youthful and even reckless approach to study: meetings were often canceled, punctuality was a problem, and members often came to meetings unprepared to deliver lectures when it was "their turn to do so." Sometimes, members would simply not show up when they were scheduled to lecture.[46]

Douglass's lectures, teaching, and political engagements clearly anticipated the focus on social uplift in black women's activism in the Reconstruction and post-Reconstruction period. Michael Sappol reminds us that popular anatomy was inextricably linked to moralistic pedagogies of hygiene and sexual conduct, and thus to discourses of respectability that were also central to racial uplift discourses.[47] The July 23, 1859, edition of the *Weekly Anglo-African* included a brief report on Douglass's "course of lectures on Anatomy, Physiology and Hygiene" and noted that the class was for "ladies in Philadelphia." It may have been this report that prompted James McCune Smith and his committee to invite Douglass to deliver a course on physiology in New York the following year. It is also likely that Douglass met with Thomas Hamilton, the *Anglo-African's* editor, during her visit to New York: her essay on pedagogy, "A Good Habit Recommended," appeared in the May 1859 issue of the magazine.[48]

While Douglass's lectures on physiology and anatomy for black women were embedded in a moralism that fed into a "politics of respectability," respectability could also serve as a cover for other purposes and activities, much as sentimentalism could be a strategic form of "camouflage" for black women writers.[49] Indeed, the discourses of respectability often became a conduit for education, and for giving black women access to medical authority that was increasingly being denied to them in the home by midcentury amid the beginnings of medicine's professionalization. The timing of her education and lecturing engagements suggests that Douglass saw her midlife medical training as an extension of both her teaching and her social uplift work, and as an opportunity to make the medical education reserved for the wealthier classes accessible to her community. Moreover, in addition to providing introductory lectures on anatomy and physiology, Douglass also provided women with much needed health advice and counsel.

By extending medical and health education to black women of different social status and class in Philadelphia, Douglass's lectures and teaching served a community that was often barred from access to city hospitals and doctors, even as it bore increased exposure to occupational hazards and lower health outcomes due to inadequate housing, education, and the daily stresses of racism. In this way, we see Douglass engaging in something like the Black Panther Party's health activism, recently uncovered by Alondra Nelson, who places this activism in a tradition of what she calls the "Long Medical Civil Rights Movement."[50] Douglass belongs to this tradition, too, particularly insofar as her lectures and courses were powerful speech acts that challenged racist regimes of medicine and made visible structures of medical discrimination and segregation in the so-called "city of brotherly love" and "city of medicine."

While Douglass certainly engaged in the discourses of domestic science, her own public lectures undermined the tethering of female physiology to the home. Indeed, women's science was necessarily transformed when it was translated from the private to the public sphere.[51] It was further complicated by race. Where the antebellum lecture stage existed alongside other performance venues, theatrical, musical, and so on, we can glimpse Sarah Mapps Douglass performing on that stage in such a way as to transform the genteel science of female hygiene and anatomy into a popular science, accessible to women of different classes, stations, and color. While both men and women attended her lectures, she also explicitly presented a science produced *by* and *for* black women. And finally, we should consider the significance of Douglass's presence on stage as a lecturer of anatomy during an age when dissections of black "character" were rampant on the minstrel stage, just as the dissection of black bodies were in anatomical theaters. Moving from the morbid onstage autopsy of Joice Heth in 1835 to Sarah Mapps Douglass's lecture courses, we can see Douglass replacing the science of black morbidity with a performative physiology of black vitality. Thus, fugitive science, in the context of Douglass's public performances, not only refers to the scientific content of her lectures, but also illuminates how her body staged a physiology of resistance. That is, lecturing on anatomy with her own person prominently displayed, Douglass challenged the widespread pathologizing of black women's bodies and sexuality in physiological discourse. And it is this embodied intervention that constitutes what is perhaps Sarah Mapps Douglass's most important contribution to antebellum racial science.

More than challenging racial science on her own, Douglass's teaching endeavors on the stage, in the classroom, and in the parlor also sought to endow her female students and audiences with knowledge and expertise in physiology, anatomy, and even craniology. In 1861–1862, Douglass embarked on yet another community-centered teaching endeavor, teaching physiology at a monthly school for mothers in the area. In a letter to Rebecca White, one of the organizers of the "Mother's Meeting," Douglass offers a rare glimpse into her own classroom:

> I feel thankful that we had so nice a meeting. After you left us the woman to whom Mrs. Richardson loaned "Facts in Physiology" took up the skull and hunted for the place where the eyestrings (muscles) were fastened. She then explained several things connected with it quite satisfactorily to me, and to the wonder of her companions.[52]

This passage gives insight into a number of important aspects about Douglass's pedagogy, including the fact that women attending the class were reading texts on physiology and were reinforcing their reading through hands-on demonstrations with scientific models in class. Students who were unable to purchase textbooks were able to borrow physiology textbooks so that they could do reading outside of class. Douglass notes that students were using *Every-Day Wonders Illustrated: or, Facts in Physiology Which All Should Know*, an introductory primer in physiology, first published in London and then in an edition published by the American Sunday-School Union in the 1850s.[53] While the volume targets young girls and young women, it also includes direct messages and lessons for parents who may have read the volume to or alongside their children. For Douglass and her collaborators, the education of mothers went hand-in-hand with the education of girls and young women. In her letter to White, Douglass also signals her use of anatomical models in class— models that may have been cast in plaster, although her reference to the woman's "t[aking] up the skull" suggests that an actual skull was present—and to be used for the education and cultivation of black women, rather than to demonstrate the inferiority of the race.

Skulls, illustrations, and other models were central to Douglass's pedagogy. In addition to drawings and other visual aids, Douglass also used a "French manikin" for demonstration purposes.[54] Douglass's possession and use of such a human model for educational demonstrations are fascinating and important. Marie Lindhorst notes that Paulina Wright, a white abolitionist and suffragist who, like Douglass, was a physiology lecturer and member of the Philadelphia Female Anti-Slavery Society, lectured with an anatomical manikin that she had imported from Paris.[55] The fact that Douglass also used a "French manikin" to illustrate her lectures opens up a number of possibilities regarding her acquisition and use of such a model. For example, did Douglass have her own French manikin imported from abroad or did she secure one in Philadelphia? While medical professionals, teachers, and lecturers routinely used such anatomical models, "manikins" could also refer to wooden models of the human form used by visual artists. Perhaps, then, Sarah's artist brother, Robert, owned such a manikin, and shared it with his sister. But then "manikins" can also refer to forms used for dress-making and dress display. In this context, Douglass may have repurposed a tool that was at the heart of women's work in Philadelphia. It is even possible that the manikin came from her mother, who worked as a milliner. In this speculative history, a tradeswoman's tool became the inheritance of her scientifically inclined daughter, who transformed the dress-form into a scientific model. Given that three members of the Douglass family—mother, daughter, and son—used some type of human model in their work, the manikin emerges as an object that signals the rich convergences of art, science, and trade in antebellum black Philadelphia.

Douglass's female students may have also served as scientific models for themselves. Indeed, *Every-Day Wonders* encourages readers to reinforce their learning by locating anatomical structures on their own bodies. Such acts of self-demonstration were particularly important for black women in the context of a whitewashed and racist textbook industry. Indeed, no black women appear in texts like *Every-Day Wonders*. When people of color were represented in scientific textbooks, they were portrayed as evolutionarily inferior to European people, or they were depicted for their deviations from the normative white body. Geography and natural history textbooks of the period, including some contained in the holdings at the Institute for Colored Youth, also contained virulently racist discourses on Africa. In this light, it is likely that Douglass's pedagogy depended on selective reading and use of teaching materials as she shaped a curriculum tailored to black women. In addition to excising racist teaching materials, she also used the bodies and the embodied experiences of her students to compensate for the lack of positive visual representations of black subjects—and complete absence of African American women—in the popular textbook trade.

While visitors to the Academy of Natural Sciences could view Morton's skulls to verify the inferiority of black and other non-white people, Sarah Mapps Douglass was teaching black women to pick up and manipulate skulls to increase their knowledge of physiology and comparative anatomy. And when comparative specimens or fancy French manikins were not available, Douglass taught black women that they could use their own bodies as sites of scientific and therapeutic investigation. This politics of self-care and self-investigation was powerful in the context of a popular science and culture intent on making claims on and to black women's bodies.

Butterflies in the Parlor

The parlor was also an important space of intellectual culture and exchange for Philadelphia's black women. In an essay that productively expands the history of science in the early United States, Sally Gregory Kohlstedt establishes the parlor as a crucial, yet neglected, space of scientific education in the nineteenth century. Arguing that the history of science in America cannot be adequately chronicled through the biographies of individual, usually male scientists, she recovers a vibrant scientific culture in the early nineteenth century by looking at a number of informal settings such as amateur groups and experiments,

conversations, and popular print culture, while emphasizing the importance that primary education and children themselves played in the rise
of a burgeoning scientific culture. In her account, the parlor emerges
as a central site "for scientific demonstrations, for cabinets of natural
history specimens, and for discussions of the newest scientific books."
It was also a site where women had access to science and mothers routinely served as the first science teachers to their children.[56]

Jasmine Nichole Cobb notes that "small, but significant communities of free Blacks established their own parlors by the early nineteenth
century."[57] These included families of the "black elite" in antebellum
Philadelphia. Black women used the parlor for a variety of purposes: for
entertaining, communing with family and friends, practicing domestic
activities like sewing, reading, and painting, and displaying furniture,
books, and other consumer items. African Americans additionally used
the semi-private space of the parlor to escape white hostilities and aggres-
sions in public life, and to engage in forms of learning and activity made
unavailable to them elsewhere. Along with her public lectures and teaching, Douglass's parlor was an important site of scientific learning and
teaching. There, she continued to offer courses on physiology to women
after retiring from her teaching career, and it is likely that this space was
particularly amenable to discussions about sexuality and reproduction.

While evidence of black women's scientific engagements in the parlor
are scant, three black women's friendship albums owned by Douglass's
students and friends provide a glimpse of the forms of scientific education and activity in which these women engaged in and beyond the
parlor. Many of the contributions in the albums were surely made in
the home, and the albums themselves, especially the handsome, com-
mercially produced albums like those discussed below, were meant to
be displayed in the owner's parlor. While couched in the sentimental
discourses and visual rhetoric of friendship, flowers, and feeling, these
documents simultaneously reflect black women's intellectual interests
and attainments, including those related to natural science. Replete with
flowers, butterflies, and other natural history specimens, the albums additionally served as a subtle intervention into scientific discourses about
race, physiology, and gender in the period.

Friendship albums were often collected and compiled by middle-class
women.[58] First emerging in the late eighteenth century, they grew in

popularity into the nineteenth century with the expansion of the book trade and especially as machine-produced leather-bound and gold-stamped albums became more widely available.[59] In them contributors inscribed original and selected poetry, sketches, moralistic tales, and affectionate dedications to the album owner. Contributions also included drawings and watercolors, especially floral paintings. Although inscriptions were often directly addressed to the album owner and included intimate sentiments, or "friendship offerings," the genre was only partly private, given that contributors anticipated a readership composed of other people who received the album. Women were most often the owners of such albums, but men did make contributions to women's friendship albums—contributions that were alternatively sentimental, performatively masculine, flirtatious, and condescending, as in satirical sketches and poems on the properly submissive place of women in society. Many friendship albums followed the form of "poesy/posey," in which sentimental poems on flowers and their symbolic meanings appeared alongside illustrations of flowers and bouquets.

Flower-themed poetry and floral paintings were part of a broader women's sentimental floral culture of the period, and such poems and images were routinely copied into friendship albums from popular floral dictionaries and "language of flower" books. Flower language books and floral dictionaries often included hand-colored lithographs and engravings of flowers that could be used as templates for women's floral painting, in friendship albums and elsewhere. Such floral themes and images were also common in gift books, volumes of sentimental poetry, illustrations, and prose, which were meant to be given as gifts during the holiday season, and many women copied selections from these gift books into their friendship albums.[60] Mirroring the affection, sentiments, and "tokens of friendship" in this popular printed genre, friendship albums often looked like manuscript versions of gift books.

A cursory overview of friendship albums may reveal them to be nothing more than a quaint, sentimental genre of women's writing, focused more on the act of transcribing poetry and copying images than on literary and artistic production. Moreover, the use of pseudonyms by album contributors and the pervasiveness of unsigned contributions make the attribution of authorship in friendship albums a difficult task. Given their privileging of the private and the imitative, these albums do not fit easily within traditional models of American literary studies that focus on authorship and publication. However, a closer look at the genre reveals a number of important writerly, social, and cultural contexts, including women's manuscript cultures, women's education, networks of female friendship and homoeroticism, burgeoning involvement in the visual arts, and challenges to the strictures of literary originality, individual authorship, and authorial attribution.

Friendship albums also register the important intersections between women's sentimental flower culture and the science of botany in the nineteenth century. Floral dictionaries and flower language books, for example, usually included introductions to Linnaean taxonomy as well as directions on collecting floral specimens in the field and curating herbariums, or collections of dried and catalogued plant specimen. In educational contexts, women teachers also drew on the conventions of sentimental flower culture in order to attract their female students to the serious study of botany and to illustrate key concepts.[61] Thus, in classrooms, textbooks, popular books, and friendship albums, the sentiment and science of flowers often overlapped. The friendship albums not only reflect the flowery sentiments of friendship culture and gift books, but also register the contours of women's education and their engagements with botany and natural history.

In this way, Douglass's contributions to the friendship albums joined the aesthetics of flower culture to the science of natural history. While middle-class white women often collected such albums, three surviving friendship albums owned by African American women in Philadelphia, collected at the Library Company of Philadelphia, and a fourth at Howard University, indicate that black women also engaged in this literary-artistic practice.[62] While only four identified albums survive, other African American women certainly compiled such albums. The albums collected at the Library Company of Philadelphia include the album of Amy Matilda Cassey (see Figure 5.2), a friend and contemporary of Douglass, and two of Douglass's students, sisters Martina and Mary Anne Dickerson. Like Douglass, Amy Cassey was a member of Philadelphia's black elite. She was also a co-founder of the Philadelphia Female Anti-Slavery Society and participated in a number of political organizations and societies, including the Female Literary Association

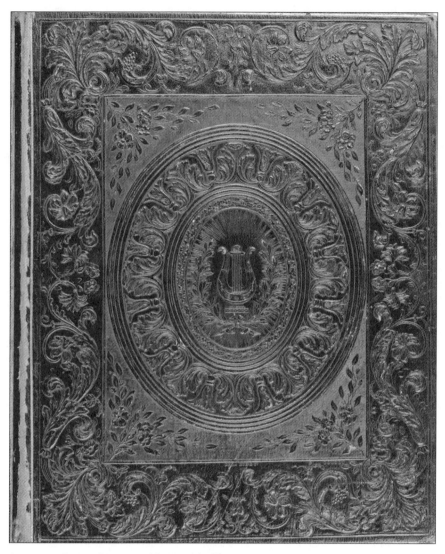

Figure 5.2. Cover of Amy Matilda Cassey's album, ca. 1833–1856, embossed and gilt morocco binding. Courtesy of The Library Company of Philadelphia.

and the Gilbert Lyceum, a coeducational literary and science society. Cassey's friendship album shares the sentimental and flower conventions outlined above, but it is also a stunning record of abolitionism in Philadelphia and across the Northeast, collecting together essays, poetry, sketches, and dedications from a number of noted activists and educators, including Frederick Douglass, William Lloyd Garrison, James McCune Smith, Daniel Alexander Payne, Wendell Phillips, and Robert Purvis. The album also maps the intimate networks of black women abolitionists in Philadelphia through its inclusion of contributions from Margaretta Forten, Mary Forten, Sarah Forten Purvis, and Douglass herself.

The Dickerson albums were begun when the sisters were young women, and they served, among other things, as pedagogical tools and models for penmanship, writing, drawing, painting, and other forms of cultivated expression. A number of adults made contributions to both albums, including their teacher, Sarah Douglass, and Douglass's brother, Robert Douglass, who also taught painting and drawing to area youth. In addition to their pedagogical functions, the Dickerson albums register the young women's intellectual proclivities and aspirations. For example, Mary Anne's album includes a number of impressive artistic contributions, including an ink wash painting of a kneeling female slave by Robert Douglass. Paired with the motto "Am I Not a Woman and a Sister?" this emblem of the female supplicant was popularized and widely circulated by abolitionists who sought to bring attention to the specific experiences and traumas of women under slavery (see Figure 5.3).[63] Douglass's image is taken after the frontispiece of Lydia Maria Child's 1833 *An Appeal in Favor of that Class of Americans Called Africans*, which was itself taken from an 1827 painting by the English artist Henry Thomson titled the *Booroom Slave*. Douglass's entry notes that his rendering of the kneeling enslaved woman was "copied by request"—that is, by the request of Mary Anne, the album owner.

Sarah Mapps Douglass made several contributions to the Cassey and Dickerson albums, including poems, floral paintings, a pencil sketch, and a short essay. Her poetic contributions stick close to the sentimental flower tradition. For example, in Amy Cassey's album a transcribed poem signed "Selected by S. M. Douglass" compares women to flowers,

When the grim lion urged his cruel chace.
When the stern panther, sought his midnight prey
What fate reserved me for this Christian race?
A race more polished, more severe than they.

Shenstone,

Copied by request

Figure 5.3. Robert Douglass, Jr., "The Booroom Slave," Mary Anne Dickerson album, ca. 1833–1882, ink wash. Courtesy of The Library Company of Philadelphia.

suggesting that like flowers, women need to be supported and cherished, lest they fade and die "beneath neglect":

> No marvel woman should love flowers, they bear
> So much of fanciful similitude
> To her own history; like herself repaying
> With such sweet interest all the cherishing
> That calls their beauty or their sweetness forth;
> And like her too—dying beneath neglect.[64]

Douglass's floral paintings in the friendship albums were connected to the flowers represented in verses like this one, but they were also part of a pedagogical tradition surrounding floral artistry, as one of the "polite" activities taught to middle-class girls and women in the home and at school. Although Cassey was a contemporary of Douglass's, rather than her student, Douglass's contributions to her album also held a pedagogical function similar to that of paintings in her classroom, which modeled skills for her students to develop. Accordingly, in the space of the album, adult women practiced and modeled artistry, writing, and penmanship for their friends, who would themselves be engaged in comparable practices. Thus, while Douglass's painting of a fuchsia in Mary Anne's album, dated July 15, 1846 (see Figure 5.4), was contributed when Mary Anne was already in her early twenties and no longer a formal student of Douglass's, the presence of the painting indicates Douglass's continuing role as a mentor for her former students. The fuchsia watercolor also captures Douglass's own practice of self-education: the flower was copied from James Andrews's *Lessons in Flower Painting* (183?), one of the many popular books that both men and women used to learn and practice floral watercolor painting. Through the copied fuchsia, Douglass displays her ongoing commitments to autodidactic learning. In this way, the friendship album both reflects and exceeds the institutional matrices of black women's education in the nineteenth century.

Beyond engaging in the polite tradition of watercolor painting, Douglass's contributions to the friendship albums reveal her pedagogical investments in natural history. One of the most stunning of these is a watercolor and gouache painting of a butterfly on a floral branch that appears at the beginning of Amy Cassey's album (see Figure 5.5). While

Figure 5.4. Sarah Mapps Douglass, Fuchsia watercolor, Mary Anne Dickerson album. Courtesy of The Library Company of Philadelphia.

Figure 5.5. Sarah Mapps Douglass, "A token of love from me, to thee," Amy Matilda Cassey album, watercolor and gouache. Courtesy of The Library Company of Philadelphia.

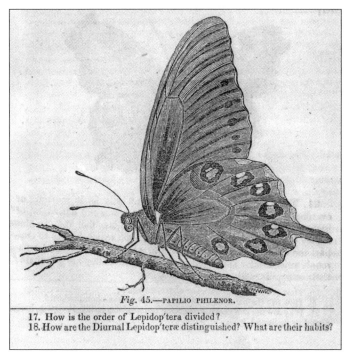

Fig. 45.—PAPILIO PHILENOR.

17. How is the order of Lepidop'tera divided?
18. How are the Diurnal Lepidop'teræ distinguished? What are their habits?

Figure 5.6. Butterfly illustration in W. S. W. Ruschenberger, *Elements of Entomology* (Philadelphia, 1845), a textbook used at the Institute for Colored Youth. Courtesy of The Library Company of Philadelphia.

the floral branch matches the style of Douglass's other floral illustrations, the butterfly is a bit of a mystery, since insects were not usually included in flower drawing books. Illustrations of butterflies combined with foliage were, however, common in natural history books, especially those devoted to the study of insects. The Institute for Colored Youth had many such books in its own library, including several used to teach insect life cycles, taxonomy, anatomy, and physiology to young people. Douglass's butterfly, which looks similar to those represented in the ICY's textbook collection (see Figure 5.6), further reflects Douglass's interest in bringing a level of scientific and technical specificity to her painting. Careful attention has been paid to illustrating specific anatomical details, including the butterfly's segmented abdomen and especially its antennae, which, following science books and textbooks during the time, are clubbed at their tops.

The friendship albums further served as common-place books that supplemented natural history textbooks. For example, Douglass appended a short essay that traverses the realms of botany and moral didacticism to her fuchsia watercolor. Included in it is an excerpt, likely selected from a floral dictionary, which points to the drooping blooms of the fuchsia, reading them as a "modest bending of the head" through which they conceal the "singular and peculiar beauty" of the flower's reproductive organs—a euphemism, no doubt, for women's sexuality and sexual organs. Accordingly, in her explication of this excerpt, Douglass says that the fuchsia "beautifully and significantly typify[ies] modesty." But Douglass's excerpt also includes technical language related to flower anatomy: the fuchsia's head droops in order to cover its "calyx." Thus, at the same time as this excerpt inculcates Mary Anne into feminine virtue and modesty, it offers a short botany lesson.

In a broader context, black women's floral painting and study of botany signifies on a variety of scientific subjections of enslaved people in the period, especially the representation of enslaved women as "specimens" of natural history. In *Uncle Tom's Cabin* (1852), Topsy's famous statement, "I spect I grow'd," in response to Miss Ophelia's query, "Do you know who made you?," indicates the cruelties and blasphemies of a slave system that withholds Christian education and scripture from the enslaved. But beyond Stowe's moral lesson, Topsy's speculation that she spontaneously sprouted from the Southern soil simultaneously places the enslaved child within an economy of natural history and agriculture on the plantation: planted in the plantation ground, Topsy becomes a natural history specimen for careful study and dissection by Southern slaveholders and Northern reformers alike.

A 1796 hand-drawn silhouette of an enslaved woman in Connecticut, which was attached to her bill of sale, further illuminates the figuration of enslaved women as plants in the period, this time in Northern contexts. The woman's name is given as "Flora" on the bill of sale, and her image, pressed between two sheets, looks like a floral specimen. Gwendolyn DuBois Shaw notes that Flora's profile is "distinguished by the soft features of the face abruptly juxtaposed with the spiky, abstract rendering of hair," which look like the "petals of a flower." The image thus marks the "visual and verbal amalgamation of 'Flora' and 'flower,' of woman and object. Her image, like a pressed blossom, is sandwiched into the two dimensions of the paper."[65] The silhouette was, furthermore, used as identification and a tool of surveillance, should Flora had ever decided to run away. Likened to a floral specimen, Flora's silhouette illustrates that black women were objectified and surveilled through the methods and naming conventions of natural history, as well as through the common cultural analogies made between women and flowers. While the connections between flowers and free black women were made through the space of the friendship album—reflecting, in a subtle way, on the confinements of both womanhood and an attenuated freedom for African American women in the North—Flora's name, and silhouette, are a reminder of an even darker side of natural history, linked to a slave system that mitigated its regimes of confinement and surveillance through flowery references to genteel, sentimental culture. This feminine, flowery name attempts to connect slavery to systems of benevolence and gentility, rather than to profit and violence.

These literary and artistic representations of enslavement open up ways of understanding the friendship albums beyond the refined traditions of middle-class life in black Philadelphia. African American women's friendship albums, and floral painting more generally, reflect not only an interest and engagement with natural history, but also re-signify the floral objectifications of both free and enslaved women, which fixed and contained women as so many floral specimens, in the home and on the plantation. In this way, the friendship albums make an important connection between natural history and physiology, returning us to black women's oblique, though crucial, interventions into nineteenth-century racial science, interventions that made imagined connections far beyond the parlor. Cobb comments on the almost complete absence of visual representations of black women's bodies in the friendship albums and argues that flowers and other natural history objects became figures for black women's bodies within the space of the album.[66] In this context, the "blackness" of Douglass's butterfly is re-signified as another "camouflaged" representation of black women's embodiment and beauty, forged in response to degrading representations of black womanhood in transatlantic popular science and visual culture.[67]

S. M. Douglass and S. G. Morton

Throughout the 1870s and into the final years before her death in 1882, Douglass continued to offer classes on physiology to black women in her home.[68] Because she suffered from rheumatism, these home lectures allowed her to continue teaching without the pain and difficulty of traveling to a school or meeting place. While challenging the public display of black women's bodies in the name of racist science, Douglass's teaching and lecturing also undid the divide between and gendering of the public and private sphere. Her navigation of black spaces, including churches, social clubs, schools, activist organizations, and voluntary associations, further raises the question of whether these were public or private spaces. Routinely excluded, through both formal and informal mechanisms, from public institutions in the city, black Philadelphians created a number of institutions that sought to protect African Americans from the cruelties and violences of a racist public sphere. Schools like the ICY also shielded black students from the indignities of public schools for students of color and in this way, sought to create a "protected space" for the education and growth of young black men and women.[69] For Douglass and other black women activists in Philadelphia, domestic spaces such as parlors could also serve as hidden domains in which science could be taught, explored, and experimented with, without the surveillance of male authority. In effect then, the parlor was a potential threat to male authority, white supremacy, and the hegemonic organization of knowledge production. While the home could protect women from the supposed vices and "masculinization" of the public sphere, parlors could also be shrouded spaces of collectivity and experimentation for black women.

Cobb has helpfully conceptualized the nineteenth-century parlor as a space that while domestic and private, was nonetheless connected to the networks of empire and nation-building across the Atlantic World, especially through its display of consumer goods and transatlantic, imperial visual culture.[70] Douglass's painting of the black butterfly was a domestic gesture ensconced in the parlor, but as a figuration of a black, feminine body, fixed on a branch and yet perhaps about to take flight, it also subtly represents black women in Philadelphia, in the Southern United States, and in various spaces across the Atlantic. We might further take a speculative leap by imagining Sarah Mapps Douglass beyond black Philadelphia, connecting her work to performance venues in transatlantic spaces, to the circuits of national and international racial science, and to experiments with black women's bodies across the Atlantic World. What would it mean to supplement the Hottentot paradigm with the speculative, fragmented history of black women engaging with natural science in this period, including teachers like Douglass who taught black girls about the politics of self-care through physiology and anatomy? Is it possible to connect the lecturing platform, the classroom, and the black parlor to the transatlantic stages upon which Heth and Baartman were exhibited and brutalized?

The story of Sarah Mapps Douglass surely supplements the history of black women's exploitation at the hands of racial science, but it is not ultimately able to fully redress that history or serve as symbolic restitution. For one thing, there were important and irresolvable tensions between the free "black elite" and the black working class, as well as between the black elite and the enslaved. Even as enslaved and nominally free people were bound together by the precariousness of black life under the conditions of racial terror and white supremacy, antagonisms nonetheless persisted. When Frederick Douglass contributed to Amy Cassey's album, he reminded her that, unlike her and the other young women who participated in album culture, he had been born a slave.[71] "Black freedom" is revealed as an indeterminate concept when it can describe both the experiences of aspiring bourgeois black women in antebellum Philadelphia and the British court's affirmation of Baartman's status as a "free" worker, a "freedom" that actually *enabled* her subjection and exploitation at the hands of her employers/captors.[72] In the context of the horrific public exploitations of women like Baartman and Heth, the black elite's construction of various "protected spaces" is recast as a relative privilege. Given such antagonisms produced at the intersection of race and class, Douglass's teachings on physiology and hygiene raise a potentially irresolvable yet important question: Did her work anticipate the health activism of the Black Panther Party or, alternatively, the hygiene movement at Tuskegee? Douglass's life and career raise a further question that is variously negotiated by the figures in this book: Is racial science ultimately salvageable? From Martin Delany's observation that Robert Benjamin Lewis's *Light and Truth* paralleled racist ethnology to

Sarah Mapps Douglass's trafficking in physiology's discourse of hygiene, African American engagements with racial science sometimes walked a dangerous line.

And yet, despite the dangers of reparative readings and valorizing an aspiring black bourgeoisie, Douglass's story still matters to the project of telling a new and different story about racial science. For example, given that Philadelphia was the birthplace of craniology in the United States, Douglass's use of skulls and other anatomical models in her classes for black women makes an important intervention into the history of racial science. In fact, Douglass's family residence and business were on Arch Street, the same street where Samuel George Morton lived and worked, obsessively amassing his collection of human skulls, entertaining scientific naturalists from across the country and world, and penning his magnum opus, *Crania Americana*. One can't help wonder if Morton ever passed Sarah on the street, if he knew about the existence of a black women who lectured on anatomy in his own neighborhood, or if he heard about a man who arrived by post at the Anti-Slavery Office on Arch Street in 1849 and renamed himself Henry Box Brown. In addition to the influence of various scientific theories and ideas on Morton's work, the presence of a vibrant black community in the city, including Douglass and her associates, surely also inflected and haunted Morton's own writings on race and science. And this is where the elusive traces of fugitive science might be found not just challenging, but infiltrating racial science itself.

Conclusion

From Sarah Mapps Douglass's use of skulls as pedagogical aids to Frederick Douglass's mobilization of phrenology *against* craniology, the history of fugitive science unsettles narratives that presume the unquestioned hegemony of racist science in the nineteenth century. This study has explored the many ways that African Americans negotiated racial science in the age of comparative anatomy: they crafted sophisticated critiques of it, approached it with caution, occasionally embraced it, eschewed it for other forms of science, used it as fodder for fiction and other types of imaginative prose, and subjected it to mockery and derision. Some racialized subjects of science and medicine also found ways to resist and challenge the regimes of experimentation to which they were subjected.[1]

At the same time, the history of fugitive science illuminates the risks of engaging with racial science from within its own methods and discourse. James McCune Smith's sensational account of St. Philip's cannibalistic sexton unintentionally raised the specter of his own use of human subjects for the benefit of science. His therapeutic treatment of African Americans in New York was supplemented by clinical investigations of patient diseases and conditions that appeared as case studies in US medical journals.[2] This is not to vilify or cast suspicion on McCune Smith, but to point out medicine's reliance on experiments with human subjects. Sarah Mapps Douglass's lectures on anatomy and physiology, while potentially empowering for her female students and audiences, also trafficked in a proto-eugenicist discourse of hygiene. Just as the American school of ethnology produced complex responses from African Americans in the antebellum period, so, too, did the emergence of social Darwinism and eugenics in the late nineteenth and early twentieth century. The racial uplift movement, for example, trafficked in a discourse of racial fitness that was often antagonistic to the poor, especially poor women.[3] Eugenic discourses of racial hygiene and sexual control would go on to shape the Tuskegee Institute's complicity with the US Public Health Service's Tuskegee Syphilis Experiments beginning in the 1930s.[4] Racial uplift's relationship to eugenics and reproductive surveillance thus cautions us against understanding African American engagements with science as wholly emancipatory, or as something unfreighted by the complications posed by class and gender.

Beyond entanglements with racial hygiene and eugenics, other flirtations with race science occurred among black writers, intellectuals, and a growing group of professionally trained doctors and scientists at the turn of the century. Khalil Gibran Muhammad notes that in the post-Emancipation era, theories of race rooted in biology and comparative anatomy began to migrate from the natural to the social sciences. Muhammad chronicles a number of black pioneers who turned the emerging statistics of race against itself, including Ida B. Wells's use of the tools of social science in documenting lynching practices and Du Bois's deployment of a radical statistics in the *Philadelphia Negro*.[5] This, then, is where we might locate the primary movement of fugitive science in the late-nineteenth century: from the natural sciences to the social sciences.

By the early twentieth century, theories of cultural relativism and the production of race through culture rather than biology gained ascendency under the growing reputation of Franz Boas and the founding of cultural anthropology, a field that built on but also departed from the armchair ethnology of the previous century.[6] This new "American school" made the inflexible, biological theories of its nineteenth-century predecessors appear hopelessly out of step with the coming of racial modernity in the new century. At the same time, though, cultural anthropology continued to rely on comparative anatomy and thus on the racial logics that survived the paradigm shift from natural history to comparative anatomy.

African Americans also turned to emerging anthropological theories and ethnographic methods to theorize the transformations of racial identity in modernity and to capture folk practices and rural cultures thought to be on the verge of extinction. The Harlem Renaissance writer and social critic Zora Neale Hurston trained as an anthropologist with Boas at Barnard College and Columbia University and conducted fieldwork on black folkways in the Caribbean and across the Deep South, including in her home state of Florida.[7] Hurston also came from a long line of black craniologists. Like the sexton who performed on-the-ground work with skulls and bones in the graveyard in Lower Manhattan, Hurston was known to measure skulls on the streets of Harlem. In *The Big Sea,* Langston Hughes commented, "Almost nobody else could stop the average Harlemite on Lenox Avenue and measure his head with a strange-looking, anthropological device and not get bawled out for the attempt, except Zora, who used to stop anyone whose head looked interesting and measure it."[8] Like the sexton's, Hurston's intentions and relationship to New York's black residents are evasive. Did her craniological measurements in Harlem represent a radical extension of science to the people, a strategic subversion of the tools of anthropology, or a perfectly sincere process of data collection in the field? And what did Hughes's "Harlemites" think of having their heads measured? While Hurston's tough-to-pin-down politics and aesthetics have been well documented, her relationship to (social) science is less clear.[9] In this case, measuring skulls might be classed with Hurston's ongoing flirtation with essentialism in her writing, a dynamic that continues to make her one of the most provocative and vexing figures in African American literary history. At the same time, a reading of Hurston as a kind of "trickster" scientist risks delegitimizing her training, expertise, and contributions as an anthropologist. In the end, fugitive science does not name a simply subversive relationship to science: in fact, it is fugitive science's history of sincerity that has occasionally placed it in a compromising relationship with racial science itself. Like Hurston, many nineteenth-century practitioners of fugitive science took the "risk of essentialism" through their close engagement with the science of race, a dynamic that should not be valorized or vilified, but should be certainly noted.[10]

Whereas antebellum African American literature was shaped by a dynamic exchange with natural science, by the twentieth century, African American writing displayed a more cautious relationship to science. This transformation may be attributed in part to the professionalization of literary authorship in the twentieth century, a period that also witnessed the professionalization of science and medicine. Thus, the conditions of professionalization muted an earlier genealogy of writing that easily moved between literature and science. While nineteenth-century black intellectuals dabbled in fiction writing, history, science, politics, and other fields, it would become rarer for black writers to publish across the increasingly specialized fields of literature and science, though figures like Du Bois and Hurston did consistently resist the specialization of knowledge production. The increasing gulf between African American literature and science across the twentieth century thus fits with C. P. Snow's notion of the "two cultures" of the sciences and the humanities as they developed in the post–World War II era.[11]

At the same time, African American literature in the twentieth century remained a key site of resistance to ongoing regimes of racial science. Black writers were especially good at illuminating the longue durée of racial science, the vicious cycles of stereotype in which it trapped black subjects, and the uncanny sense that nineteenth-century race science continued to exert on the present. Diverse works of fiction, poetry, and drama registered the dark history of experiments conducted on African American and Afro-diasporic people, from turn-of-the-century efforts like Sutton Griggs's *Imperium in Imperio* (1899) and George Schuyler's *Black No More* (1931) to late twentieth-century works like Elizabeth Alexander's "Venus Hottentot" (1990) and Suzan-Lori Parks's *Venus* (1996). Even Ralph Ellison's *Invisible Man* (1952) prophetically anticipates the 1972 discovery of the government's use of Alabama sharecroppers as an experimental population in the Tuskegee syphilis experiments. Long before Tuskegee became a national headline, African Americans knew that the Deep South's old plantation districts served as "laboratories" for the US government, philanthropic organizations, and social reformers.[12]

Ann Petry is one writer who carried the spirit and interests of fugitive science into the mid-twentieth century. Her 1947 short story, "The Bones of Louella Brown," is especially attuned to the haunting reanimations of racial science under the rule of Jim Crow segregation. "The Bones of Louella Brown" centers on a burial mishap and scandal involving Old Peabody and Young Whiffle, two business partners who "owned the oldest and most exclusive undertaking firm" in Boston.[13] Old Peabody uses an order to exhume an aristocratic Boston family from a local cemetery and rebury them in a new family abbey as an opportunity to dig up the body of Louella Brown from the same cemetery. Louella was an African American woman who had worked as a laundress for Peabody's family when he was a child: she was buried in the designated white cemetery because of a request made by Peabody's mother. Although Louella was first buried in a "very undesirable place" in the cemetery, her grave plot turned into one of its "choicest spots" after years of enlargement to the property. Peabody seeks to correct the outrage that a working-class black woman is buried in the middle of a cemetery reserved for wealthy white people. But digging up Louella Brown ends up digging up a repressed history as well, and once she is taken out of the ground, Peabody starts being haunted by startling visions of Louella, who appears before him "with an amazing sharpness."[14]

"The Bones of Louella Brown" places Petry herself in the genealogy of black craniology and anatomy this book has traced from the St. Philip's sexton to Zora Neale Hurston. Petry studied physiology and medicine while training as a pharmacist; she received her degree in 1931 and worked for many years in her family's pharmacy in Connecticut. As the title "The Bones of Louella Brown" suggests, Petry's story engages the history and long afterlives of nineteenth-century racial science. After Louella's body is exhumed by Peabody and Whiffle, she is subjected to the research whims of Stuart Reynolds, a "Harvard medical student who did large-scale research jobs for the [undertaking] firm." Reynolds is excited to have access to Louella's bones since "he was making a private study of bone structure in the Caucasian female as against the bone structure in the female of the darker race, and Louella Brown was an unexpected research plum."[15] Here, tired out, antiquated theories of the insurmountable differences between the races inscribed on the body are revealed to be part of the ideological justification for Jim Crow segregation. Revealing the troubling continuities between slavery and segregation, Reynolds's research into "black" and "white" bones amounts to a reprisal of the investigations of Agassiz, Nott, Gliddon, and other nineteenth-century scientists of race.

"The Bones of Louella Brown" thus illuminates the science of segregation while exposing the sheer absurdity and groundlessness of race science. Petry's story is alternatively funny and macabre; its comic-gothic mode goes all the way back to the writings of Washington Irving, as well as to James McCune Smith and Edgar Allan Poe's comic-horror stories of science published in the antebellum period.[16] Like E. S. Abdy's own comic-horror recounting of the sexton's craniological trick in the 1830s, Petry's story revolves around a mix-up between the bones of the black washerwoman and those of the Countess of Castro, a member of the elite Bedford family whose remains Whiffle and Peabody have been charged with moving. Reynolds's shocking discovery is that there is absolutely no difference between the bones of Louella and the bones of the countess. But the true horror for the white characters in the story is that once the remains of Louella and the countess are confused, it is unclear who should be buried in the Bedford Abbey. Their great fear is that a working-class black woman might, once again, be buried next to rich white people. Once the problem turns into a nationwide newspaper story and scandal, Whiffle and Peabody are horrified to learn that "people are saying it's some kind of trick, that we're proving there's no difference between the races."[17] Of course, the mix-up reveals a second scandal as well: that Whiffle and Peabody's firm has handled the body of an African American, a serious social and business transgression within the segregated world of burial practices in Jim Crow America. [18]

In addition to providing social commentary on the desire of white society to maintain the racial divisions of segregation even in death, Petry goes to great lengths to establish the similarities between the bones of the countess and the laundress. In this way, she uses fiction to insist on the biological sameness between the races, an argument that still needed to be made in the 1940s, as it had in the 1840s. In "The Bones of Louella Brown," she has several white characters discover and then unwittingly reveal the absurdity of rooting claims of racial difference in the supposed differences between human bones. For example, when the governor of Massachusetts is called to positively identify his relative, the countess, he is dismayed and overcome: "Why they be nothing but bones here! . . . Nothing but bones! Nobody could tell who this be!"[19] Thus, despite themselves, the white characters in the tale belie the secret of segregation: that there are no real differences between the races. Moreover, "The Bones of Louella Brown" echoes what many figures in this book also claimed: that racial science was often just bad science. If Reynolds, the young Harvard researcher, had not known Louella was a black woman, he would have assumed from her placement in the cemetery that she was a "Caucasian female," and added her to his data as such. A similar dynamic shaped the Tuskegee syphilis experiments: they were not only undeniably racist and unethical experiments, but also poorly run.

In the end, the story of Louella's bones turns into a story about racial reconciliation. Old Peabody comes to understand his visions of Louella as an act of haunting in which Louella's spirit seeks either revenge or justice for how she was wronged in life and in death. Peabody seems to think that by putting Louella's name on a headstone in the abbey he will appease her ghost, make peace with history, and put her spirit to rest. As soon as the headstone is placed in the abbey, her sprit stops haunting him. The inclusion of the headstone at the very end of the story power-fully reinforces the absurdity of race science through a comic irony. Un-able to solve the mystery of the mixed-up bones, the headstone ends up emphasizing the morphological commonness between the "black laun-dress" and the "white Countess": "HERE LIES ELIZABETH, COUNT-ESS OF CASTRO OR LOUELLA BROWN, GENTLEWOMAN, 1830–1902, REBURIED IN BEDFORD ABBEY JUNE 21, 1947."[20]

Despite Peabody's attempt at restitution, Louella's laugh is not easily forgotten: it is a persistent and haunting sound that reverberates across the story and beyond the final act of reburial, suggesting that the road to racial reconciliation may not be as easy as carving some words in a marble slab. In this way, Louella's laugh might be placed next to the sexton's laugh, or next to the sound of Frank Johnson's trumpet blaring over top of George Combe's phrenology lectures: as fleeting acts that challenge racist science through an aural reminder of black knowledge and knowingness.

Petry's story thus registers the extension of nineteenth-century racial science into the era of Jim Crow, but the haunting of Louella's spirit and the lingering of her laugh can also be linked to more contemporary de-bates over the politics of repatriation. In recent years, institutions and governments have sought to ameliorate the disturbing history of scien-tific and medical experiments conducted on racialized and colonized populations through the repatriation of remains to the communities from which they were stolen. The return of bodies—as well as material artifacts and art works—has become common practice, as museums, cultural institutions, and governments have been called to make res-titution for colonialism's plunder across the world. At the same time, fugitive science raises a red flag about attempts to shore up histories of experimentation within narratives of racial progress and amelioration. Christina Sharpe has argued that rather than putting her to rest, the re-patriation of Sarah Baartman to South Africa actually put her body *back* in the service of a "number of national and political agendas," including forms of national healing and nation-building that allowed white South Africans to claim political freedom and racial progress through the post-mortem repatriation of a black woman's remains.[21]

Repatriation is also a symbolic act that seeks to mark the end of a particular episteme: the return of Baartman's remains is thus also a declaration that the past of racial science, is in fact, past. Given the horrors of this history, the desire to establish a clean break from the past is understandable. For example, it is tempting to tell a story about polygenesis that tracks its demise to the end of the Civil War, at the moment when slavery no longer required ideological justification. Unfortunately, that narrative does not exactly fit reality. After the Civil War, the theory of polygenesis did receive a swift blow from two fronts: the publication of Charles Darwin's *On the Origin of Species* (1859), which provided a powerful argument for the theory of monogenesis, and the empirical evidence for black intellectual capacity and humanity provided by emancipation itself. But polygenesis did not simply go away in the face of paradigm shifts in science and society: it was transformed into new and often more insidious forms. The continued salience of polygenetic theories in a post-slavery state offers further evidence that there were more continuities than breaks between the age of slavery and so-called freedom; the country's economic mode of production was not transformed with Emancipation, and neither was its structure of (racial) knowledge.[22] The postbellum history of polygenesis further suggests that racial science was perhaps more concerned with managing a free black population than actually enslaved people. In this way, it may be the case that racial science's real object of analysis was never really the slave, but the country's nominally free population.

In 1879, Martin Delany saw fit to respond to postbellum ethnology through the publication of his own account of the origin and descent of the races. The very existence of Delany's *Principia of Ethnology* (1879) points to the ongoing relevance of polygenesis in the second-half of the nineteenth century.[23] In the contemporary moment, misunderstandings about the supposed verification of the genetic basis of race indicate that the presumed biological differences between black and white people still animates the cultural imaginary. Biological understandings of race continue to structure scientific and medical research agendas, and are also used to sell pharmaceuticals.[24] Moreover, the inroads that Creationist curriculums have made against the teaching of Darwinian evolution in schools across the country suggest that reversions to pre-Darwinian theories of evolution, including polygenesis, may not be far behind.

***

While writing this book, I have kept a running list of histories of human experimentation that have been uncovered and made public in recent years. That list has grown and grown: it includes the mustard gas experiments performed on black soldiers in World War II; the sister experiments to the Tuskegee Syphilis Experiments in 1940s Guatemala; various clinical trials on international populations who will never benefit from new medicines and treatments developed in the United States; the harvesting of human organs and tissues from people across the Global South; and the use of Henrietta Lacks's cancer cells to create the first immortal human cell line without her consent or knowledge.[25] However, this book has privileged the dynamic history of fugitive science over the dark history of medical and scientific experimentation on people of African descent. At times, I have pushed the actual history of experiments conducted on black subjects to the background, not to obscure that crucial history, but to clear a space for a lesser-known history of race and science. *Fugitive Science* has traced the ways that African Americans resisted and critiqued racial science throughout the nineteenth century, but it has also taken energy from fugitive science's sometimes strategic refusal to engage with biased science.

Insofar as it is linked to the freedom struggles of African Americans in the nineteenth century, fugitive science is situated within a delimited historical context. But I have also intended this concept to move, and as an itinerant or portable concept, fugitive science appears in twentieth century and contemporary contexts as well, from the Black Panther Party's instantiation of a sickle-cell anemia research program to the diverse engagements with and uses of genetic ancestry testing among black communities in our present moment.[26] Indeed, the skull is one object that we might follow from nineteenth-century contexts to the present, from the sexton's vernacular craniology to Zora Neale Hurston measuring skulls on the streets of Harlem to contemporary methods of medical anthropology and the use of facial angles for some genetic ancestry tests.

Just as Petry detailed in "The Bones of Louella Brown" in 1947, nineteenth-century racial science's relationship to contemporary science is one of connection, but also of haunting and disavowal.[27] These dynamics are particularly visible in a growing genetic ancestry market and in population genetics, which tracks gene alleles across global populations and often unwittingly reproduces a hierarchy of racial difference at the same time that it insists that "we are all" from Africa. In the past decade, a commercial industry has also emerged around direct-to-consumer (DTC) DNA ancestry testing.[28] This growing industry includes companies that target African American consumers curious to know more about their African roots. For a fee, customers send a cheek swab to a lab that extracts a DNA sequence and compares it to a large reference library of sequences; weeks later, they receive notification of the results, which may include a certificate naming their present-day country of origin or African ethnic group. The genetic search for ancestral roots is, of course, part of a long history of African American interest in genealogy, a history that stretches back to the arrival of Africans in the New World. Genealogy took on a particular urgency for enslaved and formerly enslaved people searching for biological and chosen kin and is also reflected in the reparative articulations of speculative kinship in nineteenth-century black ethnology.

The founding of DTC ancestry services that target black consumers as well as popular interest in both genetic and historical genealogical research spawned in large part by Henry Louis Gates, Jr.'s PBS television series and documentaries point to both the promises and pitfalls of genomics for African-descended people in the twenty-first century. Access to science through clinical and consumer participation is also something that should give pause. Scholars have warned that emerging fields like stem cell research and personalized medicine reproduce exclusions and exploitations at the same time as they celebrate models of inclusion and participation in science.[29] Clinical or consumer "participation" can thus be a subtle tool for exploitation under the (neo)liberal fictions of consent and contract.

Today, we are witnessing a further entrenchment of biology, biotechnology, genomics, and other sciences within the structures of global capital and neoliberalism. The global valences of DTC ancestry testing also point us back to the Atlantic currents of racial science, including those experiments conducted on Afro-diasporic people for the benefit of Western knowledge, commerce, science, and ideology. Today's global search for experimental subjects is perhaps even more nefarious as it occurs under the guises of global philanthropy, NGOs, and neoliberal ideologies like the empowerment of participating in the free market of science and commerce.

It is indeed difficult, in the age of the further institutionalization and privatization of science within the walls of the neoliberal university, the pharmaceutical industry, and multinational corporations, to imagine something like an oppositional science emanating from the people. However, the history of fugitive science illuminates the ways in which scientific knowledge continues to be made, creatively used, and circulated from below, even under the most extreme conditions of oppression, repression, and hopelessness. When we look back at the nineteenth century, we bear witness to the scientific disciplining of blackness, a biologization of race that continues to structure modern scientific and social thinking. But at the same time as the nineteenth century witnessed the ossification of blackness at the hands of racial science and related epistemologies, the as-yet noninstitutional and nonprofessional nature of science opened up a space for a surprising number of bold and necessary experiments with natural science among African Americans. Sometimes practitioners of fugitive science sought to upend the science of racism, slavery, and exploitation through direct critiques and interventions. Others largely ignored the hateful vitriol of racist science and instead turned to other fields of natural science to produce theories of blackness that could not be reduced to an impoverished biological concept of race. This history, in the spirit of fugitivity, remains elusive and partially hidden to us. And behind the creative practice of fugitive science by Martin Delany, Sarah Mapps Douglass, James McCune Smith, Frederick Douglass, and other black intellectuals in the North, lie the unrecorded histories of slaves, workers, self-taught medicine men and women, amateurs, and other ordinary people who used and mobilized science and medicine in larger emancipation struggles as well as in more mundane contexts, for increasing activity and knowledge in the world, for the sake of pleasure and leisure, and for the practices of everyday resistance. From Frederick Douglass's radical repurposing of scientific texts to Sarah Mapps Douglass's health activism in Philadelphia, the literary, cultural, and performative histories of fugitive science reveal that the twentieth- and twenty-first century struggle against racist science, medical exploitation, and health disparities has roots in the long nineteenth century. Fugitive science thus anticipates negotiations of science in the contemporary moment, even as its legacy refuses to be captured and contained by the logics of the present.

NOTES

INTRODUCTION

1 For more on St. Philip's Church and some of the families in its congregation, see Carla L. Peterson, *Black Gotham: A Family History of African Americans in Nineteenth-Century New York City* (New Haven, CT: Yale University Press, 2011).

2 E. S. Abdy, *Journal of a Residence and Tour in the United States of North America, from April 1833 to October 1834* (London: John Murray, 1835), 1:341–42.

3 Ibid., 342.

4 Peterson, *Black Gotham*, 45. St. Philip's cemetery on Chrystie Street belonged to the African American congregants of Trinity Church before they were given a building for their own church in 1818. On the African Burial Ground, a site that was designated as a national landmark in 1993, see Michael L. Blakey, "The New York African Burial Ground Project: An Examination of Enslaved Lives, a Construction of Ancestral Ties," *Transforming Anthropology* 7.1 (1998): 53–58.

5 On the grave-robbing practices of physicians, physiologists, and medical students in the period, see Michael Sappol, *A Traffic of Dead Bodies: Anatomy and Embodied Social Identity in Nineteenth-Century America* (Princeton, NJ: Princeton University Press, 2002).

6 Abdy, *Journal*, 342.

7 Ibid.

8 Classic studies on the origins of racial science in the United States include William R. Stanton, *The Leopard's Spots: Scientific Attitudes toward Race in America, 1815–1859* (Chicago: University of Chicago Press, 1960); Thomas F. Gossett, *Race: The History of an Idea in America* (Dallas: Southern Methodist University Press, 1963); Winthrop Jordan, *White over Black: American Attitudes toward the Negro, 1550–1812* (Chapel Hill: University of North Carolina Press, 2012); George M. Frederickson, *The Black Image in the White Mind: The Debate on Afro-American Character and Destiny, 1817–1914* (New York: Harper and Row, 1971); Stephen Jay Gould, *The Mismeasure of Man*, rev. ed. (New York: W. W. Norton, 1996). More recent studies include Mia Bay, *The White Image in the Black Mind: African-American Ideas about White People, 1830–1925* (New York: Oxford University Press, 2000); Bruce Dain, *A Hideous Monster of the Mind: American Race Theory in the Early Republic* (Cambridge, MA: Harvard University Press, 2002); Audrey Smedley, *Race in North America: Origin and Evolution of a Worldview*, 3rd ed. (Boulder, CO: Westview Press, 2007); Ann Fabian, *The Skull Collectors: Race, Sci-*

ence, and America's Unburied Dead (Chicago: University of Chicago Press, 2010); Katy L. Chiles, *Transformable Race: Surprising Metamorphoses in the Literature of Early America* (New York: Oxford University Press, 2014).

9 On amateur and popular science in American and British nineteenth-century contexts see Sally Gregory Kohlstedt, "Parlors, Primers, and Public Schooling: Education for Science in Nineteenth-Century America," *Isis* 81.3 (September 1990): 424–45; Geoffrey Cantor and Sally Shuttleworth, eds., *Science Serialized: Representations of the Sciences in Nineteenth-Century Periodicals* (Cambridge, MA: MIT Press, 2004); Bernard Lightman, *Victorian Popularizers of Science: Designing Nature for New Audiences* (Chicago: University of Chicago Press, 2007); Iwan Rhys Morus, *Frankenstein's Children: Electricity, Exhibition, and Experiment in Early-Nineteenth-Century London* (Princeton, NJ: Princeton University Press, 1998).

10 Histories of experiments conducted on African Americans are chronicled in Harriet A. Washington, *Medical Apartheid: The Dark History of Medical Experimentation on Black Americans from Colonial Times to the Present* (New York: Doubleday, 2006); Sappol, *A Traffic of Dead Bodies*; Margaret Humphreys, *Intensely Human: The Health of the Black Soldier in the American Civil War* (Baltimore: Johns Hopkins University Press, 2008); James H. Jones, *Bad Blood: The Tuskegee Syphilis Experiment*, rev. ed. (New York: Free Press, 1993); Susan M. Reverby, *Examining Tuskegee: The Infamous Syphilis Study and Its Legacy* (Durham, NC: Duke University Press, 2011); Susan M. Reverby, ed., *Tuskegee's Truths: Rethinking the Tuskegee Syphilis Study* (Chapel Hill: University of North Carolina Press, 2000); Allen M. Hornblum, *Acres of Skin: Human Experiments at Holmesburg Prison* (New York: Routledge, 1998); Dorothy Roberts, *Killing the Black Body: Race, Reproduction and the Meaning of Liberty* (New York: Vintage, 1999); Rebecca Skloot, *The Immortal Life of Henrietta Lacks* (New York: Broadway Books, 2011).

11 Michel Foucault, *The Order of Things: An Archaeology of the Human Sciences* (New York: Vintage 1994), 379; originally published in French as *Les mots et les choses* in 1966. Interestingly, and relevant to this study, Foucault counts ethnology as a counter-science.

12 Roger Cooter, *The Cultural Meaning of Popular Science: Phrenology and the Organization of Consent in Nineteenth-Century Britain* (New York: Cambridge University Press, 1984); Nathaniel Mackey, "Phrenological Whitman," *Conjunctions* 29 (Fall 1997), www.conjunctions.com; John D. Davies, *Phrenology, Fad and Science: A 19th-Century American Crusade* (New Haven, CT: Yale University Press, 1955). For an excellent example of the interdependence of phrenology and comparative anatomy, see George Combe's *The Constitution of Man: Considered in Relation to External Objects* (New York: Cambridge University Press, 2009), originally published in Edinburgh, Scotland, in 1828.

13 Cooter, *The Cultural Meaning of Popular Science*, 3.

14 Susan Scott Parrish, *American Curiosity: Cultures of Natural History in the Colonial British Atlantic World* (Chapel Hill: University of North Carolina Press, 2006).

15 On the role played by natural science and natural philosophy among white anti-slavery thinkers and activists, see Ian Frederick Finseth, *Shades of Green: Visions of Nature in the Literature of American Slavery, 1770–1860* (Athens: University of Georgia Press, 2009).

16 Kevin Young, *The Grey Album: On the Blackness of Blackness* (Minneapolis: Graywolf Press, 2012), 11–20.

17 Jordan, *White over Black*, 201–3.

18 Martin Bernal, *Black Athena: The Afroasiatic Roots of Classical Civilization* (London: Free Association Books, 1987), 1:239.

19 On the rise of polygenesis in the 1830s as a response to the emergence of the abolition movement, see Frederickson, *The Black Image in the White Mind*, 73–75.

20 Chiles, *Transformable Race*, 1–30.

21 Throughout this study, "Black" is capitalized whenever it appears next to or near "Native American" in order to place equal value on blackness alongside North American indigeneity.

22 Maureen Konkle, *Writing Indian Nations: Native Intellectuals and the Politics of Historiography, 1827–1863* (Chapel Hill: University of North Carolina Press, 2004); Robert E. Bieder, *Science Encounters the Indian, 1820–1880: The Early Years of American Ethnology* (Norman: University of Oklahoma Press, 1986).

23 Sean P. Harvey, *Native Tongues: Colonialism and Race from Encounter to the Reservation* (Cambridge, MA: Harvard University Press, 2015), 1–18.

24 Charles De Wolf Brownell, *The Indian Races of North and South America: Comprising an Account of the Principal Aboriginal Races; a Description of Their National Customs, Mythology, and Religious Ceremonies; the History of Their Most Powerful Tribes, and of Their Most Celebrated Chiefs and Warriors; Their Intercourse and Wars with the European Settlers; and a Great Variety of Anecdote and Description, Illustrative of Personal and National Character* (New York: H. E. and S. S. Scranton, 1854); J. C. Nott and Geo. R. Gliddon, *Types of Mankind: or, Ethnological Researches, Based upon the Ancient Monuments, Paintings, Sculptures, and Crania of Races, and upon their Natural, Geographical, Philological, and Biblical History* (Philadelphia: Lippincott, Grambo, 1854).

25 Gould, *The Mismeasure of Man*, 74; emphasis mine.

26 Ibid., 102–4. Samuel Cartwright is best known for his invention of a number of diseases and pathologies peculiar to enslaved persons, most famously *drapetomania*, or "the disease causing slaves to run away." See Cartwright's 1851 article in the *New Orleans Medical and Surgical Journal*, "Report on the Diseases and Physical Peculiarities of the Negro Race," reprinted in *The Nature of Difference: Sciences of Race in the United States from Jefferson to Genomics*, ed. Evelynn M. Hammonds and Rebecca M. Herzig (Cambridge, MA: MIT Press, 2008), 67–86.

27 On Agassiz in Brazil and the participation of a young William James in the expedition, see Louis Menand, *The Metaphysical Club: A Story of Ideas in America* (New York: Farrar, Straus, and Giroux, 2001), 117–48.

28 Monique-Adelle Callahan, *Between the Lines: Literary Transnationalism and African American Poetics* (New York: Oxford University Press, 2011), 8.

29 Monique Allewaert, *Ariel's Ecology: Plantations, Personhood, and Colonialism in the American Tropics* (Minneapolis: University of Minnesota Press, 2013).

30 Frederick Douglass, "The Claims of the Negro, Ethnologically Considered" (1854), in *The Frederick Douglass Papers, Series One*, ed. John W. Blassingame (New Haven, CT: Yale University Press, 1982), 2:503.

31 Nott and Gliddon, *Types of Mankind*, xi.

32 Frederick Douglass, *The Claims of the Negro, Ethnologically Considered: An Address Before the Literary Societies of Western Reserve College, at Commencement, July 12, 1854* (Rochester, NY: Lee, Mann, 1854). See Fabian, *The Skull Collectors*, 79–119, for information about the publication contexts and circulation of Morton's *Crania Americana* and Nott and Gliddon's *Types of Mankind*.

33 In his introduction to the fiftieth-anniversary edition of Thomas S. Kuhn's *The Structure of Scientific Revolutions* (Chicago: University of Chicago Press, 2012), Ian Hacking points out that Kuhn's account of paradigm shifts in science actually focuses on the second, rather than the first, scientific revolution (xiii). Kuhn coined "second scientific revolution" in "The Function of Measurement in Modern Physical Science," in *The Essential Tension: Selected Studies in Scientific Tradition and Change* (Chicago: University of Chicago Press, 1977), 178–224.

34 The first scientific revolution generally refers to the Baconian, or empirical, revolution in the seventeenth century. For more on the second scientific revolution, see Enrico Bellone, *A World on Paper: Studies on the Second Scientific Revolution*, trans. Mirella Giacconi and Riccardo Giacconi (Cambridge, MA: MIT Press, 1980); and Stephen G. Brush, The *History of Modern Science: A Guide to the Second Scientific Revolution, 1800–1950* (Ames: Iowa State University Press, 1988).

35 Finseth, *Shades of Green*, 31.

36 On the entrenchment of bioscience and medicine in the networks of global capital, see Kaushik Sunder Rajan, ed., *Lively Capital: Biotechnologies, Ethics, and Governance in Global Markets* (Durham, NC: Duke University Press, 2012); Adriana Petryna, *When Experiments Travel: Clinical Trials and the Global Search for Human Subjects* (Princeton, NJ: Princeton University Press, 2009); Nikolas Rose, *The Politics of Life Itself: Biomedicine, Power, and Subjectivity in the Twenty-First Century* (Princeton, NJ: Princeton University Press, 2006); Melinda E. Cooper, *Life as Surplus: Biotechnology and Capitalism in the Neoliberal Era* (Seattle: University of Washington Press, 2008), Kaushik Sunder Rajan, *Biocapital: The Constitution of Postgenomic Life* (Durham, NC: Duke University Press, 2006); Catherine Waldby and Robert Mitchell, *Tissue Economies: Blood, Organs, and Cell Lines in Late Capitalism* (Durham, NC: Duke University Press, 2006). See Christopher Newfield, *Unmaking the Public University: The Forty-Year Assault on*

the Middle Class (Cambridge, MA: Harvard University Press, 2008), on science in the neoliberal university.

37 In Francis Bacon's *The Advancement of Learning* (1605), for example, science (*scientia*) refers to all branches of knowledge. See Bacon, *Major Works* (New York: Oxford University Press, 2002), 120–299.

38 On the transition from natural history to comparative anatomy, and other wide-scale transformations of the human sciences in the nineteenth century, see Foucault, *The Order of Things.*

39 Troy Duster, *The Backdoor to Eugenics*, 2nd ed. (New York: Routledge, 2003); Jenny Reardon, *Race to the Finish: Identity and Governance in an Age of Genomics* (Princeton, NJ: Princeton University Press, 2004); Barbara A. Koenig, Sandra Soo-Jin Lee, and Sarah S. Richardson, eds., *Revisiting Race in a Genomic Age* (New Brunswick, NJ: Rutgers University Press, 2008); Keith Wailoo, Alondra Nelson, and Catherine Lee, eds., *Genetics and the Unsettled Past: The Collision of DNA, Race, and History* (New Brunswick, NJ: Rutgers University Press, 2012).

40 Sigmund Freud, "The 'Uncanny,'" *The Standard Edition of the Complete Psychological Works of Sigmund Freud* (London: Vintage, 2001), 17:220.

41 Saidiya V. Hartman, *Scenes of Subjection: Terror, Slavery, and Self-Making in Nineteenth-Century America* (New York: Oxford University Press, 1997); Nathaniel Mackey, *Discrepant Engagement: Dissonance, Cross-Culturality, and Experimental Writing* (Cambridge: Cambridge University Press, 1993); Nathaniel Mackey, *Paracritical Hinge: Essays, Talks, Notes, Interviews* (Madison: University of Wisconsin Press, 2005), 181–98; Nathaniel Mackey, *Splay Anthem* (New York: New Directions, 2002); Fred Moten, *In the Break: The Aesthetics of the Black Radical Tradition* (Minneapolis: University of Minnesota Press, 2003); Fred Moten and Stefano Harney, *The Undercommons: Fugitive Planning & Black Study* (Brooklyn, NY: Autonomedia, 2013); Stephen M. Best, *The Fugitive's Properties: Law and the Poetics of Possession* (Chicago: University of Chicago Press, 2004); Daphne A. Brooks, *Bodies in Dissent: Spectacular Performances of Race and Freedom, 1850–1910* (Durham, NC: Duke University Press, 2006); Michael Chaney, *Fugitive Vision: Slave Image and Black Identity in Antebellum Narrative* (Bloomington: Indiana University Press, 2009). On the ways that the "traveling slave" disrupts narratives about fugitive slaves and the politics of fugitivity, see Edlie L. Wong, *Neither Fugitive nor Free: Atlantic Slavery, Freedom Suits, and the Legal Culture of Travel* (New York: New York University Press, 2009).

42 Stephen Best, for example, describes his method as one of "fugitive cuts," a reading practice that is purposely "wanton," "taking the idea of the fugitive both as historical substance and structure of my various arguments and as model for the text's rhetorical and intellectual strategy." Best, *The Fugitive's Properties*, 21.

43 Gilles Deleuze and Félix Guattari, *A Thousand Plateaus: Capitalism and Schizophrenia*, trans. Brian Massumi (Minneapolis: University of Minnesota Press, 1987), 361. *A Thousand Plateaus* was originally published as *Mille plateaux: Capi-*

talisme et schizophrénie 2 in 1980; Volume 1, *L'Anti-Œdipe* (*Anti-Oedipus*), was first published in 1972.

44 Ibid., 373.

45 John Ernest, *Chaotic Justice: Rethinking African American Literary History* (Chapel Hill: University of North Carolina Press, 2009).

46 Hartman, *Scenes of Subjection*, 51.

47 Paul Gilroy, cited in ibid., 62. See Bruno Latour, *The Pasteurization of France*, trans. Alan Sheridan and John Law (Cambridge, MA: Harvard University Press, 1993), 142, 229. I riff here on Latour's conception of science as a "politics by other means." But I also mean to critique Latour's understanding of the political as an easily discernable and transparent domain. In other words, Latour does not follow Hartman's astute questioning of what counts as the political itself.

48 Parrish, *American Curiosity*, 8.

49 Sandra Harding, ed., *The Feminist Standpoint Theory Reader: Intellectual and Political Controversies* (New York: Routledge, 2003), provides a helpful overview of standpoint theory's development and interventions in debates about epistemology, empiricism, and subjectivity.

50 Gilles Deleuze, *Empiricism and Subjectivity: An Essay on Hume's Theory of Human Nature*, trans. Constantin V. Boundas (New York: Columbia University Press, 1991).

51 See Laura Dassow Walls on the fluidity between literature and science in the eighteenth and early nineteenth century in her study of Alexander von Humboldt's *Cosmos* in *The Passage to Cosmos: Alexander von Humboldt and the Shaping of America* (Chicago: University of Chicago Press, 2009).

52 Moving beyond earlier dismissals of *Clotel* because of its liberal appropriation from published sources, recent evaluations of the politics of citation and narrative experimentation in *Clotel* include Geoffrey Sanborn, "'People Will Pay to Hear the Drama': Plagiarism in *Clotel*," *African American Review* 45.1–2 (Spring/Summer 2012): 65–82; Lara Langer Cohen, "Notes from the State of Saint Domingue: The Practice of Citation in *Clotel*," in *Early African American Print Culture*, ed. Lara Langer Cohen and Jordan Alexander Stein (Philadelphia: University of Pennsylvania Press, 2012), 161–77; Ezra Greenspan, *William Wells Brown: An African American Life* (New York: W. W. Norton, 2014), 288–300.

53 William Wells Brown, *Clotel; or, The President's Daughter* (New York: Penguin, 2004), 208.

54 See Francis Bacon, *The Advancement of Learning*, book 2, in *Major Works*, 184.

55 Studies of early African American book history and print culture include Cohen and Stein, eds., *Early African American Print Culture*; Elizabeth McHenry, *Forgotten Readers: Recovering the Lost History of African American Literary Societies* (Durham, NC: Duke University Press, 2002); Frances Smith Foster, "A Narrative of the Interesting Origins and (Somewhat) Surprising Developments of African-American Print Culture," *American Literary History* 17.4 (Winter 2005): 714–40; Jeannine Marie DeLombard, "African American Cultures of Print," in *A History*

of the Book in America, Volume 3: The Industrial Book, 1848–1880, ed. Scott E. Casper, Jeffrey D. Groves, Stephen W. Nissenbaum, and Michael Winship (Chapel Hill: University of North Carolina Press, 2007), 360–72; Leon Jackson, "The Talking Book and the Talking Book Historian: African American Cultures of Print— The State of the Discipline," *Book History* 13 (2010): 251–308; Lara Langer Cohen, *The Fabrication of American Literature: Fraudulence and Antebellum Print Culture* (Philadelphia: University of Pennsylvania Press, 2011), 65–132; Trish Loughran, *The Republic in Print: Print Culture in the Age of U.S. Nation Building, 1770–1870* (New York: Columbia University Press, 2009), 303–440. The following body of scholarship includes important work on the early black press: Eric Gardner, *Unexpected Places: Relocating Nineteenth-Century African American Literature* (Jackson: University Press of Mississippi, 2011); Eric Gardner, *Black Print Unbound: The "Christian Recorder," African American Literature, and Periodical Culture* (New York: Oxford University Press, 2015); Robert S. Levine, "Circulating the Nation: David Walker, the Missouri Compromise, and the Rise of the Black Press," in *The Black Press: New Literary and Historical Essays,* ed. Todd Vogel (New Brunswick, NJ: Rutgers University Press, 2001), 17–36; Ivy Wilson, "The Brief Wondrous Life of the *Anglo-African Magazine*; or, Antebellum African American Editorial Practice and Its Afterlives," in *Publishing Blackness: Textual Constructions of Race Since 1850,* ed. George Hutchinson and John K. Young (Ann Arbor: University of Michigan Press, 2013), 18–38. Recent studies of race, visuality, and visual culture in the nineteenth century include Jasmine Nichole Cobb, *Picture Freedom: Remaking Black Visuality in the Early Nineteenth Century* (New York: New York University Press, 2015); Maurice O. Wallace and Shawn Michelle Smith, eds., *Pictures and Progress: Early Photography and the Making of African American Identity* (Durham, NC: Duke University Press, 2012); Deborah Willis and Barbara Krauthamer, *Envisioning Emancipation: Black Americans and the End of Slavery* (Philadelphia: Temple University Press, 2012); Molly Rogers, *Delia's Tears: Race, Science, and Photography in Nineteenth-Century America* (New Haven, CT: Yale University Press, 2010); Chaney, *Fugitive Vision*; Gwendolyn DuBois Shaw, *Portraits of a People: Picturing African Americans in the Nineteenth Century* (Seattle: University of Washington Press, 2006). On black performance in nineteenth-century contexts, see Brooks, *Bodies in Dissent*; Jayna Brown, *Babylon Girls: Black Women Performers and the Shaping of the Modern* (Durham, NC: Duke University Press, 2008); Tavia Nyong'o, *The Amalgamation Waltz: Race, Performance, and the Ruses of Memory* (Minneapolis: University of Minnesota Press, 2009); and the special issue of *African American Review* 45.3 (Fall 2012), "On Black Performance," edited by Soyica Diggs Colbert. Colbert's *The African American Theatrical Body: Reception, Performance, and the Stage* (New York: Cambridge University Press, 2011), suggests how our understanding of African American literature may be transformed and expanded through a deeper engagement with African American drama and performance traditions that have fundamentally shaped the literary tradition.

56 Cohen and Stein, eds., *Early African American Print Culture*; Gardner, *Unexpected Places*; Gardner, *Black Print Unbound*. On oral literacy and the history of black literary societies, see McHenry, *Forgotten Readers*. On print literacy, see Gene Andrew Jarrett, *Representing the Race: A New Political History of African American Literature* (New York: New York University Press, 2011). On social and community literacy, see P. Gabrielle Foreman, *Activist Sentiments: Reading Black Women in the Nineteenth Century* (Urbana: University of Illinois Press, 2009). Other scholars think historically about style and aesthetic practices that were forged through the mediums and formats of nineteenth-century print, including practices of reprinting and copying. See Meredith L. McGill, *American Literature and the Culture of Reprinting, 1834–1853* (Philadelphia: University of Pennsylvania Press, 2007), as well as Cohen, *The Fabrication of American Literature*. Most recently, scholars have turned to a broader category of early African American writing, recovering, for example, the rich manuscript cultures of the enslaved and recently freed. See Christopher Hager, *Word by Word: Emancipation and the Act of Writing* (Cambridge, MA: Harvard University Press, 2013). Important earlier studies insisted on the literariness of nineteenth-century African American writing. See, for example, Henry Louis Gates, Jr., *The Signifying Monkey: A Theory of African-American Literary Criticism* (New York: Oxford University Press, 1989); Hazel V. Carby, *Reconstructing Womanhood: The Emergence of the Afro-American Woman Novelist* (New York: Oxford University Press, 1987); Priscilla Wald, *Constituting Americans: Cultural Anxiety and Narrative Form* (Durham, NC: Duke University Press, 1995).

57 McHenry, *Forgotten Readers*, 12; Gardner, *Unexpected Places*, 9–10. On the importance of expanding the field's objects of study to include many different types of texts and publication formats, as well as places of production and reception, see Ernest, *Chaotic Justice*, 17–19; Cohen and Stein, eds., *Early African American Print Culture*; Gardner, *Unexpected Places*, 3–21.

58 On the publishing initiatives of the Civil Rights and Black Power movements, as well as those enabled by black amateur historians, book collectors, bookstore owners, and activists, see Ernest, *Chaotic Justice*, 1–33, and George Hutchinson and John K. Young, eds., *Publishing Blackness: Textual Constructions of Race Since 1850* (Ann Arbor: University of Michigan Press, 2013), 1–17.

59 On the "ideology of the book" in the colonization of North America, but also how books and other forms of print were used by Native Americans to resist Euro-American settler colonialism, see Phillip H. Round, *Removable Type: Histories of the Book in Indian Country, 1663–1880* (Chapel Hill: University of North Carolina Press, 2010). On the role played by language ideology, alphabetic literacy, and books in the conquest of indigenous peoples in the Americas, especially in central Mexico, see Walter D. Mignolo, *The Darker Side of the Renaissance: Literacy, Territoriality, & Colonization* (Ann Arbor: University of Michigan Press, 1995).

60 Diana Taylor, *The Archive and the Repertoire: Performing Cultural Memory in the Americas* (Durham, NC: Duke University Press, 2003), 1, 18.

61 Shawn Michelle Smith, *Photography on the Color Line: W. E. B. Du Bois, Race, and Visual Culture* (Durham, NC: Duke University Press, 2004), 2.

62 On the refusal to represent the black female body in the friendship albums, see Cobb, *Picture Freedom*, 91–3, 108–10.

63 Hartman, *Scenes of Subjection*; Christina Sharpe, *Monstrous Intimacies: Making Post-Slavery Subjects* (Durham, NC: Duke University Press, 2010).

64 Cobb, *Picture Freedom*, 8–10, 19–27.

65 On the limits of conceptualizing this group as a "black elite," see Britt Rusert, "Disappointment in the Archives of Black Freedom," *Social Text*, 33.4 (2015): 19–33.

66 See the reprint edition of the *Anglo-African Magazine*, vol. 1 (New York: Arno Press and the New York Times, 1968).

67 James McCune Smith, "The Sexton," in *The Works of James McCune Smith: Black Intellectual and Abolitionist,* ed. John Stauffer (New York: Oxford University Press, 2006), 203–6.

68 McCune Smith's admiration for Washington Irving was enshrined in his use of "Communipaw," the pen name under which he published in the black press, including in his "Heads of the Colored People" series in *Frederick Douglass' Paper.* Communipaw, an interracial colonial settlement of Africans, Native Americans, and Dutch settlers in what is now Jersey City, was made famous by Irving's account of its resistance to British invasion in *A History of New-York, from the Beginning of the World to the End of the Dutch Dynasty* (1809). Another black New Yorker, the engraver Patrick Henry Reason, inscribed a highly stylized excerpt from Irving's "The Wife" into Amy Matilda Cassey's friendship album, an artifact of black women's intellectual culture discussed in Chapter 5.

69 On enslaved practitioners of natural history in the colonial Atlantic World, see Parrish, *American Curiosity*. On enslaved healers, see Sharla M. Fett, *Working Cures: Healing, Health, and Power on Southern Slave Plantations* (Chapel Hill: University of North Carolina Press, 2002); Marie Jenkins Schwartz, *Birthing a Slave: Motherhood and Medicine in the Antebellum South* (Cambridge, MA: Harvard University Press, 2006). On slavery and conchology, see Cameron Strang, "Entangled Knowledge, Expanding Nation: Science and the United States Empire in the Southeast Borderlands, 1783–1842," PhD diss. (University of Texas at Austin, 2013). Studies on Atlantic science and slavery include James Delbourgo and Nicholas Dew, eds., *Science and Empire in the Atlantic World* (New York: Routledge, 2008); Kathleen S. Murphy, "Collecting Slave Traders: James Petiver, Natural History, and the British Slave Trade," *William and Mary Quarterly* 70.4 (October 2013): 637–70; Walls, *The Passage to Cosmos*; Mary Louise Pratt, *Imperial Eyes: Travel Writing and Transculturation* (New York: Routledge, 1992).

CHAPTER 1. THE BANNEKER AGE

1 The publication history of *Notes on the State of Virginia* is complex. Jefferson, then governor of Virginia, first penned the manuscript in 1781 in Paris, in response to a

request from François Marbois, the secretary of the French legation to the United States. The first edition was a small French printing in 1785 and the first English edition was printed by John Stockdale in 1787. The first American edition, printed in Philadelphia, did not appear until 1788. Here, I cite from the Penguin edition (New York, 1999), which reprints the 1787 Stockdale edition.

2 Gene Andrew Jarrett, *Representing the Race: A New Political History of African American Literature* (New York: New York University Press, 2011).

3 Henry Louis Gates, Jr., "Preface to Blackness: Text and Pretext," in *Afro-American Literature: The Reconstruction of Instruction*, ed. Dexter Fisher and Robert B. Stepto (New York: Modern Language Association of America, 1979), 44–69; Henry Louis Gates, Jr., *Figures in Black: Words, Signs, and the "Racial" Self* (New York: Oxford University Press, 1987); Henry Louis Gates, Jr., *The Trials of Phillis Wheatley: America's First Black Poet and Her Encounters with the Founding Fathers* (New York: Basic Books, 2003).

4 Jarrett, *Representing the Race.*

5 On eighteenth-century racial science and the widespread belief in the fungible, changeable nature of race in the period, see Katy L. Chiles, *Transformable Race: Surprising Metamorphoses in the Literature of Early America* (New York: Oxford University Press, 2014). In *A Hideous Monster of the Mind: American Race Theory in the Early Republic* (Cambridge, MA: Harvard University Press, 2002), Bruce Dain writes about the ongoing interest in environmental theories of race among nineteenth-century African Americans. Stephen G. Hall's *A Faithful Account of the Race: African American Historical Writing in Nineteenth-Century America* (Chapel Hill: University of North Carolina Press, 2009), 62–65, addresses African Americans's return to eighteenth-century universal histories amid the rise of aggressively imperial and racist US history writing in the nineteenth century.

6 Chiles, *Transformable Race*; Frederick Douglass, "The Claims of the Negro, Ethnologically Considered," in *The Frederick Douglass Papers, Series One*, ed. John W. Blassingame (New Haven, CT: Yale University Press, 1982), 2:507.

7 On the politics and power of black study, see Stefano Harney and Fred Moten, *The Undercommons: Fugitive Planning & Black Study* (Brooklyn, NY: Autonomedia, 2013).

8 Charles Darwin, *The Voyage of the Beagle: Journal of Researches into the Natural History and Geology of the Countries Visited during the Voyage of H.M.S. Beagle round the World* (New York: Modern Library, 2001).

9 Jefferson's comments on the despotism of the slaveholder and the inevitable end to the age of slavery both appear in Query XVIII, which addresses the "unhappy" influence of slavery on the manners of citizens in the state of Virginia. In a much-cited passage, Jefferson writes, "The whole commerce between master and slave, is a perpetual exercise of the most boisterous passions, the most unremitting despotism on one part, and degrading submissions on the other. . . . and with what execration should the statesman be loaded, who permitting one half of the citizens thus to trample on the rights of the other, transforms those into despots,

and these into enemies, destroys the morals of the one part, and the amor patriae [patriotism] of the other." He goes on to write, "I think a change [is] already perceptible, since the origin of the present revolution. The spirit of the master is abating, that of the slave [is] rising from the dust, his condition mollifying, the way I hope preparing, under the auspices of heaven, for a total emancipation, and that this is disposed, in the order of events, to be with the consent of the masters, rather than by their extirpation." Jefferson, *Notes on the State of Virginia* (New York: Penguin, 1999), 168–9.

10 *Colored American*, May 20, 1837.

11 On the concept of "redress" in black performance and theater, see Soyica Diggs Colbert, *The African American Theatrical Body: Reception, Performance, and the Stage* (New York: Cambridge University Press, 2011), 1–20.

12 Silvio A. Bedini's *The Life of Benjamin Banneker: The First African-American Man of Science* (New York: Scribner, 1971), remains the most complete account of Banneker's life and his scientific work. Other studies include Charles A. Cerami, *Benjamin Banneker: Surveyor, Astronomer, Publisher, Patriot* (New York: John Wiley & Sons, 2002); William L. Andrews, "Benjamin Banneker's Revision of Thomas Jefferson: Conscience Versus Science in the Early American Antislavery Debate," in *Genius in Bondage: Literature of the Early Black Atlantic*, ed. Vincent Carretta and Philip Gould (Lexington: University of Kentucky Press, 2001), 218–41.

13 Jefferson, *Notes on the State of Virginia*, 146–47.

14 Bedini, *The Life of Benjamin Banneker*, 158. A transcription of Banneker's letter and an image of the letter in manuscript appear in Bedini, 158–62. See also *Copy of a Letter from Benjamin Banneker to the Secretary of State with His Answer* (Philadelphia: Daniel Lawrence, 1792). The Jefferson correspondence was also reprinted in Banneker's almanac for 1793 (published in 1792), which included poetry by Phillis Wheatley.

15 Jefferson, *Notes on the State of Virginia*, 146.

16 Michel Foucault, *The Archaeology of Knowledge and the Discourse on Language*, trans. A. M. Sheridan Smith (New York: Pantheon, 1972), 129.

17 Ibid., 130–31.

18 Ibid., 130.

19 Martha Ellicott Tyson, *A Sketch of the Life of Benjamin Banneker: From Notes Taken in 1836. Read by J. Saurin Norris, before the Maryland Historical Society, October 5, 1854* (Baltimore: Printed for the Maryland Historical Society by John D. Toy, 1854), 7. See also an expanded sketch, based on further research by Tyson and arranged for publication by her daughter, in Anne T. Kirk., ed., *Banneker, The Afric-American Astronomer: From the Posthumous Papers of Martha E. Tyson* (Philadelphia: Friends' Book Association, 1884).

20 Tyson, *A Sketch of the Life of Benjamin Banneker*, 7, 18, 20.

21 Ibid., 15–16.

22 Banneker's circulation among white women resonates with Joanna Brooks's tracing of Phillis Wheatley's prominence in white women's reading and affective net-

works in colonial Boston, networks forged through Wheatley's careful cultivation of relationships with elite women. See Brooks, "Our Phillis, Ourselves," *American Literature* 82.1 (March 2010): 1–28.

23 Elias Ellicott to James Pemberton, July 21, 1791, in Banneker Institute Records, Constitution, Minutes, Reports, Bills and Receipts, Printed Material, Lectures, 1790–1865 and undated, Leon Gardiner collection of American Negro Historical Society Records, Historical Society of Pennsylvania.

24 On Banneker's possible Dogon family history, see Cerami, *Benjamin Banneker*, 7, 15; Ron Eglash has provided evidence for Banneker's descent from the Wolof in Senegal on his maternal grandfather's side and states that his father was from "Guinea," a designation that refers to present-day Ghana or Nigeria. Eglash suggests that African systems of numerology, passed down through his family, shaped Banneker's mathematical thinking. See Eglash, "The African Heritage of Benjamin Banneker," *Social Studies of Science* 27 (1997): 308–10.

25 On the retention and adaptation of African scientific and agricultural knowledge in the Americas, see Judith A. Carney, *Black Rice: The African Origins of Rice Cultivation in the Americas* (Cambridge, MA: Harvard University Press, 2002).

26 Peter P. Hinks, *To Awaken My Afflicted Brethren: David Walker and the Problem of Antebellum Slave Resistance* (University Park: Pennsylvania State Press, 1997), 116–72; Robert S. Levine, "Circulating the Nation: David Walker, the Missouri Compromise, and the Rise of the Black Press," in *The Black Press: New Literary and Historical Essays*, ed. Todd Vogel (New Brunswick: Rutgers University Press, 2001), 17–36.

27 Eric Williams, *Capitalism & Slavery* (1944; Chapel Hill: University of North Carolina Press, 1994); C. L. R. James, *The Black Jacobins: Toussaint L'Ouverture and the San Domingo Revolution* (1963; New York: Vintage, 1989); Walter Rodney, *How Europe Underdeveloped Africa* (1972; Cape Town: Pambazuka Press, 2012); Paul Gilroy, *The Black Atlantic: Modernity and Double Consciousness* (Cambridge, MA: Harvard University Press, 1993); Robin Blackburn, *The Making of New World Slavery: From the Baroque to the Modern, 1492–1800* (London: Verso, 1997).

28 Peter P. Hinks, ed., *David Walker's Appeal to the Coloured Citizens of the World* (University Park: Pennsylvania State University Press, 2000), 28.

29 Ibid., 17, 29.

30 Ibid., 30.

31 Ibid., 17.

32 Harney and Moten, *The Undercommons*. On autodidacticism and intellectual emancipation, see Jacques Rancière's *The Ignorant Schoolmaster: Five Lessons in Intellectual Emancipation*, trans. Kristin Ross (Stanford, CA: Stanford University Press, 1991).

33 For more on the intellectual background of the *Appeal*, see Hinks, *To Awaken My Afflicted Brethren*, 173–95.

34 Hinks, ed., *David Walker's Appeal*, 29. In "'Look!! Look!!! At This!!!!': The Radical Typography of David Walker's *Appeal*," *PMLA* 126.1 (January 2011): 55–72, Marcy

Dinius argues that the radical typography of the *Appeal* visually directs readers to transmit Walker's message to the illiterate, that "readers can virtually hear his rising voice and anger in his text's italics, capitalized words, and multiple exclamation points," and that these marks also encourage readers to read the *Appeal* aloud while directing them on how to "properly voice" the text (56).

35 Hinks, ed., *David Walker's Appeal*, 20; italics are Walker's.

36 Letter from William G. Allen, *Frederick Douglass' Paper*, April 29, 1852.

37 Michael Sappol, *A Traffic of Dead Bodies: Anatomy and Embodied Social Identity in Nineteenth-Century America* (Princeton, NJ: Princeton University Press, 2002); Harriet A. Washington, *Medical Apartheid: The Dark History of Medical Experimentation on Black Americans from Colonial Times to the Present* (New York: Doubleday, 2006); Margaret Humphreys, *Intensely Human: The Health of the Black Soldier in the American Civil War* (Baltimore: Johns Hopkins University Press, 2008).

38 Hinks, ed., *David Walker's Appeal*, 16.

39 Ibid., 2.

40 James W. C. Pennington, *A Text Book of the Origin and History, &c. &c. of the Colored People* (Hartford, CT: L. Skinner, 1841), 52–53.

41 Ibid., 53.

42 Ibid., 7.

43 Ibid., 14; emphasis in original.

44 Ibid., 92.

45 Ibid., 4.

46 Ibid., 5.

47 Pennington, *The Fugitive Blacksmith: or, Events in the History of James W. C. Pennington* (Westport, CT: Negro Universities Press, 1971), vi, xii.

48 Ibid., xii.

49 Ibid; emphasis in original.

50 Ibid., 57; emphasis in original.

51 Ibid., 64.

52 Ibid.

53 Jefferson claims that the "Oranootan" prefers "black women over those of his own species." Jefferson, *Notes on the State of Virginia*, 145.

54 For more on McCune Smith's life, see John Stauffer's introduction to *The Works of James McCune Smith: Black Intellectual and Abolitionist* (New York: Oxford University Press, 2006), xiii–xl.

55 James McCune Smith, "On the Fourteenth Query of Thomas Jefferson's Notes on Virginia," *Anglo-African Magazine*, vol. 1 (New York: Arno Press and the New York Times, 1968), 225–38.

56 McCune Smith, "Civilization: Its Dependence on Physical Circumstances," *Anglo-African Magazine*, 5–17.

57 Ibid., 15–16.

58 Stauffer, ed., *The Works of James McCune Smith*, 264.

59 McCune Smith, "On the Fourteenth Query," 234.

60 Ibid., 233.

61 Ibid., 227.

62 McCune Smith, "Civilization," 5.

63 McCune Smith, "The Black News-Vender," in Stauffer, ed., *The Works of James McCune Smith*, 191.

64 Ibid.

65 Ibid.

66 David Kazanjian, *The Colonizing Trick: National Culture and Imperial Citizenship in Early America* (Minneapolis: University of Minnesota Press, 2003), 32.

67 Jefferson, *Notes on the State of Virginia*, 145. The concept of faces as "visual archives" in "The Heads of the Colored People" comes from Susan Scott Parrish, "Response to Race, Science, and Representation in Early America Panel," MLA Annual Convention, January 6, 2013.

68 "Letter from the Editor," *Frederick Douglass' Paper*, May 27, 1853.

69 Italics are mine.

70 In this way, McCune Smith makes visible the "race/reproduction bind" that Alys Eve Weinbaum has argued structures the episteme of the modern transatlantic world, if often obliquely. Weinbaum, *Wayward Reproductions: Genealogies of Race and Nation in Transatlantic Modern Thought* (Durham, NC: Duke University Press, 2004).

71 Sharon Patricia Holland, *The Erotic Life of Racism* (Durham, NC: Duke University Press, 2012).

72 Jefferson, *Notes on the State of Virginia*, 146.

73 Stauffer, ed., *The Works of James McCune Smith*, xxix; quotations are Stauffer's.

74 Specifically, McCune Smith cites James Cowles Prichard's multi-volume work, *Researches into the Physical History of Mankind* (1813–1847).

75 McCune Smith, "Civilization" 11.

76 Darwin's *On the Origin of Species* was not published until 1859, but proto-evolutionary discourses, as well as Darwin's own theories, circulated in the cultural ether much earlier than 1859. On the wide circulation of the proto-evolutionary discourse of vestiges throughout the 1840s, see James A. Secord's *Victorian Sensation: The Extraordinary Publication, Reception, and Secret Authorship of "Vestiges of the Natural History of Creation"* (Chicago: University of Chicago Press, 2000).

77 Frederick Douglass, *My Bondage and My Freedom*, in *Frederick Douglass: Autobiographies* (New York: Library of America, 1994), 132.

78 Ibid.

79 See, for example, "Slander Refuted," *Colored American*, May 20, 1837; Letter from William G. Allen, *Frederick Douglass' Paper*, April 29, 1852; *Weekly Anglo-African*, November 24, 1860; William Wells Brown, *The Black Man: His Antecedents, His Genius, and His Achievements* (New York: Thomas Hamilton, 1863). An account

of Douglass's public reading of the Banneker's letter appears in a November 1859 letter to the editor in *Douglass' Monthly*.

80 Announcements of the Banneker birthday celebrations hosted by the Banneker Institute appear in *Douglass' Monthly*, December 1859; *Philadelphia Inquirer*, November 8, 1858, and November 13, 1861; *Liberator*, January 6, 1860, and elsewhere.

81 Banneker's column in the *Weekly Anglo-African* was also referred to as "Our Philadelphia Letter" in the newspaper. In it, the institute's secretary, Jacob C. White, Jr., provided updates on the activities of the institute and information on scientific lectures and other intellectual gatherings in black Philadelphia.

82 On performative acts of surrogation, see Joseph Roach, *Cities of the Dead: Circum-Atlantic Performance* (New York: Columbia University Press, 1996)

83 Banneker Correspondence, May 6, 1790–September 5, 1791, Banneker Institute records, Historical Society of Pennsylvania.

84 Plans to erect monuments in memory of Banneker and John Russwurm appear, for example, in the April 1, 1852, issue of the *National Era*.

85 Andrews, "Benjamin Banneker's Revision of Thomas Jefferson," 233.

86 Lisa Yaszek, "The Bannekerade: Genius, Madness, and Magic in Black Science Fiction," in *Black and Brown Planets: The Politics of Race in Science Fiction*, ed. Isiah Lavender III (Jackson: University Press of Mississippi, 2014), 15–30.

87 Caroline Levander reads *Imperium in Imperio* as a borderlands text that registers a much longer history of the Texas-Mexico border as a site of intense geopolitical contest among Mexicans, Mexican Americans, African Americans, and Anglo-American settlers. Levander, "Sutton Griggs and the Borderlands of Empire," in *Jim Crow, Literature, and the Legacy of Sutton E. Griggs*, ed. Tess Chakkalakal and Kenneth W. Warren (Athens: University of Georgia Press, 2013), 21–48.

88 Although the novel ends on a politically moderate note, conveying the importance of African Americans continuing to fight for full citizenship rights rather than resorting to violence and separatism, the radical vision forwarded by the Imperium seems to have long distracted readers from Griggs's actual message in his uplift narrative. Even scholarly descriptions of the text often focus on Griggs's imagination of a fantastical black empire in Texas, rather than the author's ultimate message that such separatist schemes were destructive and unpatriotic.

89 Sutton E. Griggs, *Imperium in Imperio* (New York: Arno Press and the New York Times, 1969), 191. The Arno Press edition reprints the 1899 novel, which was printed for Griggs by a small Cincinnati publisher and sold door to door by the author.

90 "Black founding fathers" refers to black leaders in the early republic, especially those individuals who built institutions and rallied communities in the decades following American independence. In *Imperium in Imperio*, Griggs transforms Banneker into such a builder of black institutions. See Richard S. Newman, *Freedom's Prophet: Bishop Richard Allen, the AME Church, and the Black Founding Fathers* (New York: New York University Press, 2008); Richard S. Newman and

Roy E. Finkenbine, "Black Founders in the New Republic: Introduction," *William and Mary Quarterly* 64.1 (January 2007): 83–94.

91 Griggs, *Imperium in Imperio*, 191.

92 Ibid., 179, 191. The novel's references to Jefferson and UVA may have been shaped by Griggs's residence in Jefferson's home state of Virginia when he was writing the novel.

93 Ibid., 191.

CHAPTER 2. COMPARATIVE ANATOMIES

1 Maurice O. Wallace and Shawn Michelle Smith, eds., *Pictures and Progress: Early Photography and the Making of African American Identity* (Durham, NC: Duke University Press, 2012), 9.

2 Shawn Michelle Smith, *Photography on the Color Line: W. E. B. Du Bois, Race, and Visual Culture* (Durham, NC: Duke University Press, 2004), 44. For a comprehensive treatment of Du Bois's photography exhibit, see the entirety of Smith's monograph.

3 Ibid., 2.

4 On black visual, sartorial, and expressive responses to racist forms of representation in the nineteenth century, see Jasmine Nichole Cobb, *Picture Freedom: Remaking Black Visuality in the Early Nineteenth Century* (New York: New York University Press, 2015); Wallace and Smith, eds., *Pictures and Progress*; Monica L. Miller, *Slaves to Fashion: Black Dandyism and the Styling of Black Diasporic Identity* (Durham, NC: Duke University Press, 2009). On the visual interventions and visual culture of the abolitionist movement, see Radiclani Clytus, "'Keep It Before the People': The Pictorialization of American Abolitionism," in *Early African American Print Culture*, ed. Lara Langer Cohen and Jordan Alexander Stein (Philadelphia: University of Pennsylvania Press, 2012), 290–317; Phillip Lapsansky, "Graphic Discord: Abolitionist and Antiabolitionist Images," in *The Abolitionist Sisterhood: Women's Political Culture in Antebellum America*, ed. Jean Fagan Yellin and John C. Van Horne (Ithaca, NY: Cornell University Press, 1994), 201–30.

5 Cobb, *Picture Freedom*, 6–11, 19–21. On blackness, gender, and visuality, see also Nicole R. Fleetwood, *Troubling Vision: Performance, Visuality, and Blackness* (Durham, NC: Duke University Press, 2011); Daphne A. Brooks, *Bodies in Dissent: Spectacular Performances of Race and Freedom* (Durham, NC: Duke University Press, 2006); Michele Wallace, *Dark Designs and Visual Culture* (Durham, NC: Duke University Press, 2004); and bell hooks, *Black Looks: Race and Representation* (Boston: South End Press, 1992).

6 Alondra Nelson, "Reconciliation Projects: From Kinship to Justice," in *Genetics and the Unsettled Past: The Collision of DNA, Race, and History*, ed. Keith Wailoo, Alondra Nelson, and Catherine Lee (New Brunswick, NJ: Rutgers University Press, 2012), 20-21. On these and other politically and socially oriented uses of genetics, see also Alondra Nelson, *The Social Life of DNA: Race, Reparations, and Reconciliation after the Genome* (Boston: Beacon Press, 2016).

7   Nancy Bentley, "The Fourth Dimension: Kinlessness and African American Narrative," *Critical Inquiry* 35.2 (Winter 2009): 292.

8   On the study of Native tribes and languages in federal ethnology, see Sean P. Harvey, *Native Tongues: Colonialism and Race from Encounter to the Reservation* (Cambridge, MA: Harvard University Press, 2015).

9   On the widescale economic transformations of the period, see Charles Sellers, *The Market Revolution: Jacksonian America, 1815–1846* (New York: Oxford University Press, 1991). Earlier, Jefferson had declared the United States an "empire for liberty" while the Louisiana Purchase of 1802 put the young nation on a course to conquer and colonize the entire North American continent. See Daniel Walker Howe, *What Hath God Wrought: The Transformation of America, 1815–1848* (New York: Oxford University Press, 2007), 2.

10 On this period in US history, see David S. Reynolds, *Waking Giant: America in the Age of Jackson* (New York: Harper, 2008); Howe, *What Hath God Wrought*; Sean Wilentz, *The Rise of American Democracy: Jefferson to Lincoln* (New York: W. W. Norton, 2006). On the culmination of Manifest Destiny ideology in the 1845 annexation of Texas and the Mexican-American War, as well as the subsequent extension of US empire to the West Coast, see Robert W. Johannsen, *To the Halls of the Montezumas: The Mexican War in the American Imagination* (New York: Oxford University Press, 1985).

11 Reynolds, *Waking Giant,* 91.

12 Maureen Konkle, *Writing Indian Nations: Native Intellectuals and the Politics of Historiography, 1827–1863* (Chapel Hill: University of North Carolina Press, 2004), 8–17.

13 Reynolds, *Waking Giant,* 90–95.

14 On the anti-colonization movement among African Americans, see Ousmane Power-Greene, *Against Wind and Tide: The African American Struggle against the Colonization Movement* (New York: New York University Press, 2014).

15 Harvey, *Native Tongues*; Sean P. Harvey, "'Must Not Their Languages Be Savage and Barbarous Like Them?': Philology, Indian Removal, and Race Science," *Journal of the Early Republic* 30.4 (Winter 2010): 505–32.

16 On the diverse sources studied and used by black ethnologists, see Stephen G. Hall, *A Faithful Account of the Race: African American Historical Writing in Nineteenth-Century America* (Chapel Hill: University of North Carolina Press, 2009), 49–85; and John Ernest, *Liberation Historiography: African American Writers and the Challenge of History, 1794–1861* (Chapel Hill: University of North Carolina Press, 2004).

17 Hall, *A Faithful Account of the Race*, 62.

18 Ibid., 65.

19 On the controversy and scandal surrounding the publication of Walker's *Appeal*, see Peter P. Hinks, *To Awaken My Afflicted Brethren: David Walker and the Problem of Antebellum Slave Resistance* (University Park: Pennsylvania State University Press, 1997), 116–72.

20 *Productions of Mrs. Maria W. Stewart, Presented to the First African Baptist Church and Society of the City of Boston* (Boston: Friends of Freedom and Virtue, 1835); Marilyn Richardson, ed., *Maria W. Stewart, America's First Black Woman Political Writer: Essays and Speeches* (Bloomington: Indiana University Press, 1987).

21 On Apess's life and activism, as well as an account of his relationship to David Walker and black Boston, see Philip F. Gura, *The Life of William Apess, Pequot* (Chapel Hill: University of North Carolina Press, 2014), 52–76.

22 David M. Goldenberg, *The Curse of Ham: Race and Slavery in Early Judaism, Christianity, and Islam* (Princeton, NJ: Princeton University Press, 2003), 168.

23 Ibid., 168–77.

24 Ibid, 178–82.

25 Peter P. Hinks, ed., *David Walker's Appeal to the Coloured Citizens of the World* (University Park: Pennsylvania State University Press, 2000), 63.

26 James W. C. Pennington, *A Text Book of the Origin and History, &c. &c. of the Colored People* (Hartford, CT: L. Skinner, 1841), 7.

27 On the blending of "revisionist ethnology" and messianism in black ethnology, see Mia Bay, *The White Image in the Black Mind: African-American Ideas about White People, 1830–1925* (New York: Oxford University Press, 2000), 48.

28 On the role of providential history in these texts, see Ernest, *Liberation Historiography.* See also Eddie S. Glaude, Jr., *Exodus!: Religion, Race, and Nation in Early Nineteenth-Century Black America* (Chicago: University of Chicago Press, 2000), on black salvific history, those "accounts of the experiences of African Americans viewed from the perspective of the Bible that make sense of their conditions of living" (4).

29 Hall, *A Faithful Account of the Race*, 55.

30 Ibid., 6.

31 In his 1972 study, Walter Rodney argued that European imperialism was so destructive to African economies because it interrupted an economic transition from communalism to feudalism that was happening in various ways in states and societies across the continent. The depopulation caused by the slave trade also had devastating consequences on local and regional economies, as well as the development of the continent as a whole. Walter Rodney, *How Europe Underdeveloped Africa* (Cape Town: Pambazuka Press, 2012), 38–9; 95–146.

32 See Glaude, *Exodus!*, 4, on the similar historical compression work of the Exodus story among black congregations in the nineteenth century.

33 Lydia Maria Child, *An Appeal in Favor of that Class of Americans Called Africans* (Boston: Allen and Ticknor, 1833), 155.

34 Ibid., 156; emphasis in original.

35 Robyn Wiegman, *American Anatomies: Theorizing Race and Gender* (Durham, NC: Duke University Press, 1995), 21–42.

36 See Michel Foucault, *The Order of Things: An Archaeology of the Human Sciences* (New York: Vintage Books, 1994). While eighteenth-century natural history

imagined itself as a science of surfaces (though dissection and invasive experimentation were still very much a part of this tradition), comparative anatomy and the proto-discourses and methods of biology were rooted in making internal structures visible and comparable.

37 Julien-Joseph Virey's *Histoire naturelle du genre humain* was first published in 1801, and subsequent editions appeared in the 1820s. Virey's illustrations relied on Dutch anatomist and artist Petrus Camper's drawings of comparative facial angles of Africans and apes. See *The Works of the Late Professor Camper, on the Connexion between the Science of Anatomy and the Arts of Drawing, Painting, Statuary, &c., &c.* (London: C. Dilly, 1794). On Virey and his use of Camper's African facial angle, see Albert Alhadeff, "US and THEM: Camper's odious *ligne faciale* and Géricault's beseeching black," in *Blacks and Blackness in European Art of the Long Nineteenth Century*, ed. Adrienne L. Childs and Susan H. Libby (New York: Routledge, 2014), 47–68.

38 See J. C. Nott and G. R. Gliddon, *Types of Mankind: or, Ethnological Researches, Based Upon the Ancient Monuments, Paintings, Sculptures, and Crania of Races, and upon their Natural, Geographical, Philological, and Biblical History* (Philadelphia: J. B. Lippincott, 1857), 202–3. Prisse's original portraits, two painted and one in pencil, are collected in Samuel George Morton's "Ethnological Notebook," a manuscript item held in the collection of the Library Company of Philadelphia. The interest in the visual evidence being produced by European ethnologists among the American school of ethnology is evident throughout Morton's "scrapbook," which includes many plates from the works of the French Egyptologist Jean-François Champollion.

39 Cobb, *Picture Freedom*, 193–220.

40 Ann Fabian, *The Skull Collectors: Race, Science, and America's Unburied Dead* (Chicago: University of Chicago Press, 2010), 81–91. Fabian notes that Morton struggled to secure subscriptions for the volume and eventually resigned himself to distributing complimentary copies to friends, colleagues, and various learned societies.

41 On the circulation of anti-black imagery in this period, see Lapsansky, "Graphic Discord"; Corey Capers, "Black Voices, White Print: Racial Practice, Print Publicity, and Order in the Early American Republic," in *Early African American Print Culture*, ed. Lara Langer Cohen and Jordan Alexander Stein (Philadelphia: University of Pennsylvania Press, 2012), 107–26. On the transatlantic dimensions and circuits of anti-black imagery, see Radiclani Clytus, "At Home in England: Black Imagery across the Atlantic," in *Black Victorians: Black People in British Art, 1800–1900*, ed. Jan Marsh (Aldershot, UK: Lund Humphries, 2005), 23–34. On the broader visual archive of slavery, see Marcus Wood, *Blind Memory: Visual Representations of Slavery in England and America, 1780–1865* (Manchester: Manchester University Press, 2000).

42 For example, illustrations titled "Hottentot Wagoner—Caffre War" and "Hottentot from Somerset" in *Types of Mankind* were taken from images of South Africans

published in the *Illustrated London News* in 1851; those images were based on a series of original paintings by artist and British settler-colonist Frederick Timpson l'Ons.

43 Hosea Easton, *A Treatise on the Intellectual Character, and Civil and Political Condition of the Colored People of the U. States; and the Prejudice Exercised towards Them* (Boston: Isaac Knapp, 1837), 41–42.

44 R. B. Lewis, *Light and Truth, from Ancient and Sacred History* (Portland, ME: D. C. Colesworthy, 1836).

45 Based on correspondence with Lewis's eldest daughter, Mary Augusta Lewis Johnson, the African American bibliographer and librarian Daniel Murray's short biography of Lewis refers to him as the "village tinkerer," who supported his family through a variety of odd jobs. He "whitewashed, kalsomined, painted and papered houses, covered and mended parasols and umbrellas, cleaned carpets, while his wife and such of the children as were old enough, assisted in making baskets and caning chairs." "Robert Benjamin Lewis," Daniel Murray Papers, 1851–1955, State Historical Society of Wisconsin, Wisconsin Historical Society, Madison, Reel 6. Lewis was also an inventor who held two patents. See Reginald H. Pitts, "Robert Benjamin Lewis," in *Maine's Visible Black History: The First Chronicle of Its People*, ed. H. H. Price and Gerald E. Talbot (Gardiner, ME: Tilbury House, 2006), 235-40. Biographical entries on Lewis also appear in Reginald H. Pitts, "Robert Benjamin Lewis," in *African American National Biography*, ed. Henry Louis Gates, Jr., and Evelyn Brooks Higginbotham (New York: Oxford University Press, 2013), 7: 296–97; Bay, *The White Image in the Black Mind*, 44–46.

46 Pitts, "Robert Benjamin Lewis," 235–36.

47 Mary Augusta Lewis Johnson to Daniel Murray, May 11, 1900, Daniel Murray Papers, Reel 1.

48 R. B. Lewis, *Light and Truth: Collected from the Bible and Ancient and Modern History, Containing the Universal History of the Colored and the Indian Race, from the Creation of the World to the Present Time* (Boston: Published by a Committee of Colored Men; Benjamin F. Roberts, 1844). A notice of publication in the November 3, 1843, issue of the *Liberator* indicates that 3,000 copies were printed of the new edition of *Light and Truth*.

49 The publishing committee, Thomas Dalton, Charles H. Roberts, James Scott, and Andress V. Lewis (no relation to Robert Benjamin), were all black business owners in Boston.

50 R. B. Lewis, *Light and Truth: Collected from the Bible and Ancient and Modern History, Containing the Universal History of the Colored and the Indian Race, from the Creation of the World to the Present Time* (Boston: Published by a Committee of Colored Men; Benjamin F. Roberts, 1849).

51 Bay, *The White Image in the Black Mind*, 44–46.

52 Martin Robison Delany, *Condition, Elevation, Emigration and Destiny of the Colored People of the United States* (Philadelphia: Published for the Author, 1852), 128.

53 Ibid.

54 Ibid., 129.

55 "A New History," *Liberator,* June 11, 1852; the prospectus appeared again in the June 18, 1852 issue of the *Liberator,* and then again in the May 13, 1853 issue of *Frederick Douglass' Paper.*

56 Harry T. Peters, *America on Stone: The Other Printmakers to the American People* (New York: Arno Press, 1976); Erika Piola, *Philadelphia on Stone: Commercial Lithography in Philadelphia, 1828–1878* (University Park: Pennsylvania State University Press, 2012).

57 For an overview of early African American portraiture, see Gwendolyn DuBois Shaw, *Portraits of a People: Picturing African Americans in the Nineteenth Century* (Seattle: University of Washington Press, 2006). African Americans also turned to photography to produce representations of themselves on their own terms; see Wallace and Smith, eds., *Pictures and Progress.* On the complexities of self-representation for enslaved and formerly enslaved people photographed by white photographers, see Deborah Willis and Barbara Krauthamer, *Envisioning Emancipation: Black Americans and the End of Slavery* (Philadelphia: Temple University Press, 2012).

58 See also Richard S. Newman's analysis of the portraits of Richard Allen, the founder of the African Methodist Episcopal (AME) Church, in *Freedom's Prophet: Bishop Richard Allen, the AME Church, and the Black Founding Fathers* (New York: New York University Press, 2008).

59 Although it is not clear whether Lewis was a freemason, he was certainly constructed as such in this image. His *Light and Truth* also circulated in black Masonic circles: the publishing "committee of colored gentlemen" were all Boston freemasons and an 1856 publication in Delaware further suggests a connection between *Light and Truth* and freemasonry. Echoing Lewis's title, a committee appointed by the Hiram Grand Lodge in Delaware published *Lux et veritas: Light and Truth, or, The Origin of Ancient Freemasonry, among Colored Men, in the State of Delaware* (Wilmington: Henry Eckel, 1856).

60 On Orientalist styles of painting in the nineteenth century, see James Thompson, *The East: Imagined, Experienced, Remembered: Orientalist Nineteenth Century Painting* (Dublin: National Gallery of Ireland, 1988). Orientalist garb and props were often taken back to Europe from North Africa and the Middle East for use in artist studios. For examples of Orientalist images of Africans in the history of Western Art, see *The Image of the Black in Western Art* series, ed. David Bindman and Henry Louis Gates, Jr. (Cambridge, MA: Harvard University Press), and Vincent Boele, ed., *Black is Beautiful: Rubens to Dumas* (Amsterdam: De Nieuwe Kerk, 2008).

61 Lewis, *Light and Truth* (1844), iii.

62 On the exchange and intermingling between African Americans and Native Americans in eighteenth- and early-nineteenth-century New England, see Ron Welburn, *Hartford's Ann Plato and the Native Borders of Identity* (Albany: State University of New York Press, 2015); Katy L. Chiles, *Transformable Race: Sur-*

prising Metamorphoses in the Literature of Early America (New York: Oxford University Press, 2015), 31–63; Gura, *The Life of William Apess, Pequot*; Gretchen Holbrook Gerzina, *Mr. and Mrs. Prince: How an Extraordinary Eighteenth-Century Family Moved out of Slavery and into Legend* (New York: Amistad, 2008).

63 Lara Langer Cohen talks about the "patchwork aesthetic" in the writing of William Wells Brown and notes that Lewis's *Light and Truth* shares Brown's citational practice and the patchwork style it produces. Lara Langer Cohen, "Notes from the State of Saint Domingue: The Practice of Citation in *Clotel*," in *Early African American Print Culture*, ed. Lara Langer Cohen and Jordan Alexander Stein (Philadelphia: University of Pennsylvania Press, 2012), 164, n. 374.

64 On the opacities and absences of African American genealogy, see Saidiya Hartman, *Lose Your Mother: A Journey along the Atlantic Slave Route* (New York: Farrar, Straus and Giroux, 2007). See also Carla Peterson, *Black Gotham: A Family History of African Americans in Nineteenth-Century New York City* (New Haven, CT: Yale University Press, 2011), on the difficulties of tracing African American family history in antebellum archives.

65 Lewis, *Light and Truth* (1844), 400.

66 Ibid.

67 William Apess, *A Son of the Forest: The Experience of William Apes[s], A Native of the Forest* (New York: G. F. Bunce, 1831). The first edition appeared in 1829 and was printed for Apess by an unnamed printer in New York.

68 Apess's appendix draws extensively from Elias Boudinot's *A Star in the West; or, An Humble Attempt to Discover the Long Lost Ten Tribes of Israel, Preparatory to Their Return to Their Beloved City, Jerusalem* (1816).

69 Gura, *The Life of William Apess*, 44–45.

70 *The Light and Truth of Slavery: Aaron's History* (Worcester, MA: Printed for Aaron, ca. 1845).

71 John W. Blassingame, ed., *Slave Testimony: Two Centuries of Letters, Speeches, Interviews, and Autobiographies* (Baton Rouge: Louisiana State University Press, 1977), xxviii.

72 *The Light and Truth of Slavery*, 1.

73 Ibid., 3.

74 Ibid., 14.

75 Ibid., 3.

76 Marcus Wood, *Black Milk: Imagining Slavery in the Visual Cultures of Brazil and America* (Oxford: Oxford University Press, 2013), 112.

77 Frank B. Wilderson III, *Red, White & Black: Cinema and the Structure of U.S. Antagonisms* (Durham, NC: Duke University Press, 2010).

78 Paul Reddin, *Wild West Shows* (Urbana: University of Illinois Press, 1999), 1–26; L.G. Moses, *Wild West Shows and the Images of American Indians, 1883–1933* (Albuquerque: University of New Mexico Press, 1996); Ann Fabian, *The Skull Collectors*, 50–51.

79 Easton, *Treatise*, 36–37.

80 Ibid., 44.

81 Lewis, *Light and Truth* (1844), 330. Other writers in this tradition also suffered early deaths, under unclear circumstances: David Walker passed away in 1830 at the age of thirty-four, just after the publication of the third edition of his *Appeal*, and William Apess passed away in 1839 at the age of forty.

82 Easton, *Treatise*, 43.

83 Ibid.; emphasis mine.

84 The 1830s witnessed a veritable astronomy craze: observatories were constructed across the United States, and everyday Americans lusted after the possibility of owning a telescope of their own. In 1830, Andrew Jackson funded a project that led to the founding of a national observatory. The renowned British astronomer and son of Sir William Herschel, John Herschel, published *A Treatise on Astronomy* in London in 1833, and an American edition was printed in Philadelphia in 1834.

85 "Water Telescope," *Liberator*, February 4, 1832; "Miscellaneous—Light," *Liberator*, September 28, 1833; "I Am an Anti-Slavery Man Myself," *Liberator*, December 20, 1834; "A New Use of the Microscope," *Liberator*, September 10, 1841.

86 "Mr. Carey, the Original Constructor of the Oxy-Hydrogen Microscope," *Liberator*, March 26, 1836. See also "Argument to Clean the Teeth," *Liberator*, December 13, 1834. The unsettling and sometimes grotesque images produced by the microscope and other optical instruments also shaped Edgar Allan Poe's macabre aesthetics. On Poe's engagement with the optical sciences, see John Tresch, "Estrangement of Vision: Edgar Allan Poe's Optics," in *Observing Nature–Representing Experience: The Osmotic Dynamics of Romanticism, 1800–1850*, ed. Erna Fiorenti (Berlin: Reimer Verlag, 2007), 125–57.

87 Easton, *Treatise*, 21.

88 Ibid., 23–24.

89 Ibid.

90 Ibid., 53.

91 Walter Johnson, "On Agency," *Journal of Social History* 37.1 (Fall 2003): 113–24, provides a helpful overview.

92 Easton, *Treatise*, 26.

93 Jared Sexton, "Ante-Anti-Blackness: Afterthoughts," *Lateral* 1 (2012), www.lateral.culturalstudiesassociation.org. For an introduction to Afro-pessimism, see Wilderson, *Red, White & Black*, and Jared Sexton, *Amalgamation Schemes: Antiblackness and the Critique of Multiracialism* (Minneapolis: University of Minnesota Press, 2008). See also Orlando Patterson, *Slavery and Social Death: A Comparative Study* (Cambridge, MA: Harvard University Press, 1985).

94 See Fred Moten's challenge to Afro-pessimism's denial of the social to black subjects in "Blackness and Nothingness (Mysticism in the Flesh)," *South Atlantic Quarterly* 112.4 (2013): 737–80.

95 In Chapter 8, "The Present State of Judah & Israel," Lewis includes a list of authors "adduced to prove the Tribes of Israel in America." The list includes page citations

for works by Columbus, William Penn, Edward Long, Lewis and Clark, William Bartram, Alexander von Humboldt, and many others, including the Mohegan intellectual and minister Samson Occom, whom Lewis lists as "colored" in parenthesis. Lewis does not cite Apess as an authority on the topic, but he would have certainly encountered extracts from Boudinot's *A Star in the West; or, An Humble Attempt to Discover the Long Lost Ten Tribes of Israel* in Apess's Appendix. Boudinot is cited several times in *Light and Truth*, providing ethnographic details about Native tribes and information establishing Native peoples's descent from the Israelites. In the brief section on Apess in the 1844 edition of *Light and Truth*, Walker refers to Apess as an Indian and Israelite, who cries out against the subjection of his people in the Americas and their scattering (removal) from their homeland, which the Israelites had also experienced in Egypt.

96 George R. Price and James Brewer Stewart, eds., *To Heal the Scourge of Prejudice: The Life and Writings of Hosea Easton* (Amherst: University of Massachusetts Press, 1999), 3–6.

97 James McCune Smith, "Civilization: Its Dependence on Physical Circumstances," *Anglo-African Magazine*, vol. 1 (New York: Arno Press and the New York Times, 1968), 12.

98 On the history of black representations of Native Americans in the antebellum period, see Arika Easley-Houser, "The Indian Image in the Black Mind: Representing Native Americans in Antebellum African American Public Culture," PhD diss. (Rutgers University, 2014).

99 "Afric-American Picture Gallery," *Anglo-African Magazine*, 53.

100 For example, Wilson's description of a "Head of Phillis Wheatley" most certainly referred to the iconic engraving of Wheatley that served as a frontispiece to her 1773 book of *Poems on Various Subjects, Religious and Moral.* Wilson's source may have been one of the many reproductions of Wheatley's portrait that appeared in print in 1855, just three years before the "Afric-American Picture Gallery" was published in the *Anglo-African*. Versions of Wheatley's 1773 portrait published in 1855 appeared in Sarah Hale, *Woman's Record; or, Sketches of all Distinguished Women, from the Creation to A.D. 1854* (New York: Harper and Brothers, 1855), 553; A. D. Jones, *The Illustrated American Biography* (New York: J. Milton Emerson, 1855), 3:147; Evert A. and George L. Duyckinck, eds., *Cyclopaedia of American Literature* (New York: Charles Scribner, 1855), 2:367. These 1850s images of Wheatley were likely drawn from the frontispiece of the 1834 publication of *Memoir and Poems of Phillis Wheatley*, which included a reproduction of the 1773 frontispiece. Coincidentally, the 1834 frontispiece, as well as the frontispiece that appeared in the third edition of Wheatley's memoir in 1838, were both engraved at Pendleton's Lithography in Boston, where the Robert Benjamin Lewis lithograph was also produced in the early 1830s. See *Memoir and Poems of Phillis Wheatley: A Native African and a Slave* (Boston: Geo. W. Light, 1834), and 3rd ed. (Boston: Isaac Knapp, 1838). Many thanks to Allison Lange and Connie King for their assistance in locating antebellum images of Wheatley.

101 Studies of nineteenth-century African American art and artists include Steven
Loring Jones, "'A Keen Sense of the Artistic': African American Material Cul-
ture in 19th Century Philadelphia," *International Review of African American
Art* 12.2 (1995): 4–29; Aston Gonzalez, "The Art of Racial Politics: The Work of
Robert Douglass, Jr., 1833–46," *Pennsylvania Magazine of History and Biography*
138.1 (January 2014): 5–37. See also Romare Beardon and Harry Henderson,
A History of African-American Artists from 1792 to the Present (New York:
Pantheon Books, 1993); Samella Lewis, *African American Art and Artists*, rev.
ed. (Berkeley: University of California Press, 2003); Lynda Roscoe Hartigan,
Sharing Traditions: Five Black Artists in Nineteenth-Century America (Washing-
ton, DC: Smithsonian Institution Press, 1985); Lisa Farrington, *Creating Their
Own Image: The History of African-American Women Artists* (New York: Oxford
University Press, 2005).

102 On Lewis's life, career, and work, see Kirsten Pai Buick, *Child of the Fire: Mary Ed-
monia Lewis and the Problem of Art History's Black and Indian Subject* (Durham,
NC: Duke University Press, 2010); Hartigan, *Sharing Traditions*, 85–98; Beardon
and Henderson, *A History of African-American Artists*, 54–77; Charmaine A. Nel-
son, *The Color of Stone: Sculpting the Black Female Subject in Nineteenth-Century
America* (Minneapolis: University of Minnesota Press, 2007). In Europe, Edmonia
Lewis was preceded by the mixed-race sculptor Eugène Warburg. See Paul H.
D. Kaplan, "'A mulatto sculptor from New Orleans': Eugène Warburg in Europe,
1853–59," *Blacks and Blackness in European Art of the Long Nineteenth Century,* ed.
Adrienne L. Childs and Susan H. Libby (Surrey, UK: Ashgate, 2014), 69–104.

103 While there is no known connection between Edmonia Lewis and Robert Benjamin Lewis, a September 1873 issue of the *Bath Times* (Bath, Maine) engaged in the
practice of speculative kinship by claiming that Edmonia Lewis was R. B. Lewis's
daughter.

104 Buick says that the 1870 cartes de visite of Lewis by Henry Rocher embody a certain "risk" since the artist's image "is one that rests in tension between her status
as celebrity and her status as specimen." Buick, *Child of the Fire*, 1.

CHAPTER 3. EXPERIMENTS IN FREEDOM

1 Ann Fabian, *The Skull Collectors: Race, Science, and America's Unburied Dead*
(Chicago: University of Chicago Press, 2010), 81–91.

2 Diana Taylor, *The Archive and the Repertoire: Performing Cultural Memory in the
Americas* (Durham, NC: Duke University Press, 2003).

3 Drawing from Walter Benjamin's notion that "the past can be seized only as an
image which flashes up [*aufblitzt*]" in a brief moment of recognition, David Kazanjian defines flashpoints as "the process by which someone or something emerges
or bursts into action or being, not out of nothing but transformed from one form
to another; *and*, it refers to the powerful effects of that emergence or transformation" (27). See Kazanjian, The *Colonizing Trick: National Culture and Imperial
Citizenship in Early America* (Minneapolis: University of Minnesota Press, 2003),

1–34, for a fuller account of historical and textual flashpoints and their significance for writing about emergent phenomena and historical transformation.

4 Michel Foucault, *The Order of Things: An Archaeology of the Human Sciences* (New York: Vintage, 1994), 268.

5 Jayna Brown, *Babylon Girls: Black Women Performers and the Shaping of the Modern* (Durham, NC: Duke University Press, 2008), 77. Brown's observations draw from Robert Young's argument that racial theories were "fundamentally populist in tone" (Brown, 92). See Young, *Colonial Desire: Hybridity in Theory, Culture and Race* (London: Routledge, 1995).

6 While there remains an unfortunate dearth of scholarship addressing science on the American stage during the period, a rich literature has addressed the importance of popular theater and public spectacle in the formation and dissemination of British popular science in the nineteenth century. See, for example, Iwan Rhys Morus, *Frankenstein's Children: Electricity, Exhibition, and Experiment in Early-Nineteenth-Century London* (Princeton, NJ: Princeton University Press, 1998); Bernard Lightman, *Victorian Popularizers of Science: Designing Nature for New Audiences* (Chicago: University of Chicago Press, 2007); Alison Winter, *Mesmerized: Powers of Mind in Victorian Britain* (Chicago: University of Chicago Press, 1998). James Delbourgo's study of electricity experiments and the performance of Enlightenment on the transatlantic stage does offer insight into some of the performative elements of early American science. See Delbourgo, *A Most Amazing Scene of Wonders: Electricity and Enlightenment in Early America* (Cambridge, MA: Harvard University Press, 2006).

7 Michael Sappol, *A Traffic of Dead Bodies: Anatomy and Embodied Social Identity in Nineteenth-Century America* (Princeton, NJ: Princeton University Press, 2002), 90–5, 168–75.

8 Ibid., 91.

9 See Sappol's chronology of "Popular Anatomical Museums and Exhibitions in America, 1774–1930," in *A Traffic of Dead Bodies*, 310–12.

10 On the freak show's establishment of bodily normativity through the production of the abnormal, see Rosemarie Garland Thomson, ed., *Freakery: Cultural Spectacles of the Extraordinary Body* (New York: New York University Press, 1996).

11 For a full account of Barnum's exhibition of Heth as well as her public autopsy, see Benjamin Reiss, *The Showman and the Slave: Race, Death, and Memory in Barnum's America* (Cambridge, MA: Harvard University Press, 2001). Reiss notes that nearly 1,500 people showed up to witness Heth's autopsy and that the audience was composed of medical students, editors, clergymen, and New York residents (135).

12 Quoted in "Great Attraction Just Arrived at Concert Hall. For a Short Time Only. Joice Heth, Nurse to Gen. George Washington," *Columbian Centinel*, September 19, 1835.

13 For an earlier example of the dissection and medical exploitation of a slave in late eighteenth-century New England, see the case of "Fortune's Bones," in P. Gabrielle Foreman, "New England's Fortune: An Inheritance of Black Bodies and Bones,"

Journal of American Studies, 49.2 (May 2015): 287–303. Until recently, Fortune's skeleton was still on exhibit at the Mattatuck Museum in Waterbury, Connecticut.

14 "Great Attraction Just Arrived at Concert Hall."

15 On "soundness" in plantation medicine and slave management, see Sharla M. Fett, *Working Cures: Healing, Health, and Power on Southern Slave Plantations* (Chapel Hill: University of North Carolina Press, 2002), 15–35.

16 Quoted in Anonymous, *The Life of Joice Heth* (New York, 1835), 10. A copy of this rare biography is available at the American Antiquarian Society.

17 On racialization through the visual field, see Frantz Fanon's formative account of being "sealed into that crushing objecthood" by the white gaze in *Black Skin, White Masks* (New York: Grove Press, 1994), 109. On race, visuality, and the power of spectacle, see also Kobena Mercer, *Welcome to the Jungle: New Positions in Black Cultural Studies* (New York: Routledge, 1994), and bell hooks, *Black Looks: Race and Representation* (Boston: South End Press, 1992). Here, I focus on the ways in which performances of race—by both race scientists and black performers—were just as likely to destabilize blackness and the location of its "essence" in or on the body being displayed.

18 Daphne A. Brooks, *Bodies in Dissent: Spectacular Performances of Race and Freedom, 1850–1910* (Durham, NC: Duke University Press, 2006), 8.

19 On the key role that sexual difference—and black women's bodies—played in the construction of scientific theories of race, see Robyn Wiegman, *American Anatomies: Theorizing Race and Gender* (Durham, NC: Duke University Press, 1995), 21–78; Siobhan B. Somerville, *Queering the Color Line: Race and the Invention of Homosexuality in American Culture* (Durham, NC: Duke University Press, 2000), 26; and Nancy Leys Stepan's influential article, "Race and Gender: The Role of Analogy in Science," *Isis* 77.2. (June 1986): 261–77.

20 Brooks, *Bodies in Dissent*, 162.

21 Joseph Roach's *Cities of the Dead: Circum-Atlantic Performance* (New York: Columbia University Press, 1996), explores how performance refuses origin stories, showing instead that, as Foucault writes in "Nietzsche, Genealogy, History," "[w]hat is found at the historical beginning of things is not the inviolable identity of their origin; it is the dissension of other things. It is disparity" (qtd. in Roach, 25). In other words, performance traffics in difference rather than inviolable origins.

22 Nathaniel Mackey, "Phrenological Whitman," *Conjunctions* 29 (Fall 1997), www.conjunctions.com.

23 Ibid. Mackey notes that Spurzheim's highly public funeral at Harvard and burial in Boston helped to further popularize his and Galls's ideas.

24 C. H. Fox, *Charley Fox's Sable Songster, Containing Many of the Best Banjo Songs, Jokes, and Germs of Wit* (New York: Frederic A. Brady, 1859), 24. American Minstrel Show Collection, Princeton University Rare Books and Special Collections.

25 On the disciplinary functions of literacy movements and black education in the nineteenth and early twentieth century, see Laura Wexler, *Tender Violence:*

Domestic Visions in an Age of U.S. Imperialism (Chapel Hill: University of North Carolina Press, 2000), 94–126, and Donald Spivey, *Schooling for the New Slavery: Black Industrial Education, 1868–1915* (Westport, CT: Greenwood Press, 1978).

26 On phrenology as a science that was practiced across social classes and by women, see Angela Willey, "'Christian Nations', 'Polygamic Races' and Women's Rights: Toward a Genealogy of Non/Monogamy and Whiteness," *Sexualities* 9.5 (2006): 533–34.

27 Fabian, *The Skull Collectors*, 49.

28 On the affiliations between phrenology and antebellum social reform, as well as Walt Whitman's practical and poetic interests in phrenology, see Mackey, "Phrenological Whitman." On the focus in phrenology on character building as a rejection of racial science's attempt to fix race to biology, see James Salazar, *Bodies of Reform: The Rhetoric of Character in Gilded Age America* (New York: New York University Press, 2010), 24–5.

29 Mia Bay notes that scientific theories of race were of enduring interest to Douglass and that his speech "The Races of Men," on Samuel George Morton and the heretical implications of polygenesis, was one of the few that he delivered on a regular basis; see Bay, *The White Image in the Black Mind: African-American Ideas about White People, 1830–1925* (New York: Oxford University Press, 2000), 68. On Douglass's speech, see also Jared Gardner, *Master Plots: Race and the Founding of an American Literature, 1787–1845* (Baltimore: John Hopkins University Press, 1998), 178–85.

30 Samuel Stanhope Smith, *An Essay on the Causes of the Variety of Complexion and Figure in the Human Species* (Philadelphia: Robert Aitken, 1787).

31 Frederick Douglass, "The Claims of the Negro, Ethnologically Considered," in *The Frederick Douglass Papers, Series One*, ed. John W. Blassingame (New Haven, CT: Yale University Press, 1982), 2:507.

32 Douglass, "Claims of the Negro," 519, 507, 503.

33 Ibid., 503; emphasis in original text.

34 R. J. M. Blackett, *Building an Antislavery Wall: Black Americans in the Atlantic Abolitionist Movement, 1830–1860* (Baton Rouge: Louisiana State University Press, 1983), 3–46.

35 Lisa Merrill, "Exhibiting Race 'under the World's Huge Glass Case': William and Ellen Craft and William Wells Brown at the Great Exhibition in Crystal Palace, London, 1851," *Slavery & Abolition* 33.2 (June 2012): 321–336.

36 William Wells Brown, *Three Years in Europe: or, Places I Have Seen and People I Have Met* (London: C. Gilpin, 1852), 224.

37 Merrill, "Exhibiting Race 'under the World's Huge Glass Case.'"

38 Carla Peterson, *Black Gotham: A Family History of African Americans in Nineteenth-Century New York City* (New Haven, CT: Yale University Press, 2011), 190–94.

39 Ibid., 193; "Crystal Palace," *Black Gotham Archive*, blackgothamarchive.org.

40 William Wells Brown, *My Southern Home: or, The South and Its People*, in *Slave Narratives after Slavery*, ed. William L. Andrews (New York: Oxford University Press, 2011), 163. On Brown's work as a medical assistant for his first owner, the physician and planter James Young, see Ezra Greenspan, *William Wells Brown: An African American Life* (New York: W. W. Norton, 2015), 34.

41 Brown, *Three Years in Europe*, 309–10.

42 Brooks, *Bodies in Dissent*, 11, 68.

43 Ibid., 69.

44 John Sekora, "Black Message/White Envelope: Genre, Authenticity, and Authority in the Antebellum Slave Narrative," *Callaloo* 32 (Summer 1987): 482–515. Sekora argues that slave autobiographies double as institutional biographies since their editorial framings and mediations by white editors register the power that white antebellum institutions, including mainstream abolition, held over black subjects.

45 Fred Moten, *In the Break: The Aesthetics of the Black Radical Tradition* (Minneapolis: University of Minnesota Press, 2003), 305; Fred Moten, "The Case of Blackness," *Criticism* 50.2 (Spring 2008): 179.

46 John Ernest, ed., *Narrative of the Life of Henry Box Brown, Written By Himself* (Chapel Hill: University of Carolina Press, 2008), 51. All quotations from Brown's narrative are taken from this edition of the text, which reprints the 1851 Manchester edition of Brown's narrative.

47 See Moten's critique and complication of the concept of self-possession in *In the Break*, 1–24.

48 Blackett, *Building an Antislavery Wall*, 32–33.

49 Ibid., 195–208, on the enthusiastic reception of black lecturers and performers among British working-class audiences. See Jayna Brown, *Babylon Girls*, 38–47, on the antagonisms between the mainstream abolitionist movement and labor struggles in England, as well as the bonds of solidarity that British labor activists and former slaves forged through shared discourses of subjugated labor.

50 Ernest, ed., *Narrative of the Life of Henry Box Brown*, 43.

51 Ibid., 48. On the growth of the global cotton industry in the nineteenth century and cotton's role in the expansion of US slavery, see Sven Beckert, *Empire of Cotton: A Global History* (New York: Knopf, 2014); Walter Johnson, *River of Dark Dreams: Slavery and Empire in the Cotton Kingdom* (Cambridge, MA: Belknap Press, 2013); Edward E. Baptist, *The Half Has Never Been Told: Slavery and the Making of American Capitalism* (New York: Basic Books, 2014).

52 Despite the fact that the introduction to the 1851 English edition of Brown's narrative has been attributed to Reverend Thomas Gardiner Lee of Salford, England, I want to maintain Brown's control over this later iteration of his narrative. By soliciting and incorporating an introduction from a local authority, while incorporating advertisements, songs, and other media in the revised text, Brown took on an authoritative role: that of the editor of his own slave narrative. Moreover, Brown's English readers would have read the narrative, including the introduction, as Brown's own writing.

53 Ernest, ed., *Narrative of the Life of Henry Box Brown*, 55.

54 Ibid., 62.

55 Samuel Fielden, *Autobiography of Samuel Fielden*, in *The Autobiographies of the Haymarket Martyrs*, ed. Philip S. Foner (New York: Humanities Press, 1969), 142.

56 Ibid.

57 Ibid.

58 *West London Observer*, March 19, 1859, quoted in Jeffrey Ruggles, *The Unboxing of Henry Brown* (Richmond: Library of Virginia, 2003), 151.

59 *Cardiff Times*, March 11, 1864.

60 Morus, *Frankenstein's Children*, 70.

61 Ibid., 70–98.

62 On the refusal of work in more contemporary contexts, see Kathi Weeks, *The Problem with Work: Feminism, Marxism, Antiwork Politics, and Postwork Imaginaries* (Durham, NC: Duke University Press, 2011).

63 Quoted in Ruggles, *The Unboxing of Henry Brown*, 156.

64 Morus, *Frankenstein's Children*.

65 Bruno Latour, *Science in Action* (Cambridge, MA: Harvard University Press, 1988).

66 See www.uclan.ac.uk.

67 Kathy Chater, "From Slavery to Show Business," *Ancestors* (December 2005): 32–33; Alan Rice, *Creating Memorials, Building Identities: The Politics of Memory in the Black Atlantic* (Liverpool: Liverpool University Press, 2010), 64.

68 Martha J. Cutter, "Will the Real Henry 'Box' Brown Please Stand Up?," *Commonplace: The Journal of Early American Life* 16.1 (Fall 2015), common-place.org.

69 Ruggles, *Unboxing Henry Brown*, 159.

70 Saidiya V. Hartman, *Scenes of Subjection: Terror, Slavery, and Self-Making in Nineteenth-Century America* (New York: Oxford University Press, 1997), 51, 61. Throughout her study, Hartman challenges uncritical celebrations of agency that ignore the political, economic, legal, and other institutions that delimited the field of agency for enslaved and nominally free people during slavery and Reconstruction.

71 See John Ernest's introduction to his edition of the *Narrative of the Life of Henry Box Brown*, 27.

72 "The Hymn of Thanksgiving" also appeared in Brown's 1849 narrative.

73 Ernest, ed., Introduction, *Narrative of the Life of Henry Box Brown*, 28.

74 Ernest, ed., *Narrative of the Life of Henry Box Brown*, 89–90.

75 Ibid., 91.

76 Ibid., 91–92.

77 Many thanks to Edlie Wong for bringing this aspect of Brown's narrative to my attention.

78 Ernest, ed., *Narrative of the Life of Henry Box Brown*, 83.

79 Fabian, *The Skull Collectors*, 94.

CHAPTER 4. DELANY'S COMET

1 Lynn McDonald, "Florence Nightingale and the Early Origins of Evidence-Based Nursing," *Evidence-Based Nursing* 4 (2001): 68–9.

2 "International Statistical Congress, Proceedings of the Sanitary Section," *Lancet,* July 28, 1860. Prompted by the intolerable conditions and widespread racial terror created by the passage of the Fugitive Slave Act, Delany fled to Chatham, Canada West, in 1856 and lived there until the start of the Civil War.

3 "A Physician of Colour," *Lancet,* July 28, 1860.

4 Ibid.

5 Ibid.

6 See Richard Blackett, "In Search of International Support for African Coloniza-tion: Martin R. Delany's Visit to England, 1860," *Canadian Journal of History / Annales canadiennes d'histoire* 10.3 (December 1975): 316–19.

7 *Manchester Weekly Advertiser,* July 21, 1860.

8 "Dallas and Delany," *Douglass' Monthly,* September 1860.

9 A. B. Longstreet, Letter in the *Morning Chronicle,* July 23, 1860.

10 Frantz Fanon, *Black Skin, White Masks,* trans. Charles Lam Marmann (New York: Grove Press, 1967), 109.

11 Ibid.

12 Frank [Frances] A. Rollin, *Life and Public Services of Martin R. Delany* (1868, 1883), in *Two Biographies by African-American Women,* ed. Henry Louis Gates, Jr. (New York: Oxford University Press, 1991), 118. This section of the text appears in quotations, indicating that Delany dictated the scene to Rollin.

13 Ibid., 119; emphasis in original. Richard Blackett notes that reports of the incident and Brougham's exact words to Dallas vary in different newspaper accounts. See Blackett, "In Search of International Support for African Colonization," 317. Similarly, Delany's response varies in different accounts. Here, I rely on Delany's retrospective recall of his statement at the event, since it is valuable to have access to Delany's own recollection of his activities and words at the Statistical Congress. Robert Levine also offers an account of the events surrounding Delany at the Sta-tistical Congress. See Levine, *Martin Delany, Frederick Douglass, and the Politics of Representative Identity* (Chapel Hill: University of North Carolina Press, 1997), 187–88.

14 Douglass, "Dallas and Delany."

15 Blackett offers an overview of the international newspaper coverage of Delany's involvement in the congress. See Blackett, "In Search of International Support for African Colonization," 316–19.

16 Jeffory A. Clymer, "Martin Delany's *Blake* and the Transnational Politics of Property," *American Literary History* 15.4 (2003): 709–31; Katy Chiles, "Within and without Raced Nations: Intratextuality, Martin Delany, and *Blake; or the Huts of America,*" *American Literature* 80.2 (June 2008): 323–52; Andy Doolan, "'Be Cautious of the Word Rebel': Race, Revolution, and Transnational History in

Martin Delany's *Blake; or, The Huts of America*," *American Literature* 81.1 (March 2009): 153–79; Ifeoma C. K. Nwankwo, "The Promises and Perils of US African-American Hemispherism: Latin America in Martin Delany's *Blake* and Gayle Jones's *Mosquito*," *American Literary History* 18.3 (Fall 2006): 579–99.

17 Rollin, *Life and Public Services of Martin R. Delany*, 19.

18 Andrews, Introduction, *Two Biographies by African-American Women*, xxxv.

19 Levine, *Martin Delany, Frederick Douglass*, 219–23. In his introduction to Rollin's biography, William L. Andrews seems less concerned with the biases and inaccuracies in the text, instead praising Rollin for introducing a thoroughly analytic approach into the genre of nineteenth-century African American biography. See Andrews, Introduction, *Two Biographies by African-American Women*, xxxiii–xliii.

20 Rollin, *Life and Public Services of Martin R. Delany*, 46.

21 Levine, *Martin Delany, Frederick Douglass*, 25.

22 Rollin, *Life and Public Services of Martin R. Delany*, 54.

23 On the history of the *Christian Recorder* in the nineteenth century, see Eric Gardner, *Black Print Unbound: The "Christian Recorder," African American Literature, and Periodical Culture* (New York: Oxford University Press, 2015).

24 On Delany's acceptance to Harvard Medical School and the conditions of his ejection, see Louis Menand, *The Metaphysical Club: A Story of Ideas in America* (New York: Farrar, Straus, and Giroux, 2001), 7–9.

25 Toyin Falola, Introduction, Martin R. Delany, *The Condition, Elevation, Emigration, and Destiny of the Colored People of the United States and Official Report of the Niger Valley Exploring Party* (Amherst, NY: Humanity Books, 2004), 11.

26 Rollin, *Life and Public Services of Martin R. Delany*, 69.

27 In the 1850s, African American proponents of emigration had to fight against an earlier history of pro-slavery interests in colonization. In 1816, the American Colonization Society (ACS) proposed its plan to expatriate free African Americans to the African state that would eventually become Liberia. Critics argued that the ACS was composed of slaveholders and other pro-slavery advocates who wanted to rid the country of freemen and women so that regimes of enslavement in the United States could continue undisturbed. African American proponents of emigration continued throughout the 1850s to struggle against critiques that emigration was just a scheme to depopulate African Americans from the United States.

28 Delany, *Condition*, 182; italics are mine.

29 Ibid., 186.

30 Treatments of Delany's trip to West Africa include Tunde Adeleke's *Unafrican Americans: Nineteenth-Century Black Nationalists and the Civilizing Mission* (Lexington: University Press of Kentucky, 1998), and Howard H. Bell's introduction to Delany and Robert Campbell's writings on their expeditions to Africa in *Search for a Place: Black Separatism and Africa, 1860*, ed. Howard H. Bell (Ann Arbor: University of Michigan Press, 1969), 1–22.

31 Delany, *The Official Report of the Niger Valley Exploring Party*, in Bell, ed., *Search for a Place*, 39.

32 Ibid., 132.

33 The treaty was reprinted from the *New York Daily Times* in the January 16, 1861, edition of the *Weekly Anglo-African*. This issue also ran an inflamed letter from James McCune Smith, who was furious about the Niger Valley plot because he believed that Delany and his party intended to uphold all of the Igbo's laws and customs, including slaveholding.

34 On the structuring of the world capitalist economy around cotton production in the nineteenth century, see Sven Beckert, *Empire of Cotton: A Global History* (New York: Knopf, 2014); Walter Johnson, *River of Dark Dreams: Slavery and Empire in the Cotton Kingdom* (Cambridge, MA: Belknap Press, 2013); Edward E. Baptist, *The Half Has Never Been Told: Slavery and the Making of American Capitalism* (New York: Basic Books, 2014). Karl Marx was an astute observer of the transatlantic cotton crisis of the 1860s. See his writings from the *New York Daily Tribune* and the Vienna *Presse* in Karl Marx and Frederick Engels, *The Civil War in the United States* (New York: International Publishers, 1937). Recent analyses of Marx's thinking on American slavery, its relationship to an increasingly global industrial system in the mid-nineteenth century, and the economic motivations of the Civil War include Robin Blackburn, *An Unfinished Revolution: Karl Marx and Abraham Lincoln* (New York: Verso, 2011), and Kevin B. Anderson, *Marx at the Margins: On Nationalism, Ethnicity, and Non-Western Societies* (Chicago: University of Chicago Press, 2010), 79–114.

35 Rollin, *Life and Public Services of Martin R. Delany*, 97–98.

36 Blackett, "In Search of International Support for African Colonization," 316–20.

37 *Anglo-African Magazine*, vol. 1 (New York: Arno Press and the New York Times, 1968), 20–21.

38 See the advertisement for the *Anglo-African* in the September 24, 1859, issue of the *Weekly Anglo-African*.

39 The serialization of *Blake* was indeed uneven. When it first appeared in the *Anglo-African* in January 1859, Hamilton noted that they were publishing Chapters 28–30 because they had not secured rights from Delany to publish other sections of the novel. Hamilton emphasized the fact that Delany held the copyright for the book. The rights were apparently soon secured: the February 1859 issue restarted the serial with the first chapter of the novel.

40 The newspaper's focus on science, statistics, and philosophy disappeared when the *Weekly* was sold to James Redpath at the end of 1861 and later, when the paper reverted to the ownership of Robert Hamilton, Thomas's brother.

41 Delany, "The Attraction of Planets," *Anglo-African Magazine*, 17. See also George B. Vashon, "The Successive Advances of Astronomy," *Anglo-African Magazine*, 204.

42 Ibid., 20.

43 Delany, "The Fugitives," *Anglo-African Magazine*, 20–29. Chapters 28–30 of *Blake* were the first to appear in the *Anglo-African* (in the inaugural January 1859 issue).

44 Delany, "Comets," *Anglo-African Magazine*, 59–60.

45 Eric Gardner notes that the black San Francisco newspaper, *Mirror of the Times*, complained about a lecture on "Comets" by Peter Cole in its May 30, 1857, issue. Cole, who immigrated to San Francisco sometime in the 1850s, was disparaged by the paper, which suggested he would "employ his time much better in lecturing on some subject that he knows something about." Gardner, *Unexpected Places: Relocating Nineteenth-Century African American Literature* (Jackson: University Press of Mississippi, 2011), 96.

46 On the history of national and Southern interest in annexing Cuba, see Robert E. May, *The Southern Dream of a Caribbean Empire: 1854–1861* (Baton Rouge: Louisiana State University Press, 1973).

47 Clymer, "Martin Delany's *Blake*," 719; Eric Sundquist, *To Wake the Nations: Race in the Making of American Literature* (Cambridge, MA: Harvard University Press, 1998), 11.

48 Martin Delany, *Blake; or, The Huts of America*, ed. Floyd Miller (Boston: Beacon Press, 1970), 241. All subsequent citations of the novel come from Miller's 1970 edition.

49 Placido's presence in the novel is striking since Cuban authorities executed the poet in 1844, during La Escalera, for conspiring against the state. The narrative effectively resurrects Placido and places him at the center of insurrectionary activity in 1850s Cuba.

50 Editor's Note, *Anglo-African Magazine*, 20.

51 Notable exceptions include Levine's introduction to Delany's article "Comets" in his edited volume, *Martin R. Delany: A Documentary Reader* (Chapel Hill: University of North Carolina Press, 2003), 313–14. Paul Gilroy also highlights Delany's medical career and scientific activities, including his attendance at the International Statistical Congress. See Gilroy, *The Black Atlantic: Modernity and Double Consciousness*, repr. ed. (Cambridge, MA: Harvard University Press, 1993), 17.

52 Delany, *Blake*, 66–67.

53 Ibid., 101.

54 Ibid., 16, 68.

55 Ibid., 68.

56 On the aesthetics, values, and readership practices enabled by the serial form, see Linda K. Hughes and Michael Lund, *The Victorian Serial* (Charlottesville: University of Virginia Press, 1991).

57 For an overview of exobiology, the study of life beyond the terrestrial biosphere, see Robert Markley, *Dying Planet: Mars in Science and the Imagination* (Durham, NC: Duke University Press, 2005), 9.

58 Delany, *Blake*, 98.

59 On Delany's affiliation with freemasonry, see Levine, *Martin Delany, Frederick Douglass*, 7–12, and Maurice O. Wallace, *Constructing the Black Masculine: Identity and Ideality in African American Men's Literature and Culture, 1775–1995* (Durham, NC: Duke University Press, 2002), 53–81. On the history of freemasonry in

the early United States, see Steven C. Bullock, *Revolutionary Brotherhood: Free-masonry and the Transformation of the American Social Order, 1730–1840* (Chapel Hill: University of North Carolina Press, 1998). On African American freemasonry, see Peter P. Hinks and Stephen Kantrowitz, eds., *All Men Free and Brethren: Essays on the History of African American Freemasonry* (Ithaca, NY: Cornell University Press, 2013), and Corey D. B. Walker, *A Noble Fight: African American Freemasonry and the Struggle for Democracy in America* (Urbana: University of Illinois Press, 2008).

60   Quoted in Levine, *Martin Delany, Frederick Douglass*, 292.

61   Delany, *Blake*, 132.

62   Ibid., 133.

63   Ibid., 134.

64   Ibid., 136–37.

65   Levine, *Martin Delany, Frederick Douglass*, 194.

66   Delany, *Blake*, 112, 113.

67   Ibid., 112.

68   Ibid., 114, 126.

69   Ibid.,124.

70   Ibid.

71   Ibid., 108–15.

72   Jane Bennett, *Vibrant Matter: A Political Ecology of Things* (Durham, NC: Duke University Press, 2009), viii.

73   On "actant" as a nonanthropomorphic concept of agency, see Bruno Latour, *Politics of Nature: How to Bring the Sciences into Democracy*, trans. Catherine Porter (Cambridge, MA: Harvard University Press, 2004), 75–77, 237.

74   Fred Moten, *In the Break: The Aesthetics of the Black Radical Tradition* (Minneapolis: University of Minnesota Press, 2003), 1.

75   Gilles Deleuze, *Essays Critical and Clinical,* trans. Daniel W. Smith and Michael A. Greco (Minneapolis: University of Minnesota Press, 1997). Countering the idea that the modern novel deals with the realm of the private and focuses on the interior life of its characters, Deleuze argues that all literature is a "public affair," a collective enunciation that replaces the personal and the possessive form with the impersonal: "It discovers beneath apparent persons the power of an impersonal—which is not a generality but a singularity at the highest point" (3).

76   Fred Moten, "Black Op," *PMLA* 123.5 (October 2008): 1743–47. See also Fred Moten, *In the Break*, 1–23, on how blackness disrupts the assumed equivalence between personhood and subjectivity.

77   Sylvia Wynter, "Unsettling the Coloniality of Being/Power/Truth/Freedom: Toward the Human, After Man, Its Overrepresentation—An Argument," *CR: The New Centennial Review* 3.3 (Fall 2003): 257–337.

78   Thomas Hamilton, "Apology (Introductory)," *Anglo-African Magazine*, 2.

79   Gilles Deleuze and Félix Guattari, *A Thousand Plateaus: Capitalism and Schizophrenia*, trans. Brian Massumi (Minneapolis: University of Minnesota Press,

1987), 232–309. Massumi's translation also refers to the process of individuation and becoming in the terms of fugitivity, as "fugitive beings" (271, 281).

80 On the "documentary status" of black letters, see Henry Louis Gates, Jr., *Figures in Black: Words, Signs, and the "Racial" Self* (New York: Oxford University Press, 1989), 3.

81 William L. Andrews, *To Tell a Free Story: The First Century of Afro-American Autobiography, 1760–1865* (Urbana: University of Illinois Press, 1986), 1.

82 The empirical footnotes are particularly fascinating since many of them are written from the perspective of Delany instead of Henry Holland/Blake. Levine says that these "authenticating footnotes" were added by Delany after his 1859 expedition to West Africa. See Levine, *Martin Delany, Frederick Douglass*, 179.

83 Samuel A. Cartwright, "How to Save the Republic, and the Position of the South in the Union," *De Bow's Review* 11.2 (August 1851): 184–97; emphasis in original.

84 Samuel A. Cartwright, "Report on the Diseases and Physical Peculiarities of the Negro Race," in *The Nature of Difference: Sciences of Race in the United States from Jefferson to Genomics*, ed. Evelynn M. Hammonds and Rebecca M. Herzig (Cambridge, MA: MIT Press, 2008), 67–86. An excerpt from Cartwright's report listing his taxonomy of fictive diseases also appeared in *De Bow's Review*, suggesting the wide circulation of Cartwright's diseases in popular Southern discourse. Cartwright often pointed to the "bowed" legs of slaves as proof of the biological inferiority of the black race (ergo, African and African-descended people were made by God to be slaves). James McCune Smith responded to Cartwright by asserting that bowed legs were from rickets, rampant among slaves because of their inadequate diet. See James McCune Smith, "On the Fourteenth Query of Thomas Jefferson's Notes on Virginia," *Anglo-African Magazine*, 231.

85 Cartwright, "Report on the Diseases and Physical Peculiarities of the Negro Race," 81.

86 Ibid.

87 See, for example, Frederick Douglass, "The Claims of the Negro, Ethnologically Considered," in *The Frederick Douglass Papers, Series One*, ed. John W. Blassingame (New Haven, CT: Yale University Press, 1982), 2:497–525.

88 Samuel R. Delany, "Racism and Science Fiction," in *Dark Matter: A Century of Speculative Fiction from the African Diaspora*, ed. Sheree R. Thomas (New York: Aspect Books, 2000), 383.

89 Martin Delany, *Principia of Ethnology: The Origin of Races and Color, with an Archaeological Compendium of Ethiopian and Egyptian Civilization, from Years of Careful Examination and Enquiry* (Philadelphia: Harper and Row, 1879), 92.

CHAPTER 5. SARAH'S CABINET

1 Lynda Roscoe Hartigan notes that Lydia Maria Child recommended to Lewis that she study anatomy. See Hartigan, *Sharing Traditions: Five Black Artists in Nineteenth-Century America* (Washington, DC: Smithsonian Institution Press,

1985), 90. The historical connections between art and anatomy are substantial, and that history also shaped race science: for example, the Dutch anatomist and artist Petrus Camper's African "facial angle" became central to nineteenth-century craniology's quest to establish the morphological separation of Africans from other peoples.

2 Pauline E. Hopkins, "Artists," in *Daughter of the Revolution: The Major Nonfiction Works of Pauline E. Hopkins*, ed. Ira Dworkin (New Brunswisk, NJ: Rutgers University Press, 2007), 184–92. "Artists" originally appeared as part of Hopkins's "Famous Women of the Negro Race," a series published in the *Colored American Magazine* in 1901 and 1902. Hopkins's entry on Edmonia Lewis cribs from William Wells Brown's *The Rising Son; or, The Antecedents and Advancement of the Colored Race* (1874, 1882); her emendations to Brown's text reflect her feminist sensibilities as well as the politics of her editing work. For example, Hopkins expunged Brown's note that Lewis's manners were "childlike and simple" and replaced it with "her manners are unassuming" (Hopkins 186).

3 William R. Stanton, *The Leopard's Spots: Scientific Attitudes toward Race in America, 1815–1859* (Chicago: University of Chicago Press, 1960); Winthrop Jordan, *White over Black: American Attitudes toward the Negro, 1550–1812* (Chapel Hill: University of North Carolina Press, 1968); George Frederickson, *The Black Image in the White Mind: The Debate on Afro-American Character and Destiny, 1817–1914* (New York: Harper and Row, 1971); Stephen Jay Gould, *The Mismeasure of Man*, rev. ed. (New York: W. W. Norton, 1996).

4 Gould, *The Mismeasure of Man*, 93–104.

5 Nancy Leys Stepan, "Race and Gender: The Role of Analogy in Science," *Isis* 77.2 (June 1986): 263–64.

6 Robyn Wiegman, *American Anatomies: Theorizing Race and Gender* (Durham, NC: Duke University Press, 1995), 44.

7 Ann Fabian's *The Skull Collectors: Race, Science, and America's Unburied Dead* (Chicago: University of Chicago Press, 2010) does illustrate how craniology was used to delineate human differences beyond race, including age, geographical origin, and sex.

8 Kyla C. Schuller's essay, "Taxonomies of Feeling: The Epistemology of Sentimentalism in Late-Nineteenth-Century Racial and Sexual Science," *American Quarterly* 64.2 (2012): 277–99, is an important contribution to the still under-theorized connections between sex and race in nineteenth-century scientific discourse. See also Siobhan B. Somerville, *Queering the Color Line: Race and the Invention of Homosexuality in American Culture* (Durham, N.C.: Duke University Press, 2000), 15–38, and Alys Eve Weinbaum on "the race/reproduction bind" in *Wayward Reproductions: Genealogies of Race and Nation in Transatlantic Modern Thought* (Durham, NC: Duke University Press, 2004).

9 Part of the groundbreaking nature of Darwin's *Voyage of the Beagle* as well as the ethnological writings of James McCune Smith, a fellow traveler with Darwin, is the fact that neither censored the realities of sexual desire and practice.

10 Jennifer C. Nash has compellingly argued that the continual invocation of the "Hottentot Venus" in black feminism has enabled a pernicious anti-pornography framework to take shape within black feminism itself. See Nash, "Strange Bedfellows: Black Feminism and Antipornography Feminism," *Social Text* 26.4 (2008): 52. For another trenchant critique of the politics of restaging spectacles of racialized and gendered violence, see Saidiya V. Hartman, *Scenes of Subjection: Terror, Slavery, and Self-Making in Nineteenth-century America* (New York: Oxford University Press, 1997), 3–4, 17–23.

11 For example, a recent biography of Baartman, *Sara Baartman and the Hottentot Venus: A Ghost Story and Biography* (Princeton, NJ: Princeton University Press, 2009) by Clifton Crais and Pamela Scully, presents a careful portrayal of Baartman and her life, but still falls into the trap of reifying Baartman as object, especially through the book's copious use of visual images, including several racist caricatures of Baartman taken from nineteenth-century print and visual culture. Deborah Willis's edited collection, *Black Venus 2010: They Called Her "Hottentot"* (Philadelphia: Temple University Press, 2010), which focuses on the representational history of Baartman, provides a model for how Baartman and her legacy might be more productively addressed in scholarship. In addition to essays that provide relevant nineteenth-century contexts and histories, the collection provides an overview to the myriad forms of contemporary art, film, poetry, prose, and theater that have focused on Baartman and her complicated legacies, particularly in the representation of black women's bodies and desires.

12 Soyica Diggs Colbert, *The African American Theatrical Body: Reception, Performance, and the Stage* (New York: Cambridge University Press, 2011), 1–19.

13 Carla L. Peterson, "Subject to Speculation: Assessing the Lives of African-American Women in the Nineteenth Century," in *Women's Studies in Transition: The Pursuit of Interdisciplinarity*, ed. Kate Conway-Turner, Suzanne Cherin, Jessica Schiffman, and Kathleen Doherty Turkel (Cranbury, NJ; Associated University Presses, 1998), 116, 114.

14 Tina Gianquitto, *"Good Observers of Nature:" American Women and the Scientific Study of the Natural World, 1820–1885* (Athens: University of Georgia Press, 2007); Ann B. Shteir, *Cultivating Women, Cultivating Science: Flora's Daughters and Botany in England, 1760–1860* (Baltimore: John Hopkins University Press, 1999); Susan Scott Parrish, *American Curiosity: Cultures of Natural History in the Colonial British Atlantic World* (Chapel Hill: University of North Carolina Press, 2006), 174–214; Elizabeth B. Keeney, *The Botanizers: Amateur Scientists in Nineteenth-Century America* (Chapel Hill: University of North Carolina Press, 1992), 69–82.

15 Kim Tolley, *The Science Education of American Girls: A Historical Perspective* (New York: Routledge, 2002); Mary Kelley, *Learning to Stand and Speak: Women, Education, and Public Life in America's Republic* (Chapel Hill: University of North Carolina Press, 2006), 66–111.

16 On the construction of black counterpublics as protections against a racist public sphere, see Joanna Brooks, "The Early American Public Sphere and the Emer-

gence of a Black Print Counterpublic," *William and Mary Quarterly* 62.1 (January 2005): 67–92.

17 Julie Winch, *Philadelphia's Black Elite: Activism, Accommodation, and the Struggle for Autonomy, 1787–1848* (Philadelphia: Temple University Press, 1988).

18 On African American employment and work conditions in antebellum Philadelphia, see Julie Winch, Introduction, *The Elite of Our People: Joseph Willson's Sketches of Upper-class Black Life in Antebellum Philadelphia* (University Park: Pennsylvania State University Press, 2000), 10–25.

19 See *Register of Trades of the Colored People in the City of Philadelphia and Districts* (Philadelphia: Merrihew and Gunn, 1838). Henry M. Minton offers an early analysis of the 1838 register in *Early History of Negroes in Business in Philadelphia, Read before the American [Negro] Historical Society, March, 1913.* This text is available at the Library Company of Philadelphia.

20 On the "black elite" in antebellum Philadelphia, see Winch, *Philadelphia's Black Elite*; Winch, *The Elite of Our People*; and Erica Armstrong Dunbar, *A Fragile Freedom: African American Women and Emancipation in the Antebellum City* (New Haven, CT: Yale University Press, 2008).

21 Dunbar, *A Fragile Freedom*, 99. There was a handful of other black churches in Philadelphia, but Dunbar notes that almost 50 percent of the black community attended Mother Bethel.

22 Banneker Institute Records, Lectures and Debates Book, 1859–1861, Leon Gardiner Collection of American Negro Historical Society Records, Historical Society of Pennsylvania (HSP).

23 Jacob C. White, Jr., "Phrenology," Banneker Institute Records, Constitution, Minutes, Reports, Bills and Receipts, Printed Material, Lectures, 1790–1865 and undated, Leon Gardiner Collection of American Negro Historical Society Records, HSP. Roger Lane notes that in the late 1890s, Jacob White and William Dorsey, who was an artist and amateur historian of black Philadelphia, served as consultants to W. E. B. Du Bois while he was writing *The Philadelphia Negro*. White and Dorsey were also co-founders of the American Negro Historical Society. Lane, *William Dorsey's Philadelphia & Ours: On the Past and Future of the Black City in America* (New York: Oxford University Press, 1991), 107.

24 Delany, *Condition*, 133. Bias's pamphlet does not appear to have survived.

25 Winch, *The Elite of Our People*, 21–22, 127 n. 19.

26 Brenda Stevenson, ed., *The Journals of Charlotte Forten Grimké* (New York: Oxford University Press, 1988), 105, 107, 152–53. On Forten's education in Salem, see also Mary Kelley, *Learning to Stand and Speak*, 169–71. With Salem being a major port city, its schools included a strong curriculum in astronomy, mathematics, and other fields related to navigation and sailing. Local merchants and others involved with the city's seafaring trades provided financial support to Salem's schools.

27 Lane, *William Dorsey's Philadelphia & Ours*, 120. For an overview of black artists in nineteenth-century Philadelphia, including Robert Douglass and his cousin,

David Bowser, see ibid., 120–25, and Steven Loring Jones, "'A Keen Sense of the Artistic': African American Material Culture in 19th Century Philadelphia," *International Review of African American Art* 12.2 (1995): 4–29. See also Aston Gonzalez, "The Art of Racial Politics: The Work of Robert Douglass Jr., 1833–46," *Pennsylvania Magazine of History and Biography* 138.1 (January 2014): 5–37.

28 For more background on the life and activities of Douglass as well as her political family, see Dorothy Sterling, *We Are Your Sisters: Black Women in the Nineteenth Century,* rev. ed. (New York: W. W. Norton, 1997), 111–50; Marie J. Lindhorst, *Sarah Mapps Douglass: The Emergence of an African American Educator/Activist in Nineteenth-Century Philadelphia,* PhD diss. (University of Pennsylvania, 1995); Winch, *The Elite of Our People,* 1–78; Winch, *Philadelphia's Black Elite*; Martha Jones, *All Bound Up Together: The Woman Question in African American Public Culture, 1830–1900* (Chapel Hill: University of North Carolina Press, 2007). On Douglass in the context of Philadelphia abolitionism, see Jean Fagan Yellin and John C. Van Horne, eds., *The Abolitionist Sisterhood: Women's Political Culture in Antebellum America* (Ithaca, NY: Cornell University Press, 1994), and Dunbar, *A Fragile Freedom.*

29 Lindhorst, *Sarah Mapps Douglass*, 84.

30 "Seventh Annual Report," *Pennsylvania Freeman*, March 17, 1841. Douglass notes in this letter that she had been the sole teacher at her school for thirteen years, which suggests that she took it over in the late 1820s. However, it seems more plausible that Douglass did not take over the school until after returning from New York in 1834.

31 In 1837, Samuel Cornish, editor of the New York newspaper the *Colored American,* visited "Miss Sarah Douglass' school" and raved about the teacher and her students, stating that he and his group "passed two of the most gratifying, satisfactory hours of our life, with Miss Douglass and her interesting, improving scholars." Cornish noted that Douglass was teaching her class of forty in all of the branches of a "good and solid female education." See *Colored American*, December 2, 1837.

32 Margaret Hope Bacon, *Sarah Mapps Douglass, Faithful Attender of Quaker Meeting: View from the Back Bench* (Philadelphia: Quaker Press, 2003), 25.

33 *Fourth Annual Announcement of the Female Medical College of Pennsylvania, for Session 1853–1854* (Philadelphia: William S. Young, 1853); *Eighth Annual Announcement of the Female Medical College of Pennsylvania, for the Session 1857–1858* (Philadelphia: Deacon and Peterson, 1857). Margaret Bacon notes that Douglass attended lectures at the Pennsylvania Medical University in 1853, 1855, and 1858. See Bacon, *Sarah Mapps Douglass*, 24.

34 Calvin Cutter's *First Book of Anatomy and Hygiene* (1847, 1854), Jane Taylor's *Primary Lessons in Physiology* (1839, 1848), Worthington Hooker's *The Child's Book of Nature* (1857), and Asa Gray's "Gray's Botany," which likely refers either to Gray's *First Lessons in Botany and Vegetable Physiology* (1857) or his *Botany for Young People and Common Schools* (1858).

35 See *Catalogue of the Library in the Reading Room of the Institute for Colored Youth* (Philadelphia: Joseph Bakestraw, 1853).

36 *Colored American*, December 2, 1837.

37 Lindhorst, *Sarah Mapps Douglass*, 98.

38 Banneker Institute Minute Book, 1855–1859, March 16, 1859, March 30, 1859, in Leon Gardiner Collection of American Negro Historical Society Records, HSP.

39 Willson, *Sketches of the Higher Classes of Philadelphia*, in Winch, *The Elite of Our People*, 118.

40 Ibid.

41 Emma Jones Lapsansky, "The World the Agitators Made: The Counterculture of Agitation in Urban Philadelphia," in *The Abolitionist Sisterhood*, ed. Yellin and Van Horne, 97. For a comprehensive analysis of the activities of the Banneker Institute and its membership, see also Emma Jones Lapsansky, "'Discipline to the Mind': Philadelphia's Banneker Institute, 1854–1872," *Pennsylvania Magazine of History and Biography* 117.1–2 (January–April 1993): 83–102.

42 Dunbar, *A Fragile Freedom*, 123.

43 Tolley, *The Science Education of American Girls*, 1–11.

44 *Objects and Regulations of the Institute for Colored Youth* (Philadelphia: Merrihew and Thompson, 1860), 30.

45 Bacon, *Sarah Mapps Douglass*, 33. Bacon says that this and other pecuniary arrangements, including a modest sum of money left to Douglass in the will of one of members of the board of managers, suggest that Douglass struggled with financial difficulties late in her life.

46 Banneker Institute Minute Book, 1855–1859, Leon Gardiner Collection, HSP. Emma Lapsansky has a different take on the institute, considering it in terms of the rationalization of time and discipline in the mid-nineteenth century and reading it as an organization that was highly invested in forms of self-policing and self-discipline. See Lapsansky, "'Discipline to the Mind.'"

47 Michael Sappol, *A Traffic of Dead Bodies: Anatomy and Embodied Social Identity in Nineteenth-Century America* (Princeton, NJ: Princeton University Press, 2002), 172.

48 Sarah Mapps Douglass, "A Good Habit Recommended," *Anglo-African Magazine*, vol. 1 (New York: Arno Press and the *New York Times*, 1968), 154.

49 On sentimentalism as a "camouflage" for black women, see P. Gabrielle Foreman, *Activist Sentiments: Reading Black Women in the Nineteenth Century* (Urbana: University of Illinois Press, 2009), 19–21.

50 Alondra Nelson, *Body and Soul: The Black Panther Party and the Fight against Medical Discrimination* (Minneapolis: University of Minnesota Press, 2011), 5–12.

51 On the regular public performance of the private sphere in and through publication, see Elizabeth Maddock Dillon, *The Gender of Freedom: Fictions of Liberalism and the Literary Public Sphere* (Stanford, CA: Stanford University Press, 2004).

52 Sarah Mapps Douglass to Rebecca White, February 9, 1862, Box 11, Josiah White Papers, Quaker Collection, Haverford College; the parenthetical notation is found in the original letter.

53 *Every-Day Wonders Illustrated: or, Facts in Physiology which All Should Know* (Philadelphia: American Sunday-School Union, 185?).

54 On this particular course of lectures, see also "Mrs. Douglass' Lectures," *Weekly Anglo-African*, July 23, 1859.

55 Lindhorst, *Sarah Mapps Douglass*, 172.

56 Sally Gregory Kohlstedt, "Parlors, Primers, and Public Schooling: Education for Science in Nineteenth-Century America," *Isis* 81.3 (September 1990): 429.

57 Jasmine Nichole Cobb, *Picture Freedom: Remaking Black Visuality in the Early Nineteenth Century* (New York: New York University Press, 2015), 66.

58 Catherine E. Kelly, *In the New England Fashion: Reshaping Women's Lives in the Nineteenth Century* (Ithaca, NY: Cornell University Press, 1999), 77–9. Kelly also offers an overview of friendship culture among white New England women in the period.

59 James N. Green, "The Rise of Book Publishing," in *A History of the Book in America; Volume 2, An Extensive Republic: Print, Culture, and Society in the New Nation, 1790–1840*, ed. Robert A. Gross and Mary Kelley (Chapel Hill: University of North Carolina Press), 117.

60 On the emergence of the gift book industry out of transformations and improvements in antebellum print technology and bookmaking, see Lara Langer Cohen, *The Fabrication of American Literature: Fraudulence and Antebellum Print Culture* (Philadelphia: University of Pennsylvania Press, 2011), 7–10.

61 See, for example, Almira H. Lincoln, *Familiar Lectures on Botany. Including Practical and Elemental Botany, with Generic and Specific Descriptions of the Most Common Native and Foreign Plants, and a Vocabulary of Botanical Terms. For the Use of Higher Schools and Academies* (Hartford, CT: H. and F. J. Huntingdon, 1829), 23. See also Gianquitto, "*Good Observers of Nature*," 15–56.

62 Amy Matilda Cassey Friendship Album, Mary Anne Dickerson Friendship Album, Martina Dickerson Friendship Album, Library Company of Philadelphia. The friendship album held at Howard University belonged to another Philadelphian, Mary Virginia Wood Forten, the mother of Charlotte Forten Grimké. Francis J. Grimké Papers, Box 40–44, Folder 1908, Moorland-Spingarn Research Center, Howard University.

63 On the circulation and use of the emblem of the female slave supplicant by women abolitionists, see Jean Fagan Yellin, *Women & Sisters: The Antislavery Feminists in American Culture* (New Haven, CT: Yale University Press, 1989). See also Phillip Lapsansky, "Graphic Discord: Abolitionist and Antiabolitionist Images," in *The Abolitionist Sisterhood: Women's Political Culture in Antebellum America*, ed. Jean Fagan Yellin and John C. Van Horne (Ithaca, NY: Cornell University Press, 1994), 204–9.

64 Douglass, Amy Matilda Cassey Album, Library Company of Philadelphia, 24.

65 Gwendolyn DuBois Shaw, *Portraits of a People: Picturing African Americans in the Nineteenth Century* (Seattle: University of Washington Press, 2006), 49.

66 Cobb, *Picture Freedom*, 66–110.

67 On the "camouflage" provided by sentimentalism's perceived transparency and supposedly easy relationship to the "truth," see Foreman, *Activist Sentiments*, 6–8.

68 "Catharine Casey's First Fling," *Christian Recorder*, June 27, 1878; "Philadelphia Matters," *Christian Recorder*, February 19, 1880; *Christian Recorder*, September 14, 1882. Douglass's obituary, which refers to her home courses, appears in the *Christian Recorder*, December 14, 1882.

69 Dunbar, *A Fragile Freedom*, 123.

70 On the "transatlantic parlor," see Cobb, *Picture Freedom*, 16–19; 193–220.

71 Sarah Mapps Douglass, Amy Matilda Cassey Friendship Album, Library Company of Philadelphia, 35.

72 Christina Sharpe, *Monstrous Intimacies: Making Post-Slavery Subjects* (Durham, NC: Duke University Press, 2010), 82–83.

CONCLUSION

1 Gretchen Long, *Doctoring Freedom: The Politics of African American Medical Care in Slavery and Emancipation* (Chapel Hill: University of North Carolina Press, 2012); Molly Rogers, *Delia's Tears: Race, Science, and Photography in Nineteenth-Century America* (New Haven, CT: Yale University Press, 2010); Marie Jenkins Schwartz, *Birthing a Slave: Motherhood and Medicine in the Antebellum South* (Cambridge, MA: Harvard University Press, 2006); Terri Kapsalis, *Public Privates: Performing Gynecology from Both Ends of the Speculum* (Durham, NC: Duke University Press, 1997).

2 Thomas M. Morgan notes that McCune Smith was the first African American to publish in medical journals in the United States. See Morgan, "The Education and Medical Practice of Dr. James McCune Smith (1813–1865), First Black American to Hold a Medical Degree," *Journal of the National Medical Association* 95 (July 2003): 603–14.

3 On the uptake of eugenics and ideas of racial fitness in the cause of racial uplift, see Michele Mitchell, *Righteous Propagation: African Americans and the Politics of Racial Destiny after Reconstruction* (Chapel Hill: University of North Carolina Press, 2004); Shawn Michelle Smith, *American Archives: Gender, Race, and Class in Visual Culture* (Princeton, NJ: Princeton University Press, 1999), 157–205.

4 Britt Rusert, "'A Study in Nature': The Tuskegee Experiments and the New South Laboratory," *Journal of Medical Humanities* 30.3 (September 2009): 155–71; Christina Simmons, "African Americans and Sexual Victorianism in the Social Hygiene Movement, 1910–40," *Journal of the History of Sexuality* 4.1 (July 1993): 51–75.

5 Khalil Gibran Muhammad, *The Condemnation of Blackness: Race, Crime, and the Making of Modern Urban America* (Cambridge, MA: Harvard University Press, 2010).

6 On the theorization of race as a culture concept in the development of anthropology, see Lee D. Baker, *Anthropology and the Racial Politics of Culture* (Durham, NC: Duke University Press, 2010); Lee D. Baker, *From Savage to Negro: Anthropology and the Construction of Race, 1896–1954* (Berkeley: University of California Press, 1998).

7 On Hurston as ethnographer, see Sonnet H. Retman, *Real Folks: Race and Genre in the Great Depression* (Durham, NC: Duke University Press, 2011); Michael A. Elliott, *The Culture Concept: Writing and Difference in the Age of Realism* (Minneapolis: University of Minnesota Press, 2002). The results of Hurston's field work can be found in her book-length studies, *Of Mules and Men* (1935) and *Tell My Horse* (1938), and in Hurston, *Go Gator and Muddy Water: Writings from the Federal Writers' Project* (New York: W. W. Norton, 1999). *Of Mules and Men*, *Tell My Horse*, and additional works on black folklore and folk culture are collected in Hurston, *Folklore, Memoirs, & Other Writings* (New York: Library of America, 1995).

8 Langston Hughes, *The Big Sea: An Autobiography* (New York: Hill and Wang, 1993), 239.

9 Scholarly views on the nature of Hurston's relationship to anthropology—as subversive or complicit—have been split. See Elliott, *The Culture Concept*, 163.

10 On the "risk of essence," see Diana Fuss, *Essentially Speaking: Feminism, Nature, and Difference* (New York: Routledge, 1989); Naomi Schor and Elizabeth Weed, eds., *The Essential Difference* (Bloomington: Indiana University Press, 1994). On strategic essentialism, see Gayatri Chakravorty Spivak, "Subaltern Studies: Deconstructing Historiography," in her *In Other Worlds: Essays in Cultural Politics* (New York: Methuen, 1987), 197–221.

11 C. P. Snow, *The Two Cultures and the Scientific Revolution* (New York: Cambridge University Press, 1961).

12 Rusert, "'A Study in Nature.'"

13 Ann Petry, *Miss Muriel and Other Stories* (New York: Kensington, 2008), 164.

14 Ibid., 166.

15 Ibid., 165, 166–67.

16 See James McCune Smith, "The Heads of the Colored People," *Frederick Douglass' Paper*, 1852–1854; Edgar Allan Poe, "Some Words with a Mummy," *American Review: A Whig Journal*, April 1845.

17 Petry, "The Bones of Louella Brown," 172.

18 On how segregation influenced African American burial and mourning practices, see Karla Holloway, *Passed On: African American Mourning Stories, A Memorial* (Durham, NC: Duke University Press, 2003).

19 Ibid., 176.

20 Petry, "The Bones of Louella Brown," 180.

21 Christina Sharpe, *Monstrous Intimacies: Making Post-Slavery Subjects* (Durham, NC: Duke University Press, 2010), 72–4; On repatriation efforts in the United States, see David Hurst Thomas, *Skull Wars: Kennewick Man, Archaeology, and*

the Battle for Native American Identity (New York: Basic Books, 2000); "A Slave Whose Bones Helped Train Doctors Gets a Proper Burial," *Los Angeles Times*, September 14, 2013.

22 On the non-event of Emancipation, see Saidiya V. Hartman, *Scenes of Subjection: Terror, Slavery, and Self-Making in Nineteenth-Century America* (New York: Oxford University Press, 1997); Frank B. Wilderson III, *Red, White & Black: Cinema and the Structure of U.S. Antagonisms* (Durham, NC: Duke University Press, 2010); Sharpe, *Monstrous Intimacies.*

23 Martin Delany, *Principia of Ethnology: The Origin of Races and Color, with an Archeological Compendium of Ethiopian and Egyptian Civilization, from Years of Careful Examination and Enquiry* (Philadelphia: Harper and Brother, 1879).

24 W. Carson Byrd and Matthew W. Hughey, eds., *Race, Racial Inequality, and Biological Determinism in the Genetic and Genomic Era*, Special Issue of *Annals of the American Academy of Political and Social Science* 661.1 (Spring 2015); Barbara A. Koenig, Sandra Soo-Jin Lee, and Sarah S. Richardson, eds., *Revisiting Race in a Genomic Age* (New Brunswick, NJ: Rutgers University Press, 2008); Ian Whitmarsh and David S. Jones, *What's the Use of Race?: Modern Governance and the Biology of Difference* (Cambridge: MIT Press, 2010); Anne Pollock, *Medicating Race: Heart Disease and Durable Preoccupations with Difference* (Durham, NC: Duke University Press, 2012). On the case of the heart medicine BiDil and popular misconceptions of its tailoring to "black genes," see Jonathan Kahn, *Race in a Bottle: The Story of BiDil and Racialized Medicine in a Post-Genomic Age* (New York: Columbia University Press, 2014); Britt M. Rusert and Charmaine D. M. Royal, "Grassroots Marketing in a Global Era: More Lessons from BiDil," *Journal of Law, Medicine & Ethics* 39.1 (Spring 2011): 79–90.

25 "Secret World War II Chemical Experiments Tested Troops by Race," *National Public Radio*, June 22, 2015, www.npr.org; Susan L. Smith, "Mustard Gas and American Race-Based Human Experimentation in World War II," *Journal of Law, Medicine & Ethics* 36.3 (2008): 517–21; Susan M. Reverby, "'Normal Exposure' and Inoculation Syphilis: A PHS 'Tuskegee' Doctor in Guatemala, 1946–1948," *Journal of Policy History* 23.1 (2011): 6–28; Adriana Petryna, *When Experiments Travel: Clinical Trials and the Global Search for Human Subjects* (Princeton, NJ: Princeton University Press, 2009); Jeneen Interlandi, "Organ Trafficking Is No Myth," *Newsweek*, January 9, 2009; Catherine Waldby and Robert Mitchell, *Tissue Economies: Blood, Organs, and Cell Lines in Late Capitalism* (Durham, NC: Duke University Press, 2006); Melinda Cooper and Catherine Waldby, *Clinical Labor: Tissue Donors and Research Subjects in the Global Bioeconomy* (Durham, NC: Duke University Press, 2014); Ian Whitmarsh, *Biomedical Ambiguity: Race, Asthma, and the Contested Meaning of Genetic Research in the Caribbean* (Ithaca, NY: Cornell University Press, 2008); Rebecca Skloot, *The Immortal Life of Henrietta Lacks* (New York: Broadway Books, 2011).

26 Alondra Nelson, *Body and Soul: The Black Panther Party and the Fight against Medical Discrimination* (Minneapolis: University of Minnesota Press, 2011);

Alondra Nelson, "Reconciliation Projects: From Kinship to Justice," in *Genetics and the Unsettled Past: The Collision of DNA, Race, and History*, ed. Keith Wailoo, Alondra Nelson, and Catherine Lee (New Brunswick, NJ: Rutgers University Press, 2012), 20–31; Alondra Nelson, *The Social Life of DNA: Race, Reparations, and Reconciliation after the Genome* (Boston: Beacon Press, 2016).

27 On the resurrection of racial science and eugenics in population genetics and genomics, more generally, see Troy Duster, *Backdoor to Eugenics*, 2nd ed. (New York: Routledge, 2003); Jenny Reardon, *Race to the Finish: Identity and Governance in an Age of Genomics* (Princeton, NJ: Princeton University Press, 2004); Dorothy Roberts, *Fatal Invention: How Science, Politics, and Big Business Re-create Race in the Twenty-First Century* (New York: New Press, 2011); Keith Wailoo, Alondra Nelson, and Catherine Lee, eds., *Genetics and the Unsettled Past*; Kim TallBear, *Native American DNA: Tribal Belonging and the False Promise of Genetic Science* (Minneapolis: University of Minnesota Press, 2013).

28 On direct-to-consumer (DTC) ancestry testing, see Henry T. Greely, "Genetic Genealogy: Genetics Meets the Marketplace," in Koenig, Lee, and Richardson, eds., *Revisiting Race in a Genomic Age*, 215–34; Kim TallBear, "Native-American-DNA. com: In Search of Native American Race and Tribe," in ibid., 235–52; Alondra Nelson, "The Factness of Diaspora: The Social Sources of Genetic Genealogy," in ibid., 253–68.

29 Steven Epstein, *Inclusion: The Politics of Difference in Medical Research* (Chicago: University of Chicago Press, 2007). On the possibilities and perils of community participation in stem cell research, see Ruha Benjamin, *People's Science: Bodies and Rights on the Stem Cell Frontier* (Stanford, CA: Stanford University Press, 2013). See also, Kahn, *Race in a Bottle*, and Rusert and Royal, "Grassroots Marketing in a Global Age."

INDEX

Abdy, Edward Strutt (E. S.), 1–4, 29–31, 223
abolitionism: American Anti-Slavery
 Society and Garrisonians, 51, 69, 107,
 133–34; attraction of phrenology in, 125;
 in Britain, 134, 149, 159; in the friendship albums, 208; Henry Box Brown's
 relationship to, 133–41; Jefferson and,
 240–41n9; and lecture circuit, 147–48;
 and Martin Delany, 170–71, 176; and
 McCune Smith, 51; place in literary
 studies, 51; and relationship to natural
 science, 5, 15, 75, 125; women's organizations in Philadelphia, 192
Academy of Natural Sciences, 113, 194, 203
Africa, 11, 13, 34, 79, 87, 95, 225, 228; in
 abolitionist poetry, 39; in African
 American genealogy, 46–50, 70–
 71, 227–29; Banneker's intellectual
 inheritance from, 39–40; birth of arts
 and sciences in, 181; in black ethnology, 47–50, 71–74; and the colonization
 movement, 70, 262n27; and Ethiopia-
 nism, 86–87; European imperialism
 and interruption of development in,
 262n31; Martin Delany's expedition to,
 27, 129, 149, 158–59; precolonial visions
 of, 39, 74; scientific thought in, 39–40;
 study of astronomy and numerology in, 40, 242n24; in textbooks, 203;
 theories of civilization about, 1–4, 9,
 57–58, 74, 113, 130, 181. *See also* Middle
 Passage; slave trade
The Afric-American Astronomer (Kirk),
 241n19

"Afric-American Picture Gallery" (Wil-
 son), 54–55, 106–107, 145
African Burial Ground, 2, 231n4
African Methodist Episcopal (AME)
 Church: Mother Bethel in Phila-
 delphia, 189, 269n21; in Pittsburgh,
 155
African Methodist Episcopal Zion
 (AMEZ) Church, 45
Afro-pessimism, 102–3, 253nn93–94
Agassiz, Louis, 12, 126–27, 155, 223
Alexander, Elizabeth, 184, 220
amateur science, 31, 48 190, 194–95. *See
 also* vernacular science
American Anatomies (Wiegman), 182–83
American Anti-Slavery Society (AASS),
 51, 69, 107, 133–34
American Colonization Society (ACS), 70,
 262n27
American Museum, 115, 117
American Philosophical Society, 194
American school of ethnology, 9–10, 34,
 41, 45, 177, 249; Frederick Douglass's
 critique of, 41, 124–28. *See also* ethnol-
 ogy; polygenesis
America on Stone (Peters), 84, 257n19
anatomical theaters, 117–20, 200
anatomy, 116–20, 162, 181, 185–203, 219,
 266–67n1
ancestry testing, 66–67, 227–29
Ancient Egypt (Gliddon), 80
Anderson, M. B., 126
Andrews, James, 210
Andrews, William, 62, 176, 262n19

ABOUT THE AUTHOR

Britt Rusert is Assistant Professor of African American Literature and Culture in the W. E. B. Du Bois Department of Afro-American Studies at the University of Massachusetts Amherst.